The Ultimate
Instant Pot Cookbook

800+ Foolproof, Quick & Flavorful Instant Pot Recipes for Everyday Pressure Cooker

Mabel Lueck

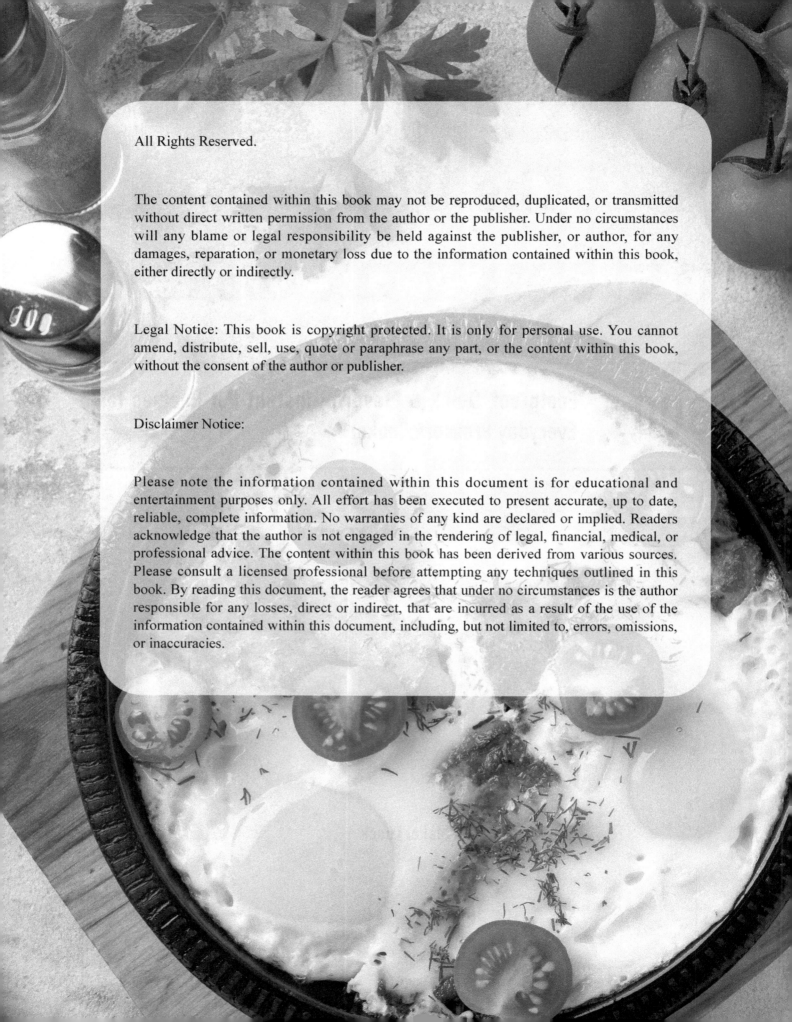

Contents

Chapter 5 : Beans, Rice, & Grains Recipes................................38

Chapter 6 : Pork, Beef & Lamb Recipes 51

Chapter 7 : Fish & Seafood Recipes 65

Chapter 10 : Desserts & Drinks Recipes 105

APPENDIX : Recipes index 120

Chapter 1 : Introduction

Whether you've just bought your Instant Pot or have been using it for years and just need some inspiration, this book is for you. You can find 800 flavorful ,quick and foolproof instant cooker recipes to give you inspiration everyday that I put my whole heart into it to make sure it's the only book you will ever need to start your journey with Instant Pot.

Hi，My name is Mabel Lueck .I am a food blogger, recipes developer and a social media influencer. I was born in Brooklyn, New York. In 2002, I began my food blog,three of my blogs had been rewarded the best recipes of year in Brooklyn.Then I began my tweeter and YouTube channel in 2005,now I am having about 80k followers. 《Air Fryer for beginner》 is my first cookbook.

I has great passion for writing and cooking when I was little. My family wanted me to be a teacher since most of my family member are teacher .Especially my father is the school principle. I got my Teacher's Diploma and taught in a primary school in Brooklyn. After one year I decided to become a food blogger and recipe developer ,I found out I hated repeating same work tasks day in and day out. Now I am very thrilled and grateful I am doing what I love.

Cooking with an Instant pot is a life-changing experience for me and for everyone I believed.Because it save a lot of time and effort for us to make great meal for our families. And It can retain most of the nutrition from the cooking. This multifunctional cooking tool allows us to sauté, brown, steam, and warm our food. It cooks soups, eggs, and even cheesecakes! whether you are making a hearty breakfast, a main dish, or a decadent dessert. So plug in your Instant Pot and get ready to enjoy some amazing, delicious, and quick and easy meals.

In this book, you'll find everything you need to know about how to use your Instant Pot, including how to use instant pot. how to clean it, how to maintain the it, and what you should have on hand to make your dishes even better.

Thank you for choosing my Instant Pot cookbook.The book designed to show you how to best use your Instant Pot to prepare simple everyday meals, most recipes use widely available ingredients to create incredible meals effortlessly and rich in flavors and textures.Hope you enjoy this cookbook!Let's get started!

Chapter 2 : Getting Started with Your Instant Pot

What is an Instant Pot?

Instant Pot is a pressure cooker -- and then some. It also sautés, slow cooks, makes rice and steams veggies and poultry. It's an all-in-one device, so you can, for instance, brown a chicken and cook it all in the same pot. In most cases, Instant Pot meals are ready to serve in less than an hour.

Its quick cook times are thanks to its pressure-cooking function, which locks steam created by liquid (even liquid released from meat and veggies), building pressure and pushing steam back into the food.

How to use Instant Pot?

How you use your Instant Pot depends on what you're cooking. But, many recipes -- especially those involving meat -- tend to follow this formula:

▪ Set the Instant Pot to Saute mode. Add oil (or other fat) and brown your protein, like beef or chicken. Aromatics, like garlic and onion, are browned in this step, too.

▪ Hit the Cancel button. Now tap Manual, followed by Pressure. Tap it again to go into High Pressure mode (which most recipes require.) Use the plus and minus buttons to set the cook time.

▪ Place the lid on the Instant Pot and lock it into place. You should hear a lovely little sound letting you know it's locked.

▪ Make sure the valve built into the lid is in the Sealing position.

When the Instant Pot builds enough pressure, the red button will pop up. Now the cook time will officially begin.

The above steps can vary quite a bit, depending on the recipe, but most of what I cook in my Instant Pot follows that sequence.

How to clean Instant Pot?

1.Unplug the appliance: Always unplug any appliance before cleaning. It's also a great time to check the cord for any damage or needed repairs.

2.Separate lid and interior pot from housing: Take these pieces apart so that you can hit every area that needs it.

3.Clean the outside: Wipe exterior of housing to remove crumbs and tough stains. Remember: The housing has electronic components and should never be immersed in water.

4.Get in the cracks: Use a small brush to remove dried food residue in the recessed area of the housing unit.

5.Hand-wash lid with warm, soapy water: If you allow your Instant Pot to cool naturally, the lid will normally be rather clean, with condensation water only. Most of the time, you won't need to unscrew anything to wash it — just simply wipe dry with a dry cloth. But the lid should also get a periodic deep-clean by removing a few key parts for proper maintenance.

5.Remove the steam-release handle: Remove the steam-release handle by pulling it off gently to check for food particles.

6.Remove the anti-block shield: Remove the anti-block shield from the underside of the lid to wipe the steam valve clean. Note: The steam valve should never be removed. Reattach the anti-block shield and tighten by hand. If you regularly use the quick release to let steam out or cook sticky foods, it's recommended to unscrew the anti-block shield for cleaning with some regularity.

7.Remove the float valve: Remove the silicone ring anchoring the float valve and clean both portions; reattach when dry. Always inspect the float valve to make sure it can move up and down easily without obstruction.

8.Remove sealing ring: The silicone sealing ring should be removed periodically to remove lingering smells and to inspect for damage. If you notice cracking, leaking, or deformation of the sealing ring, you should replace it. The silicone ring can be washed in the dishwasher or soaked in vinegar first to remove odors. The sealing ring should always be clean and well-seated before use to ensure a proper seal during pressure cooking.

9.Wash the inner pot and steam rack: The inner pot and steam rack may be hand-washed or washed in the dishwasher. You can also add the sealing ring to the top rack if you want.

10.Use vinegar to renew finish on inner pot: To remove common rain-bowing effect or discoloring on the stainless steel inner pot, wipe or soak with vinegar. Avoid using steel wool, which will scratch the surface.

11.Reassemble: Make sure all parts are securely reattached to ensure the proper seal. Double-check that the silicone sealing ring, anti-block shield, and float valve weren't forgotten! Then get back to making some dinner magic.

Maintenance tips for your Instant Pot

Step 1 : Give your pressure cooker a thorough cleaning and inspection once a year. Check the gasket, knobs and handles for cracks, loosening, or other signs of age. Replace rubber or silicon parts as necessary.

Step 2 : Clean the inside of the pressure regulator weight and the vent pipe on old-style pressure cookers with a small brush or pipe cleaner. Remove the entire valve assembly on newer pressure cookers and wash all the parts by hand in hot soapy water. Dry the parts on a clean towel and then put it back together.

Step 3 : Tighten handle and lid screws if they become loose and replace them as necessary. Add a drop of oil to the handle screws to give them a longer life.

Measurement Conversions

BASIC KITCHEN CONVERSIONS & EQUIVALENTS

DRY MEASUREMENTS CONVERSION CHART

3 TEASPOONS = 1 TABLESPOON = 1/16 CUP

6 TEASPOONS = 2 TABLESPOONS = 1/8 CUP

12 TEASPOONS = 4 TABLESPOONS = 1/4 CUP

24 TEASPOONS = 8 TABLESPOONS = 1/2 CUP

36 TEASPOONS = 12 TABLESPOONS = 3/4 CUP

48 TEASPOONS = 16 TABLESPOONS = 1 CUP

METRIC TO US COOKING CONVERSIONS

OVEN TEMPERATURES

120 °C = 250 °F

160 °C = 320 °F

180° C = 350 °F

205 °C = 400 °F

220 °C = 425 °F

LIQUID MEASUREMENTS CONVERSION CHART

8 FLUID OUNCES = 1 CUP = 1/2 PINT = 1/4 QUART

16 FLUID OUNCES = 2 CUPS = 1 PINT = 1/2 QUART

32 FLUID OUNCES = 4 CUPS = 2 PINTS = 1 QUART = 1/4 GALLON

128 FLUID OUNCES = 16 CUPS = 8 PINTS = 4 QUARTS = 1 GALLON

BAKING IN GRAMS

1 CUP FLOUR = 140 GRAMS

1 CUP SUGAR = 150 GRAMS

1 CUP POWDERED SUGAR = 160 GRAMS

1 CUP HEAVY CREAM = 235 GRAMS

VOLUME

1 MILLILITER = 1/5 TEASPOON

5 ML = 1 TEASPOON

15 ML = 1 TABLESPOON

240 ML = 1 CUP OR 8 FLUID OUNCES

1 LITER = 34 FL. OUNCES

WEIGHT

1 GRAM = .035 OUNCES

100 GRAMS = 3.5 OUNCES

500 GRAMS = 1.1 POUNDS

1 KILOGRAM = 35 OUNCES

US TO METRIC COOKING CONVERSIONS

1/5 TSP = 1 ML

1 TSP = 5 ML

1 TBSP = 15 ML

1 FL OUNCE = 30 ML

1 CUP = 237 ML

1 PINT (2 CUPS) = 473 ML

1 QUART (4 CUPS) = .95 LITER

1 GALLON (16 CUPS) = 3.8 LITERS

1 OZ = 28 GRAMS

1 POUND = 454 GRAMS

BUTTER

1 CUP BUTTER = 2 STICKS = 8 OUNCES = 230 GRAMS = 8 TABLESPOONS

WHAT DOES 1 CUP EQUAL

1 CUP = 8 FLUID OUNCES

1 CUP = 16 TABLESPOONS

1 CUP = 48 TEASPOONS

1 CUP = 1/2 PINT

1 CUP = 1/4 QUART

1 CUP = 1/16 GALLON

1 CUP = 240 ML

BAKING PAN CONVERSIONS

1 CUP ALL-PURPOSE FLOUR = 4.5 OZ

1 CUP ROLLED OATS = 3 OZ 1 LARGE EGG = 1.7 OZ

1 CUP BUTTER = 8 OZ 1 CUP MILK = 8 OZ

1 CUP HEAVY CREAM = 8.4 OZ

1 CUP GRANULATED SUGAR = 7.1 OZ

1 CUP PACKED BROWN SUGAR = 7.75 OZ

1 CUP VEGETABLE OIL = 7.7 OZ

1 CUP UNSIFTED POWDERED SUGAR = 4.4 OZ

BAKING PAN CONVERSIONS

9-INCH ROUND CAKE PAN = 12 CUPS

10-INCH TUBE PAN =16 CUPS

11-INCH BUNDT PAN = 12 CUPS

9-INCH SPRINGFORM PAN = 10 CUPS

9 X 5 INCH LOAF PAN = 8 CUPS

9-INCH SQUARE PAN = 8 CUPS

Chapter 3 :
Breakfast Recipes

Chapter 3 : Breakfast Recipes

Tofu Hash Brown Breakfast

Servings: 4 | Cooking Time: 21 Minutes

Ingredients:
- 1 cup tofu cubes
- 2 cups frozen hash browns
- 8 beaten eggs
- 1 cup shredded cheddar
- ¼ cup milk
- Salt and pepper to taste

Directions:
1. Set your Instant Pot to Sauté. Place in tofu and cook until browned on all sides, about 4 minutes. Add in hash brown and cook for 2 minutes. Beat eggs, cheddar cheese, milk, salt, and pepper in a bowl and pour over hash brown. Seal the lid, select Manual, and cook for 5 minutes on High. Once done, perform a quick pressure release. Cut into slices before serving.

Nutty Steel-cut Oats

Servings:2 | Cooking Time: 12 Minutes

Ingredients:
- 1 ½ cups steel-cut oats
- 2 cups water
- 1 cup whole milk
- ½ teaspoon vanilla extract
- 2 tablespoons packed light brown sugar
- 2 tablespoons chopped walnuts
- ⅛ teaspoon salt

Directions:
1. In the Instant Pot, add oats, water, milk, vanilla, brown sugar, walnuts, and salt. Stir to combine. Lock lid.
2. Press the Manual or Pressure Cook button and adjust time to 12 minutes. When timer beeps, quick-release pressure until float valve drops. Unlock lid.
3. Stir oatmeal, then spoon into two bowls. Serve warm.

Vanilla Chai Latte Oatmeal

Servings: 4 | Cooking Time: 35 Minutes

Ingredients:
- 3 ½ cups milk
- ½ cup raw peanuts
- 1 cup steel-cut oats
- ¼ cup agave syrup
- 1 ½ tsp ground ginger
- 1 ¼ tsp ground cinnamon
- ¼ tsp ground allspice
- ¼ tsp ground cardamom
- 1 tsp vanilla extract
- 2 tbsp chopped tea leaves
- ¼ tsp cloves

Directions:

1. With a blender, puree peanuts and milk to obtain a smooth consistency. Transfer into the cooker. To the peanuts mixture, add agave syrup, oats, ginger, allspice, cinnamon, cardamom, tea leaves, and cloves and mix well. Seal the lid and cook on High Pressure for 12 minutes. Let pressure release naturally for 10 minutes. Stir in vanilla and serve.

Georgia Peach French Toast Casserole

Servings:4 | Cooking Time: 20 Minutes

Ingredients:
- 4 cups cubed French bread, dried out overnight
- 2 cups diced, peeled ripe peaches
- 1 cup whole milk
- 3 large eggs
- 1 teaspoon vanilla extract
- ¼ cup granulated sugar
- ⅛ teaspoon salt
- 3 tablespoons unsalted butter, cut into 3 pats
- 1 cup water

Directions:
1. Grease a 7-cup glass baking dish. Add bread to dish in an even layer. Add peaches in an even layer over bread. Set aside.
2. In a medium bowl, whisk together milk, eggs, vanilla, sugar, and salt. Pour over bread; place butter pats on top.
3. Add water to the Instant Pot and insert steam rack. Place glass baking dish on top of steam rack. Lock lid.
4. Press the Manual or Pressure Cook button and adjust time to 20 minutes. When timer beeps, quick-release pressure until float valve drops. Unlock lid.
5. Remove bowl and transfer to a cooling rack until set, about 20 minutes. Serve.

Crustless Power Quiche

Servings:2 | Cooking Time: 9 Minutes

Ingredients:
- 6 large eggs
- ½ teaspoon salt
- ½ teaspoon ground black pepper
- 2 teaspoons olive oil
- ½ cup diced red onion
- 1 medium red bell pepper, seeded and diced
- ¼ pound ground pork sausage
- 1 ½ cups water
- 1 medium avocado, peeled, pitted, and diced

Directions:
1. In a medium bowl, whisk together eggs, salt, and black pepper. Set aside.
2. Press the Sauté button on the Instant Pot and heat oil. Stir-fry onion, bell pepper, and sausage 3–4 minutes until sausage starts to brown and onions are tender. Press the Cancel button.
3. Transfer sausage mixture to a greased 7-cup glass bowl. Pour whisked eggs over the mixture.

4. Add water to the Instant Pot and insert steam rack. Place bowl with egg mixture on steam rack. Lock lid.
5. Press the Manual or Pressure Cook button and adjust time to 5 minutes. When timer beeps, quick-release pressure until float valve drops. Unlock lid.
6. Remove bowl from pot. Let sit at room temperature 5–10 minutes to allow the eggs to set, then remove quiche from bowl, slice, and garnish with avocado. Serve warm.

Walnut & Pumpkin Strudel

Servings: 8 | Cooking Time: 55 Minutes

Ingredients:
- 2 cups pumpkin puree
- 1 tsp vanilla extract
- 2 cups Greek yogurt
- 2 eggs
- 2 tbsp brown sugar
- 2 tbsp butter, softened
- 2 puff pastry sheets
- 1 cup walnuts, chopped

Directions:
1. In a bowl, mix butter, yogurt, and vanilla until smooth. Unfold the pastry and cut each sheet into 4-inch x 7-inch pieces; brush with some beaten eggs. Place approximately 2 tbsp of pumpkin puree, sugar, and 2 tbsp of the yogurt mixture at the middle of each pastry, sprinkle with walnuts. Fold the sheets and brush with the remaining eggs.
2. Cut the surface with a sharp knife and gently place each strudel into an oiled baking dish. Pour 1 cup of water into the pot and insert the trivet. Place the pan on top. Seal the lid and cook for 25 minutes on High Pressure. Release the pressure naturally for about 10 minutes. Let it chill for 10 minutes. Serve.

Sunday Brunch Sausage Gravy

Servings:10 | Cooking Time: 10 Minutes

Ingredients:
- 2 tablespoons butter
- 1 pound ground pork sausage
- 1 small sweet onion, peeled and diced
- ¼ cup chicken broth
- ¼ cup all-purpose flour
- 1½ cups heavy cream
- ½ teaspoon sea salt
- 1 tablespoon ground black pepper

Directions:
1. Press the Sauté button on the Instant Pot. Add butter and heat until melted. Add pork sausage and onion. Stir-fry 3–5 minutes until onions are translucent. The pork will still be a little pink in places. Add chicken broth. Lock lid.
2. Press the Manual button and adjust time to 1 minute. When the timer beeps, quick-release the pressure until the float valve drops and then unlock the lid. Whisk in flour, cream, salt, and pepper.
3. Press the Keep Warm button and let the gravy sit for about 5–10 minutes to allow the sauce to thicken. Remove from heat and serve warm.

Nuts And Fruit Oatmeal

Servings:2 | Cooking Time: 7 Minutes

Ingredients:
- 1 cup old-fashioned oats
- 1¼ cups water
- ¼ cup freshly squeezed orange juice
- 1 medium pear, peeled, cored, and cubed
- ¼ cup dried cherries
- ¼ cup chopped walnuts
- 1 tablespoon honey
- ¼ teaspoon ground ginger
- ¼ teaspoon ground cinnamon
- Pinch of salt

Directions:
1. In the Instant Pot bowl, add the oats, water, orange juice, pear, cherries, walnuts, honey, ginger, cinnamon, and salt. Stir to combine. Lock lid.
2. Press the Manual button and adjust time to 7 minutes. When the timer beeps, let pressure release naturally until the float valve drops and then unlock the lid.
3. Stir oatmeal and spoon the cooked oats into two bowls. Serve warm.

Lazy Steel Cut Oats With Coconut

Servings: 2 | Cooking Time: 25 Minutes

Ingredients:
- 1 tsp coconut oil
- 1 cup steel-cut oats
- ¾ cup coconut milk
- ¼ cup sugar
- ½ tsp vanilla extract
- 1 tbsp shredded coconut

Directions:
1. Warm coconut oil on Sauté in your Instant Pot. Add oats and cook as you stir until soft and toasted. Add in milk, sugar, vanilla, and 2 cups water and stir. Seal the lid and press Porridge. Cook for 12 minutes on High Pressure. Set steam vent to Venting to release the pressure quickly. Open the lid. Add oats as you stir to mix any extra liquid. Top with coconut and serve.

Pumpkin Spice Latte French Toast Casserole

Servings:4 | Cooking Time: 20 Minutes

Ingredients:
- 4 cups cubed whole-wheat bread
- 1½ cups whole milk
- ¼ cup brewed coffee, cooled
- 3 large eggs
- ¼ cup pumpkin purée
- 1 teaspoon vanilla extract
- ¼ cup pure maple syrup
- 2 teaspoons pumpkin pie spice
- Pinch of sea salt
- 3 tablespoons butter, cut into 3 pats
- 1 cup water

Directions:
1. Grease a 7-cup glass dish. Add bread. Set aside.

2. In a medium bowl, whisk together milk, coffee, eggs, pumpkin purée, vanilla, maple syrup, pumpkin pie spice, and salt. Pour over bread; place pats of butter on top.
3. Pour water into Instant Pot. Set trivet in Instant Pot. Place glass dish on top of trivet. Lock lid.
4. Press the Manual button and adjust time to 20 minutes. When the timer beeps, quick-release the pressure until float valve drops and then unlock lid.
5. Remove glass bowl from the Instant Pot. Transfer to a rack until cool. Serve.

Pumpkin Muffins

Servings:6 | Cooking Time: 9 Minutes

Ingredients:
- 1 ¼ cups all-purpose flour
- 2 teaspoons baking powder
- ½ teaspoon baking soda
- 1 teaspoon pumpkin pie spice
- ⅛ teaspoon salt
- ¼ cup pumpkin purée
- ½ teaspoon vanilla extract
- 1 tablespoon unsalted butter, melted
- 2 large eggs
- ⅓ cup packed light brown sugar
- 1 cup water

Directions:
1. Grease six silicone cupcake liners.
2. In a large bowl, combine flour, baking powder, baking soda, pumpkin pie spice, and salt.
3. In a medium bowl, combine pumpkin purée, vanilla, butter, eggs, and brown sugar.
4. Pour wet ingredients from medium bowl into large bowl with dry ingredients. Gently combine ingredients. Do not overmix. Spoon mixture into prepared cupcake liners.
5. Add water to the Instant Pot and insert steam rack. Place cupcake liners on top. Lock lid.
6. Press the Manual or Pressure Cook button and adjust time to 9 minutes. When timer beeps, quick-release pressure until float valve drops. Unlock lid.
7. Remove muffins from pot and set aside to cool 30 minutes. Serve.

Italian Egg Cakes

Servings: 4 | Cooking Time: 25 Minutes

Ingredients:
- ¼ cup ricotta cheese, cubed
- ½ cup mozzarella, shredded
- 1 cup chopped baby spinach
- 6 beaten eggs
- 1 chopped tomato
- Salt and pepper to taste
- 2 tbsp basil, chopped

Directions:
1. Pour 1 cup of water into the Instant Pot and fit in a trivet. Place spinach in small cups. Combine eggs, mozzarella cheese, ricotta cheese, tomato, salt, and pepper in a bowl. Fill 3/4 of each cup with the mixture and top with basil.
2. Place the cups on top of the trivet and seal the lid. Select Manual and cook for 15 minutes on High pressure. Once ready, per-

form a quick pressure release. Serve hot.

Maple French Toast Casserole

Servings:4 | Cooking Time: 20 Minutes

Ingredients:
- 4 cups cubed French bread
- 1 cup whole milk
- 3 large eggs
- 1 tablespoon granulated sugar
- 1 teaspoon vanilla extract
- ¼ cup pure maple syrup
- ⅛ teaspoon salt
- 3 tablespoons unsalted butter, cut into 3 pats
- 1 cup water

Directions:
1. Grease a 7-cup glass baking dish. Add bread. Set aside.
2. In a medium bowl, whisk together milk, eggs, sugar, vanilla, maple syrup, and salt. Pour over bread; place butter pats on top.
3. Add water to the Instant Pot and insert steam rack. Place glass baking dish on top of steam rack. Lock lid.
4. Press the Manual or Pressure Cook button and adjust time to 20 minutes. When timer beeps, quick-release pressure until float valve drops. Unlock lid.
5. Remove bowl and transfer to a cooling rack until set, about 20 minutes. Serve.

Hard-"boiled" Eggs

Servings:6 | Cooking Time: 6 Minutes

Ingredients:
- 1 cup water
- 6 large eggs

Directions:
1. Add water to the Instant Pot and insert steamer basket. Place eggs in basket. Lock lid.
2. Press the Manual or Pressure Cook button and adjust time to 6 minutes. When timer beeps, quick-release pressure until float valve drops. Unlock lid.
3. Create an ice bath by adding 1 cup ice and 1 cup water to a medium bowl. Transfer eggs to ice bath to stop the cooking process.
4. Peel eggs. Slice each egg directly onto a plate. Serve immediately.

Strawberry Jam

Servings: 6 | Cooking Time: 30 Minutes

Ingredients:
- 1 lb strawberries, chopped
- 1 cup sugar
- ½ lemon, juiced and zested
- 1 tbsp mint, chopped

Directions:
1. Add the strawberries, sugar, lemon juice, and zest to the Instant Pot. Seal the lid, select manual, and cook for 2 minutes on High.
2. Release pressure naturally for 10 minutes. Open the lid and stir in chopped mint. Select Sauté and continue cooking until the jam thickens, about 10 minutes. Let to cool before serving.

Pumpkin Steel Cut Oats With Cinnamon

Servings: 4 | Cooking Time: 25 Minutes

Ingredients:
- 1 tbsp butter
- 2 cups steel-cut oats
- ¼ tsp cinnamon
- 1 cup pumpkin puree
- 3 tbsp maple syrup
- 2 tsp pumpkin seeds, toasted

Directions:
1. Melt butter on Sauté. Add in cinnamon, oats, pumpkin puree, and 3 cups of water. Seal the lid, select Porridge and cook for 10 minutes on High Pressure to get a few bite oats or for 14 minutes to form soft oats. Do a quick release. Open the lid and stir in maple syrup. Top with pumpkin seeds and serve.

Pecan Chocolate Chip Breakfast Oats

Servings:2 | Cooking Time: 7 Minutes

Ingredients:
- 1 cup old-fashioned oats
- 1 cup water
- 1 cup whole milk
- ¼ teaspoon vanilla extract
- 2 tablespoons packed light brown sugar
- 2 tablespoons chopped pecans
- ⅛ teaspoon salt
- 2 tablespoons mini chocolate chips

Directions:
1. In the Instant Pot, add oats, water, milk, vanilla, brown sugar, pecans, and salt. Stir to combine. Lock lid.
2. Press the Manual or Pressure Cook button and adjust time to 7 minutes. When timer beeps, quick-release pressure until float valve drops. Unlock lid.
3. Stir oatmeal, then spoon into two bowls and garnish with chocolate chips. Serve warm.

Speedy Soft-boiled Eggs

Servings: 4 | Cooking Time: 10 Minutes

Ingredients:
- 4 large eggs
- Salt and pepper to taste

Directions:
1. To the pressure cooker, add 1 cup of water and place a wire rack. Place eggs on it. Seal the lid, press Steam, and cook for 3 minutes on High Pressure. Do a quick release.
2. Allow to cool in an ice bath. Peel the eggs and season with salt and pepper before serving.

Banana & Vanilla Pancakes

Servings: 6 | Cooking Time: 15 Minutes

Ingredients:
- 2 bananas, mashed
- 1 ¼ cups milk
- 2 eggs
- 1 ½ cups rolled oats
- 1 ½ tsp baking powder
- 1 tsp vanilla extract
- 2 tsp coconut oil
- 1 tbsp honey

Directions:
1. Combine the bananas, milk, eggs, oats, baking powder, vanilla, coconut oil, and honey in a blender and pulse until a completely smooth batter. Grease the inner pot with cooking spray. Spread 1 spoon batter at the bottom. Cook for 2 minutes on Sauté, flip the crepe, and cook for another minute. Repeat the process with the remaining batter. Serve immediately with your favorite topping.

Crustless Crab Quiche

Servings:6 | Cooking Time: 10 Minutes

Ingredients:
- 6 large eggs
- ¼ cup unsweetened almond milk
- 2 teaspoons fresh thyme leaves
- ½ teaspoon sea salt
- ¼ teaspoon ground black pepper
- ½ teaspoon hot sauce
- ½ pound crabmeat
- ¼ cup crumbled goat cheese
- 2 thick slices bacon, diced
- ¼ cup peeled and diced onion
- ¼ cup seeded and diced green bell pepper
- 2 cups water

Directions:
1. In a medium bowl, whisk eggs, milk, thyme leaves, salt, pepper, and hot sauce. Stir in crabmeat and goat cheese. Set aside.
2. Grease a 7-cup glass dish. Set aside.
3. Press the Sauté button on Instant Pot. Add diced bacon and brown for 2 minutes, rendering some fat. Add onion and bell pepper and stir-fry with bacon until tender. Transfer mixture to the glass container. Pour in egg mixture.
4. Place trivet in Instant Pot. Pour in water. Place dish with egg mixture onto trivet. Lock lid.
5. Press the Manual button and adjust time to 5 minutes. When timer beeps, let pressure release naturally for 10 minutes. Quick-release any additional pressure until float valve drops and then unlock lid.
6. Remove dish from Instant Pot. Let cool for 10 minutes to allow eggs to set. Slice and serve.

Grandma's Country Gravy

Servings: 6 | Cooking Time: 16 Minutes

Ingredients:
- 2 tablespoons unsalted butter
- 1 pound ground pork sausage
- 1 small sweet onion, peeled and diced
- ¼ cup chicken broth
- ¼ cup all-purpose flour
- 1 ½ cups heavy cream
- ½ teaspoon salt
- 1 tablespoon ground black pepper

Directions:
1. Press the Sauté button on the Instant Pot. Add butter and heat until melted. Add sausage and onion and stir-fry 3–5 minutes until onions are translucent. The pork will still be a little pink in places. Add broth. Press the Cancel button. Lock lid.
2. Press the Manual or Pressure Cook button and adjust time to 1 minute. When timer beeps, quick-release pressure until float valve drops. Unlock lid. Whisk in flour, cream, salt, and pepper.
3. Press the Keep Warm button and let the gravy sit about 5–10 minutes to allow to thicken. Remove from heat. Serve warm.

Tomato Mozzarella Basil Egg Bites

Servings: 6 | Cooking Time: 8 Minutes

Ingredients:
- 4 large eggs
- 2 tablespoons grated yellow onion
- ½ teaspoon salt
- ½ teaspoon ground black pepper
- 6 cherry tomatoes, quartered
- ¼ cup grated mozzarella cheese
- 2 tablespoons chopped fresh basil
- 1 cup water

Directions:
1. Grease six silicone cupcake liners.
2. In a medium bowl, whisk together eggs, onion, salt, and pepper. Distribute egg mixture evenly among cupcake liners. Add tomatoes, cheese, and basil to each cup.
3. Add water to the Instant Pot and insert steam rack. Place steamer basket on steam rack. Carefully place cupcake liners in basket. Lock lid.
4. Press the Manual or Pressure Cook button and adjust time to 8 minutes. When timer beeps, quick-release pressure until float valve drops. Unlock lid.
5. Remove egg bites. Serve warm.

French Cheese & Spinach Quiche

Servings: 5 | Cooking Time: 20 Minutes

Ingredients:
- 1 lb spinach, chopped
- ½ cup mascarpone cheese
- ½ cup feta cheese, shredded
- 3 eggs, beaten
- ½ cup goat cheese
- 3 tbsp butter
- ½ cup milk
- 1 pack pie dough

Directions:
1. In a bowl, mix spinach, eggs, mascarpone, feta and goat cheeses. Dust a clean surface with flour and unfold the pie sheets onto it. Using a rolling pin, roll the dough to fit your Instant Pot. Repeat with the other sheets. Combine milk and butter in a skillet. Bring to a boil and melt the butter completely. Remove from the heat.
2. Grease a baking pan with oil. Place in 2 pie sheets and brush with milk mixture. Make the first layer of spinach mixture and cover with another two pie sheets. Again, brush with butter and milk mixture, and repeat until you have used all ingredients. Pour 1 cup water into your Instant Pot and insert a trivet. Lower the pan on the trivet. Seal the lid. Cook on High Pressure for 6 minutes. Do a quick release. Place parchment paper under the pie to use it as a lifting method to remove the pie. Serve cold.

Blueberry-oat Muffins

Servings: 6 | Cooking Time: 9 Minutes

Ingredients:
- 1 cup all-purpose baking flour
- ¼ cup old-fashioned oats
- 2 teaspoons baking powder
- ½ teaspoon baking soda
- ⅛ teaspoon salt
- ½ teaspoon vanilla extract
- 3 tablespoons unsalted butter, melted
- 2 large eggs
- 4 tablespoons granulated sugar
- ⅓ cup blueberries
- 1 cup water

Directions:
1. Grease six silicone cupcake liners.
2. In a large bowl, combine flour, oats, baking powder, baking soda, and salt.
3. In a medium bowl, combine vanilla, butter, eggs, and sugar.
4. Pour wet ingredients from medium bowl into the bowl with dry ingredients. Gently combine ingredients. Do not overmix. Fold in blueberries, then spoon mixture into prepared cupcake liners.
5. Add water to the Instant Pot and insert steam rack. Place cupcake liners on top. Lock lid.
6. Press the Manual or Pressure Cook button and adjust time to 9 minutes. When timer beeps, quick-release pressure until float valve drops. Unlock lid.
7. Remove muffins from pot and set aside to cool 30 minutes. Serve.

Spinach & Feta Pie With Cherry Tomatoes

Servings: 2 | Cooking Time: 35 Minutes

Ingredients:
- 4 eggs
- Salt and pepper to taste
- ½ cup heavy cream
- 1 cup cherry tomatoes, halved
- 1 cup baby spinach
- 1 spring onion, chopped
- ¼ cup feta, crumbled
- 1 tbsp parsley, chopped

Directions:
1. Grease a baking dish with cooking spray and add in the spinach and onion. In a bowl, whisk the eggs, heavy cream, salt, and pepper. Pour over the spinach and arrange the cherry tomato on top. Sprinkle with the feta.
2. Add a cup of water to the Instant Pot and insert a trivet. Place the dish on the trivet. Seal the lid, press Manual, and cook on High pressure for 15 minutes. Release pressure naturally for 10 minutes. Scatter parsley to serve.

Savory Roast Beef Sandwiches

Servings: 8 | Cooking Time: 1 Hour 30 Minutes

Ingredients:
- 2 ½ lb beef roast
- 2 tbsp olive oil
- 1 onion, chopped
- 4 garlic cloves, minced
- ½ cup dry red wine
- 2 cups beef broth stock
- 16 slices Fontina cheese
- 8 split hoagie rolls
- Salt and pepper to taste

Directions:
1. Season the beef with salt and pepper. Warm oil on Sauté and brown the beef for 2 to 3 minutes per side; reserve. Add onion and garlic to the pot and cook for 3 minutes until translucent. Set aside. Add red wine to deglaze. Mix in beef broth and take back the beef. Seal the lid and cook on High Pressure for 50 minutes. Release the pressure naturally for 10 minutes. Preheat a broiler.
2. Transfer the beef to a cutting board and slice. Roll the meat and top with onion. Each sandwich should be topped with 2 Fontina cheese slices. Place the sandwiches under the broiler for 2-3 minutes until the cheese melts.

Southern Cheesy Grits

Servings:4 | Cooking Time: 10 Minutes

Ingredients:
- ¾ plus 1½ cups water, divided
- 1 cup stone-ground grits
- 2 tablespoons butter
- 1 teaspoon sea salt
- ½ teaspoon ground black pepper
- ½ cup grated sharp Cheddar cheese

Directions:
1. Place ¾ cup water in the bottom of the Instant Pot. Insert the trivet.
2. In the stainless-steel bowl that fits down into the pot insert, stir together the grits, butter, remaining 1½ cups water, salt, and pepper. Lock lid.
3. Press the Rice button. When timer beeps, quick-release the pressure until the float valve drops and then unlock the lid. Stir in the cheese and serve warm.

Honey Butternut Squash Cake Oatmeal

Servings: 4 | Cooking Time: 35 Minutes

Ingredients:
- 3 ½ cups coconut milk
- 1 cup steel-cut oats
- 8 oz butternut squash, grated
- ½ cup sultanas
- 1/3 cup honey
- ¾ tsp ground ginger
- ½ tsp salt
- ½ tsp orange zest
- ¼ tsp ground nutmeg
- ¼ cup walnuts, chopped
- ½ tsp vanilla extract
- ½ tsp sugar

Directions:
1. In the cooker, mix sultanas, orange zest, ginger, milk, honey, butternut squash, salt, oats, and nutmeg. Seal the lid and cook on High Pressure for 12 minutes. Do a natural release for 10 minutes. Into the oatmeal, stir in the vanilla extract and sugar. Top with walnuts and serve.

Trail Mix Oatmeal

Servings:2 | Cooking Time: 10 Minutes

Ingredients:
- 1 cup steel-cut oats
- 1½ cups water
- 2 teaspoons butter
- 1 cup freshly squeezed orange juice
- 1 tablespoon dried cranberries
- 1 tablespoon raisins
- 1 tablespoon chopped dried apricots
- 2 tablespoons pure maple syrup
- ¼ teaspoon ground cinnamon
- 2 tablespoons chopped pecans
- Pinch of salt

Directions:
1. Add all ingredients to the Instant Pot bowl and stir to combine. Lock lid.
2. Press the Manual button and adjust time to 10 minutes. When timer beeps, quick-release pressure until float valve drops and then unlock lid.
3. Stir oatmeal. Spoon the cooked oats into two bowls. Serve warm.

California Frittata Bake

Servings:4 | Cooking Time: 10 Minutes

Ingredients:
- 4 large eggs
- 4 large egg whites
- ½ teaspoon sea salt
- ¼ teaspoon ground black pepper
- ¼ cup chopped fresh basil
- ½ cup chopped spinach
- 2 small Roma tomatoes, diced
- 1 medium avocado, pitted and diced
- ¼ cup grated Gruyère cheese
- 1 tablespoon avocado oil
- 1 pound ground chicken
- 1 small onion, peeled and diced
- 1 cup water

Directions:
1. In a medium bowl, whisk together eggs, egg whites, salt, and pepper. Add basil, spinach, tomatoes, avocado, and cheese. Set aside.
2. Press the Sauté button on Instant Pot. Heat the avocado oil and stir-fry chicken and onion for approximately 5 minutes or until chicken is no longer pink.
3. Transfer cooked mixture to a 7-cup greased glass dish and set aside to cool. Once cool pour whisked eggs over the chicken mixture and stir to combine.
4. Place trivet in Instant Pot. Pour in water. Place dish with egg mixture onto trivet. Lock lid.
5. Press the Manual button and adjust time to 5 minutes. When the timer beeps, let pressure release naturally until the float valve drops and then unlock the lid.
6. Remove dish from the Instant Pot and set aside for 5–10 minutes to allow the eggs to set. Slice and serve.

Strawberry Cream-filled French Toast Casserole

Servings:4 | Cooking Time: 20 Minutes

Ingredients:
- 8 ounces cream cheese, room temperature
- ¼ cup sugar
- 2 cups sliced strawberries
- 1 tablespoon orange zest
- 4 cups cubed bread, dried out overnight, divided
- 2 cups whole milk
- 3 large eggs
- 1 teaspoon vanilla extract
- ¼ cup pure maple syrup
- Pinch of ground nutmeg
- Pinch of sea salt
- 3 tablespoons butter, cut into 3 pats
- 1 cup water
- 4 teaspoons powdered sugar

Directions:
1. In a large bowl, cream together the cream cheese and sugar by mashing ingredients with the tines of a fork. Fold in strawberries and orange zest. Set aside.
2. Grease a 7-cup glass dish. Add 2 cups bread. Spoon in a layer of the strawberry mixture. Add remaining 2 cups bread. Set aside.
3. In a medium bowl, whisk together milk, eggs, vanilla, maple

syrup, nutmeg, and salt. Pour over bread; place pats of butter on top.
4. Pour water into Instant Pot. Set trivet in Instant Pot. Place glass dish on top of trivet. Lock lid.
5. Press the Manual button and adjust time to 20 minutes. When the timer beeps, quick-release pressure until float valve drops and then unlock lid.
6. Remove glass bowl from the Instant Pot. Transfer to a rack until cooled. Sprinkle with powdered sugar.

Sausage And Sweet Potato Hash

Servings:4 | Cooking Time: 10 Minutes

Ingredients:
- ½ pound ground pork sausage
- 1 large sweet potato, peeled and grated
- 1 small yellow onion, peeled and diced
- 2 cloves garlic, peeled and minced
- 1 medium green bell pepper, seeded and diced
- 1 tablespoon Italian seasoning
- ½ teaspoon salt
- ½ teaspoon ground black pepper
- 2 cups water

Directions:
1. Press the Sauté button on the Instant Pot. Stir-fry sausage, sweet potato, onion, garlic, bell pepper, Italian seasoning, salt, and black pepper 3–5 minutes until onions are translucent. Press the Cancel button.
2. Transfer mixture to a greased 7-cup glass baking dish.
3. Add water to the Instant Pot and insert steam rack. Place dish on steam rack. Lock lid.
4. Press the Manual or Pressure Cook button and adjust time to 5 minutes. When timer beeps, quick-release pressure until float valve drops. Unlock lid.
5. Remove dish from the Instant Pot. Spoon hash onto plates and serve.

Pimiento Cheese Grits

Servings:4 | Cooking Time: 10 Minutes

Ingredients:
- ¾ cup plus 1 ½ cups water, divided
- 1 cup stone-ground grits
- 2 tablespoons unsalted butter
- 1 teaspoon salt
- ½ teaspoon ground black pepper
- ½ cup grated sharp Cheddar cheese
- 1 jar diced pimientos, drained

Directions:
1. Add ¾ cup water to the Instant Pot and insert steam rack.
2. In a 7-cup glass baking dish that fits down into the pot insert, combine grits, butter, remaining 1 ½ cups water, salt, and pepper. Lock lid.
3. Press the Rice button. When timer beeps, quick-release pressure until float valve drops. Unlock lid.
4. Stir in cheese and pimientos. Serve warm.

Banana Nut Bread Oatmeal

Servings:2 | Cooking Time: 7 Minutes

Ingredients:
- 1 cup old-fashioned oats
- 1 cup water
- 1 cup whole milk
- 2 ripe bananas, peeled and sliced
- 2 tablespoons pure maple syrup
- 2 teaspoons ground cinnamon
- ¼ teaspoon vanilla extract
- 2 tablespoons chopped walnuts
- Pinch of salt

Directions:
1. In the Instant Pot bowl, add the oats, water, milk, bananas, maple syrup, cinnamon, vanilla, walnuts, and salt. Stir to combine. Lock lid.
2. Press the Manual button and adjust time to 7 minutes. When the timer beeps, let pressure release naturally until float valve drops and then unlock lid.
3. Stir oatmeal. Spoon the cooked oats into two bowls. Serve warm.

Western Omelet Casserole

Servings:4 | Cooking Time: 10 Minutes

Ingredients:
- 6 large eggs
- ½ teaspoon sea salt
- ½ teaspoon ground black pepper
- 2 dashes hot sauce
- 1 cup diced ham
- 1 small red bell pepper, seeded and diced
- 1 small green bell pepper, seeded and diced
- 1 small onion, peeled and diced
- 2 cups water

Directions:
1. In a medium bowl, whisk together eggs, salt, pepper, and hot sauce. Set aside.
2. Press the Sauté button on Instant Pot. Stir-fry ham, bell peppers, and onion for 3–5 minutes or until onions are translucent.
3. Transfer mixture to a greased 7-cup glass dish. Pour whisked eggs over the ham mixture.
4. Place trivet in Instant Pot. Pour in water. Place dish with egg mixture onto trivet. Lock lid.
5. Press the Manual button and adjust time to 5 minutes. When timer beeps, quick-release pressure until float valve drops and then unlock lid.
6. Remove dish from the Instant Pot. Let sit at room temperature for 5–10 minutes to allow the eggs to set. Slice and serve.

Brunchy Sausage Bowl

Servings:4 | Cooking Time: 10 Minutes

Ingredients:
- 1 pound pork sausage links
- 2 large potatoes, peeled and thinly sliced
- 1 medium red bell pepper, seeded and diced
- 1 medium sweet onion, peeled and diced
- 1 can creamed corn
- ½ teaspoon sea salt
- ¼ teaspoon ground black pepper
- ¾ cup tomato juice

Directions:
1. Press the Sauté button on Instant Pot. Add sausage links and brown for 4–5 minutes. Move the sausages to a plate.
2. Layer the potatoes, bell pepper, onion, and corn in the Instant Pot. Sprinkle with salt and pepper. Place sausage links on top of the corn. Pour the tomato juice over the top of the other ingredients in the Instant Pot. Lock lid.
3. Press the Manual button and adjust time to 5 minutes. When the timer beeps, let the pressure release naturally for at least 10 minutes.
4. Quick-release any additional pressure until the float valve drops and then unlock lid. Serve warm.

Peachy Cream Oats

Servings:2 | Cooking Time: 7 Minutes

Ingredients:
- 1 cup old-fashioned oats
- 1 cup water
- 1 cup whole milk
- 4 ripe peaches, peeled, pitted, and diced
- 2 tablespoons packed light brown sugar
- ¼ teaspoon vanilla extract
- 2 tablespoons chopped pecans
- Pinch of salt

Directions:
1. In the Instant Pot bowl, add the oats, water, milk, peaches, brown sugar, vanilla, pecans, and salt. Stir to combine. Lock lid.
2. Press the Manual button and adjust time to 7 minutes. When timer beeps, quick-release pressure until float valve drops and then unlock lid.
3. Stir oatmeal. Spoon the cooked oats into two bowls. Serve warm.

Chocolate Banana French Toast Casserole

Servings:4 | Cooking Time: 20 Minutes

Ingredients:
- 4 cups cubed bread, dried out overnight, divided
- 2 bananas, peeled and sliced
- 4 tablespoons chocolate syrup, divided
- 2 cups whole milk
- 3 large eggs
- 1 teaspoon vanilla extract
- ¼ cup pure maple syrup
- Pinch of ground nutmeg
- Pinch of sea salt
- 3 tablespoons butter, cut into 3 pats
- 1 cup water

Directions:
1. Grease a 7-cup glass dish. Add 2 cups bread. Arrange banana slices in an even layer over bread. Drizzle 2 tablespoons chocolate syrup over bananas. Add remaining 2 cups bread. Set aside.
2. In a medium bowl, whisk together milk, eggs, vanilla, maple syrup, nutmeg, and salt. Pour over bread; place pats of butter on top.
3. Pour water into Instant Pot. Set trivet in Instant Pot. Place

glass dish on top of trivet. Lock lid.

4. Press the Manual button and adjust time to 20 minutes. When the timer beeps, quick-release pressure until float valve drops and then unlock lid.

5. Remove glass bowl from the Instant Pot. Transfer to a rack until cooled. Top with remaining 2 tablespoons chocolate. Serve warm.

Bacon Cheddar Scrambled Egg Muffins

Servings:6 | Cooking Time: 8 Minutes

Ingredients:
- 4 large eggs
- 2 tablespoons whole milk
- 2 tablespoons grated yellow onion
- ½ teaspoon salt
- ½ teaspoon ground black pepper
- 5 slices bacon, cooked and crumbled
- ¼ cup grated Cheddar cheese
- 1 cup water

Directions:
1. Grease six silicone cupcake liners.
2. In a medium bowl, whisk together eggs, milk, onion, salt, and pepper. Distribute egg mixture evenly among cupcake liners. Add equal amounts of bacon and cheese to each cup.
3. Add water to the Instant Pot and insert steam rack. Place steamer basket on steam rack. Carefully place muffin cups in basket. Lock lid.
4. Press the Manual or Pressure Cook button and adjust time to 8 minutes. When timer beeps, quick-release pressure until float valve drops. Unlock lid.
5. Remove egg muffins. Serve warm.

Buckwheat Pancake With Yogurt & Berries

Servings: 4 | Cooking Time: 15 Minutes

Ingredients:
- 1 cup buckwheat flour
- 2 tsp baking powder
- 1 ¼ cups milk
- 1 egg
- 1 tsp vanilla sugar
- 1 tsp strawberry extract
- 1 cup Greek yogurt
- 1 cup fresh berries

Directions:
1. In a bowl, whisk milk and egg until foamy. Gradually add flour and continue to beat until combined. Add baking powder, strawberry extract, and vanilla sugar. Spoon the batter in a greased cake pan. Pour 1 cup of water into the pot. Place a trivet. Lay the pan on the trivet. Seal the lid and cook for 5 minutes on High Pressure. Do a quick release. Top pancake with yogurt and berries.

Bacon Onion Cheddar Frittata

Servings:4 | Cooking Time: 12 Minutes

Ingredients:
- 6 large eggs
- 2 teaspoons Italian seasoning
- ½ cup shredded Cheddar cheese
- ½ teaspoon salt
- ¼ teaspoon ground black pepper
- 1 tablespoon olive oil
- 4 slices bacon, diced
- 1 small yellow onion, peeled and diced
- 1 cup water

Directions:
1. In a medium bowl, whisk together eggs, Italian seasoning, cheese, salt, and pepper. Set aside.
2. Press the Sauté button on the Instant Pot and heat oil. Add bacon and onion and stir-fry 3–4 minutes until onions are translucent and bacon is almost crisp. Press the Cancel button.
3. Transfer cooked mixture to a greased 7-cup glass bowl and set aside to cool 5 minutes. Pour whisked egg mixture over the cooked mixture and stir to combine.
4. Add water to the Instant Pot and insert steam rack. Place glass bowl with egg mixture on steam rack. Lock lid.
5. Press the Manual or Pressure Cook button and adjust time to 8 minutes. When timer beeps, let pressure release naturally until float valve drops. Unlock lid.
6. Remove bowl from pot and let sit 10 minutes to allow eggs to set. Slice and serve warm.

Peanut Butter And Banana Oatmeal

Servings:2 | Cooking Time: 7 Minutes

Ingredients:
- 1 cup old-fashioned oats
- 1 ¼ cups water
- 1 large ripe banana, peeled and mashed
- 1 tablespoon packed light brown sugar
- ¼ teaspoon vanilla extract
- ¼ teaspoon ground cinnamon
- ⅛ teaspoon salt
- 2 tablespoons crunchy peanut butter

Directions:
1. In the Instant Pot, add oats, water, banana, brown sugar, vanilla, cinnamon, and salt. Stir to combine. Lock lid.
2. Press the Manual or Pressure Cook button and adjust time to 7 minutes. When timer beeps, let pressure release naturally until float valve drops. Unlock lid.
3. Stir in peanut butter, then spoon oatmeal into two bowls. Serve warm.

Sweet Potato Morning Hash

Servings:4 | Cooking Time: 10 Minutes

Ingredients:
- 6 large eggs
- 1 tablespoon Italian seasoning
- ½ teaspoon sea salt
- ½ teaspoon ground black pepper
- ½ pound ground pork sausage
- 1 large sweet potato, peeled and cubed

- 1 small onion, peeled and diced
- 2 cloves garlic, minced
- 1 medium green bell pepper, seeded and diced
- 2 cups water

Directions:
1. In a medium bowl, whisk together eggs, Italian seasoning, salt, and pepper. Set aside.
2. Press the Sauté button on Instant Pot. Stir-fry sausage, sweet potato, onion, garlic, and bell pepper for 3–5 minutes until onions are translucent.
3. Transfer mixture to a 7-cup greased glass dish. Pour whisked eggs over the sausage mixture.
4. Place trivet in Instant Pot. Pour in water. Place dish with egg mixture onto trivet. Lock lid.
5. Press the Manual button and adjust time to 5 minutes. When timer beeps, quick-release pressure until float valve drops and then unlock lid. Remove dish from Instant Pot. Let sit at room temperature for 5–10 minutes to allow the eggs to set. Slice and serve.

Tex-mex Breakfast

Servings:4 | Cooking Time: 10 Minutes

Ingredients:
- 6 large eggs
- ½ teaspoon sea salt
- ¼ teaspoon ground black pepper
- ⅛ teaspoon chili powder
- ½ cup shredded Cheddar cheese
- 1 small Roma tomato, diced
- 2 tablespoons butter
- 2 small Yukon gold potatoes, grated
- 2 cups cubed cooked ham
- 1 small onion, peeled and diced
- 1 small jalapeño, seeded and diced
- ½ cup sliced button mushrooms
- 2 cups water

Directions:
1. In a medium bowl, whisk together eggs, salt, pepper, and chili powder. Stir in cheese and tomato. Set aside.
2. Press the Sauté button on Instant Pot. Heat the butter and stir-fry potatoes, ham, onion, jalapeño, and mushrooms for approximately 5 minutes until the potatoes are tender and onions are translucent.
3. Transfer cooked mixture to a 7-cup greased glass dish. Pour whisked eggs over the potato mixture.
4. Place trivet in Instant Pot. Pour in water. Place dish with egg mixture onto trivet. Lock lid.
5. Press the Manual button and adjust time to 5 minutes. When timer beeps, quick-release pressure until float valve drops and then unlock lid.
6. Remove dish from the Instant Pot. Let sit at room temperature for 5–10 minutes to allow the eggs to set. Slice and serve warm.

Lemony Pancake Bites With Blueberry Syrup

Servings:4 | Cooking Time: 24 Minutes

Ingredients:
- 1 packet Hungry Jack buttermilk pancake mix
- ⅔ cup whole milk
- Juice and zest of ½ medium lemon
- ⅛ teaspoon salt
- 1 cup water
- ½ cup blueberry syrup

Directions:
1. Grease a seven-hole silicone egg mold.
2. In a medium bowl, combine pancake mix, milk, lemon juice and zest, and salt. Fill egg mold with half of batter.
3. Add water to the Instant Pot and insert steam rack. Place filled egg mold on steam rack. Lock lid.
4. Press the Manual or Pressure Cook button and adjust time to 12 minutes. When timer beeps, quick-release pressure until float valve drops. Unlock lid.
5. Allow pancake bites to cool, about 3 minutes until cool enough to handle. Pop out of mold. Repeat with remaining batter.
6. Serve warm with syrup for dipping.

Bacon-poblano Morning Taters

Servings:4 | Cooking Time: 10 Minutes

Ingredients:
- 1 tablespoon olive oil
- 2 slices bacon, diced
- 1 small onion, peeled and diced
- 2 small poblano peppers, seeded and diced
- 4 cups small-diced russet potatoes
- 2 tablespoons ghee
- 2–3 cloves garlic, minced
- 1 teaspoon sea salt
- ½ teaspoon ground black pepper
- ½ cup water

Directions:
1. Press Sauté button on Instant Pot and heat oil. Add bacon, onion, and peppers. Stir-fry until onions are translucent, 3–5 minutes. Transfer mixture to a 7-cup glass dish. Toss in potatoes, ghee, garlic, salt, and pepper.
2. Insert trivet into Instant Pot. Pour in water. Place dish on trivet. Lock lid.
3. Press the Manual button and adjust time to 5 minutes. When the timer beeps, let the pressure release naturally until the float valve drops. Remove dish from pot and serve.

Ham And Swiss Muffin Frittatas

Servings:3 | Cooking Time: 15 Minutes

Ingredients:
- 1 tablespoon olive oil
- ¼ cup small-diced ham
- ¼ cup diced red bell pepper, seeded
- 4 large eggs
- ½ teaspoon sea salt
- ½ teaspoon ground black pepper
- ¼ cup shredded Swiss cheese

- 1 cup water

Directions:
1. Press the Sauté button on Instant Pot. Heat olive oil. Add ham and bell pepper and stir-fry 3–5 minutes until peppers are tender. Transfer mixture to a small bowl to cool.
2. In a medium bowl, whisk together eggs, salt, pepper, and Swiss cheese. Stir in cooled ham mixture.
3. Place trivet into Instant Pot. Pour in water. Place steamer basket on trivet.
4. Distribute egg mixture evenly among 6 silicone muffin cups. Carefully place cups on steamer basket. Lock lid.
5. Press the Manual button and adjust time to 8 minutes. When timer beeps, quick-release pressure until float valve drops and then unlock lid.
6. Remove frittatas and serve warm.

Egg Muffins To Go

Servings:3 | Cooking Time: 15 Minutes

Ingredients:
- 1 tablespoon olive oil
- 3 pieces bacon, diced
- 1 small onion, peeled and diced
- 4 large eggs
- 2 teaspoons Italian seasoning
- ½ teaspoon sea salt
- ½ teaspoon ground black pepper
- ¼ cup shredded Cheddar cheese
- 1 small Roma tomato, diced
- ¼ cup chopped spinach
- 1 cup water

Directions:
1. Press the Sauté button on Instant Pot. Heat olive oil. Add bacon and onion and stir-fry 3–5 minutes until onions are translucent. Transfer mixture to a small bowl to cool.
2. In a medium bowl, whisk together eggs, Italian seasoning, salt, black pepper, cheese, tomatoes, and spinach. Stir in cooled bacon mixture.
3. Place trivet into Instant Pot. Pour in water. Place steamer basket on trivet.
4. Distribute egg mixture evenly among 6 silicone muffin cups. Carefully place cups on steamer basket. Lock lid.
5. Press the Manual button and adjust time to 8 minutes. When the timer beeps, quick-release pressure until float valve drops and then unlock lid.
6. Remove egg muffins and serve warm.

Breakfast Frittata

Servings: 4 | Cooking Time: 25 Minutes

Ingredients:
- 8 beaten eggs
- 1 cup cherry tomatoes, halved
- 1 tbsp Dijon mustard
- 1 cup mushrooms, chopped
- Salt and pepper to taste
- 1 cup sharp cheddar, grated

Directions:
1. Combine the eggs, mushrooms, mustard, salt, pepper, and ½ cup of cheddar cheese in a bowl. Pour in a greased baking pan and top with the remaining cheddar cheese and cherry tomatoes.

Add 1 cup of water to your Instant Pot and fit in a trivet. Place the baking pan on the trivet.
2. Seal the lid. Select Manual and cook for 15 minutes on High. When ready, perform a quick pressure release and unlock the lid. Slice into wedges before serving.

Cinnamon Roll Doughnut Holes

Servings:14 | Cooking Time: 16 Minutes

Ingredients:
- 1 package Krusteaz Cinnamon Roll Supreme Mix (includes icing packet)
- 6 tablespoons unsalted butter, melted
- ½ cup cold water
- ¼ cup chopped pecans
- 1 cup water

Directions:
1. In a medium bowl, combine dry mix, butter, and ½ cup cold water. Fold in pecans. Spoon half of batter into a greased seven-hole silicone egg mold. If your egg mold has a silicone top, use this. If your egg mold came with a plastic top, do not use. Instead, cover with aluminum foil.
2. Add 1 cup water to the Instant Pot and insert steam rack. Place egg mold on steam rack. Lock lid.
3. Press the Manual or Pressure Cook button and adjust time to 8 minutes. When timer beeps, quick-release pressure until float valve drops. Unlock lid.
4. Pop doughnut holes out of egg mold and repeat with remaining batter.
5. When doughnut holes are cooled, mix icing packet with 1 ½ tablespoons water and dip doughnut holes into glaze to cover. Serve.

Banana Nut Muffins

Servings:6 | Cooking Time: 9 Minutes

Ingredients:
- 1 ¼ cups all-purpose baking flour
- 2 teaspoons baking powder
- ½ teaspoon baking soda
- ⅛ teaspoon salt
- ½ teaspoon vanilla extract
- 3 tablespoons unsalted butter, melted
- 2 large eggs
- ¼ cup granulated sugar
- 2 medium ripe bananas, peeled and mashed with a fork
- ¼ cup chopped walnuts
- 1 cup water

Directions:
1. Grease six silicone cupcake liners.
2. In a large bowl, combine flour, baking powder, baking soda, and salt.
3. In a medium bowl, combine vanilla, butter, eggs, sugar, and bananas.
4. Pour wet ingredients from medium bowl into large bowl with dry ingredients. Gently combine ingredients. Do not overmix. Fold in walnuts, then spoon mixture into prepared cupcake liners.
5. Add water to the Instant Pot and insert steam rack. Place cupcake liners on top. Lock lid.
6. Press the Manual or Pressure Cook button and adjust time to 9 minutes. When timer beeps, quick-release pressure until float

valve drops. Unlock lid.
7. Remove muffins from pot and set aside to cool 30 minutes.
Serve.

Chicken Sandwiches With Barbecue Sauce

Servings: 4 | Cooking Time: 50 Minutes

Ingredients:
- 4 chicken thighs, boneless and skinless
- 2 cups barbecue sauce
- 1 onion, minced
- 2 garlic cloves, minced
- 2 tbsp minced fresh parsley
- 1 tbsp lemon juice
- 1 tbsp mayonnaise
- 2 cups lettuce, shredded
- 4 burger buns

Directions:
1. Into the pot, place the garlic, onion, and barbecue sauce. Add in the chicken and toss it to coat. Seal the lid and cook on High Pressure for 15 minutes. Do a natural release for 10 minutes. Use two forks to shred the chicken and mix it into the sauce. Press Keep Warm and let the mixture simmer for 15 minutes to thicken the sauce until the desired consistency.
2. In a bowl, mix lemon juice, mayonnaise, and parsley; toss lettuce into the mixture to coat. Separate the chicken into equal parts to match the burger buns; top with lettuce and complete the sandwiches.

Ricotta & Potato Breakfast

Servings: 4 | Cooking Time: 25 Minutes

Ingredients:
- 2 tbsp olive oil
- 1 lb potatoes, chopped
- 5 eggs, whisked
- 1 cup ricotta, crumbled
- ½ tsp dried oregano
- 1 tsp dried onion flakes
- Salt and pepper to taste

Directions:
1. Warm the olive oil in your Instant Pot on Sauté.
2. Place the potatoes and cook for 3-4 minutes. Add in eggs, ricotta cheese, oregano, dried onion flakes, ¼ cup of water, salt, and pepper.
3. Seal the lid, select Manual, and cook for 10 minutes on High pressure.
4. Once ready, perform a quick pressure release and unlock the lid. Serve immediately.

Smoked Salmon & Egg Muffins

Servings: 2 | Cooking Time: 15 Minutes

Ingredients:
- 4 beaten eggs
- 2 salmon slices, chopped
- 4 tbsp mozzarella, shredded
- 1 green onion, chopped

Directions:
1. Beat eggs, salmon, mozzarella cheese, and onion in a bowl. Share into ramekins. Pour 1 cup of water into your Instant Pot and fit in a trivet.
2. Place the tins on top of the trivet and seal the lid. Select Manual and cook for 8 minutes on High pressure. Once done, let sit for 2 minutes, then perform a quick pressure release and unlock the lid. Serve immediately.

Chapter 4 : Appetizers, Soups & Sides Recipes

Chapter 4 : Appetizers, Soups & Sides Recipes

Rosemary Potato Fries

Servings: 4 | Cooking Time: 15 Minutes

Ingredients:
- 1 lb potatoes, cut into ½ inch sticks
- Sea salt to taste
- 4 tbsp olive oil
- 2 tbsp rosemary, chopped

Directions:
1. Place 1 cup of water in your Instant Pot and fit in a steamer basket. Place the potatoes in the basket and seal the lid. Select Manual and cook for 3 minutes on High.
2. Once ready, perform a quick pressure release. Unlock the lid. Remove potatoes to a bowl and pat them dry.
3. Discard the water and dry the pot. Warm the olive oil in the pot on Sauté. Place the potato sticks and cook until golden brown. Sprinkle with salt and rosemary to serve.

Crab And Artichoke Dip

Servings:8 | Cooking Time: 10 Minutes

Ingredients:
- 16 ounces cream cheese, room temperature
- ⅛ cup sour cream, room temperature
- ½ cup minced onion
- ½ cup seeded and finely diced red bell pepper
- ½ teaspoon Worcestershire sauce
- 2 teaspoons prepared horseradish
- 1 teaspoon Old Bay Seasoning
- 1 teaspoon sriracha
- 1 cup diced canned artichoke hearts
- ¾ pounds lump crabmeat
- 2 teaspoons lemon zest
- ¼ teaspoon ground black pepper
- ¼ cup freshly grated Parmesan cheese, divided
- 2 cups water

Directions:
1. Using the tines of two forks, cream together cream cheese and sour cream in a medium bowl until smooth. Add remaining ingredients except ⅛ cup Parmesan cheese and 2 cups water and combine. Spoon into a 7-cup glass dish. Sprinkle top with remaining cheese.
2. Insert trivet into Instant Pot and pour in 2 cups water. Place glass dish on trivet. Lock lid.
3. Press the Manual button and adjust time to 10 minutes. When timer beeps, quick-release the pressure until float valve drops and then unlock lid. Remove dish and serve warm.

Split Pea Soup With Ham

Servings:4 | Cooking Time: 35 Minutes

Ingredients:
- 1 tablespoon olive oil
- 1 large sweet onion, peeled and diced
- 2 medium stalks celery, diced
- 2 large carrots, peeled and diced
- 1 ½ cups dried green split peas, rinsed
- 5 cups chicken broth
- 1 teaspoon Italian seasoning
- 1 pound smoked ham hock
- ½ teaspoon salt
- ½ teaspoon ground black pepper

Directions:
1. Press the Sauté button on the Instant Pot and heat oil. Add onion, celery, and carrots. Sauté 3–5 minutes until onions are translucent. Add split peas, broth, Italian seasoning, ham hock, salt, and pepper. Press the Cancel button. Lock lid.
2. Press the Soup button and let cook for the default time of 30 minutes. When timer beeps, release pressure naturally for 5 minutes. Quick-release any additional pressure until float valve drops. Unlock lid. Pull ham off of the bone and chop ham into soup.
3. Ladle soup into four bowls. Serve warm.

Kale & Parmesan Omelet

Servings: 6 | Cooking Time: 20 Minutes

Ingredients:
- 6 large eggs
- 2 tbsp heavy cream
- ½ tsp freshly grated nutmeg
- Salt and pepper to taste
- 1 ½ cups kale, chopped
- ¼ cup grated Parmesan

Directions:
1. In a bowl, beat eggs, heavy cream, nutmeg, salt, pepper, kale, and Parmesan. Place egg mixture into a greased baking pan. Pour in 1 cup of water and set a steamer rack over. Lay the pan onto the rack. Seal the lid and cook for 10 minutes on High. Release the pressure quickly. Serve.

Ham Omelet With Red Bell Pepper

Servings: 2 | Cooking Time: 20 Minutes

Ingredients:
- 1 red bell pepper, chopped
- 4 eggs, beaten
- 2 tbsp olive oil
- 2 garlic cloves, crushed
- ½ cup ham, chopped
- 1 tsp Italian seasoning

Directions:
1. Grease the pot with olive oil. Stir-fry the pepper and garlic for 5 minutes. Mix the eggs with ham and season with Italian seasoning. Pour the mixture into the pot and cook for 2-3 minutes, or until set. Using a spatula, loosen the edges and gently slide onto a plate. Fold over to serve.

Feta & Onion Layered Potatoes

Servings: 4 | Cooking Time: 30 Minutes

Ingredients:
- 1 tbsp butter, melted
- 1 lb potatoes, sliced
- ½ tsp garlic powder
- ½ lb onions, finely sliced
- 1 cup feta cheese, grated
- Salt and pepper to taste
- 2 tbsp scallions, chopped

Directions:
1. Pour 1 cup of water into your Instant Pot and fit in a trivet. Add a layer of potatoes on a greased baking pan, sprinkle with salt and pepper, then add onions and half of the feta cheese. Top with another layer of potatoes and finish with the remaining feta cheese. Sprinkle with garlic powder and drizzle melted butter all over.
2. Cover with aluminum foil and lower the pan onto the trivet. Seal the lid, select Manual, and cook for 20 minutes on High. When done, perform a quick pressure release and unlock the lid. Garnish with scallions and serve.

Chowder With Broccoli, Carrot & Tofu

Servings: 4 | Cooking Time: 35 Minutes

Ingredients:
- 1 head broccoli, chopped
- 1 carrot, chopped
- 2 tbsp sesame oil
- 1 onion, chopped
- 2 garlic cloves
- 1 cup soy milk
- 2 cups vegetable broth
- ¼ cup tofu, crumbled
- A pinch of salt

Directions:
1. Heat oil on Sauté. Add onion and garlic and stir-fry for 2 minutes, or until translucent. Pour in broth, a cup of water, broccoli, salt, and carrot. Seal the lid and cook on Manual/Pressure Cook for 5 minutes on High. Do a quick release. Stir in the soy milk and transfer to a food processor. Pulse until creamy. Serve with crumbled tofu.

Paprika Chicken Wings

Servings: 4 | Cooking Time: 25 Minutes

Ingredients:
- 2 lb chicken wings
- ¼ cup olive oil
- 2 garlic cloves, crushed
- 1 tbsp rosemary, chopped
- Salt and pepper to taste
- 1 tsp paprika
- 1 tbsp grated ginger
- ¼ cup lime juice
- ½ cup apple cider vinegar

Directions:
1. In a bowl, mix oil, garlic, rosemary, white pepper, salt, paprika, ginger, lime juice, and apple cider vinegar. Submerge wings into the mixture and cover. Refrigerate for one hour. Remove the wings from the marinade and pat dry.
2. Insert the steaming rack, 1 cup of water, and place the chicken on the rack. Seal the lid and cook on High Pressure for 8 minutes. Release the steam naturally for about 10 minutes. Serve with fresh vegetable salad.

Classic Baba Ghanoush

Servings:1 | Cooking Time: 10 Minutes

Ingredients:
- 1 tablespoon sesame oil
- 1 large eggplant, peeled and diced
- 4 cloves garlic, peeled and minced
- ½ cup water
- ¼ cup chopped fresh parsley, divided
- ¼ teaspoon ground cumin
- ½ teaspoon salt
- 2 tablespoons fresh lemon juice
- 2 tablespoons tahini
- 1 tablespoon olive oil
- ¼ teaspoon paprika

Directions:
1. Press the Sauté button on Instant Pot. Heat sesame oil. Add eggplant and stir-fry for 4–5 minutes until it softens. Add garlic and cook for an additional minute. Add water. Lock lid.
2. Press the Manual button and adjust time to 4 minutes. When timer beeps, let pressure release naturally until float valve drops and then unlock lid.
3. Strain the cooked eggplant and garlic. Add to a food processor or blender along with ⅛ cup parsley, cumin, salt, lemon juice, and tahini. Pulse to process. Add the olive oil and process until smooth. Transfer to a serving dish and garnish with remaining ⅛ cup chopped parsley and sprinkle with paprika.

Cheesy Jalapeño Sweet Potatoes

Servings: 4 | Cooking Time: 35 Minutes

Ingredients:
- 1 lb sweet potatoes, sliced
- 2 tbsp olive oil
- Salt to taste
- 1 jalapeño pepper, sliced

Directions:
1. Pour 1 cup of water into your Instant Pot and fit in a steamer basket. Place in the sweet potatoes and seal the lid. Select Manual and cook for 15 minutes on High.
2. Once ready, perform a quick pressure release and unlock the lid. Warm the olive oil in the pot on Sauté. Add in sweet potatoes and Sauté for 3-5 minutes. Sprinkle salt and pepper. Serve scattered with jalapeño slices.

Sparerib Nachos

Servings:8 | Cooking Time: 40 Minutes

Ingredients:
- 3 pounds pork spareribs, cut into 2-rib sections
- 2 cups beef broth
- 1 packet taco seasoning mix
- 1 bag tortilla chips
- 2 cups shredded Cheddar cheese
- 3 medium Roma tomatoes, diced

Directions:
1. Add ribs, broth, and taco seasoning to the Instant Pot. Lock lid.
2. Press the Manual or Pressure Cook button and adjust time to 40 minutes. When timer beeps, let pressure release naturally for 10 minutes. Quick-release any additional pressure until float valve drops. Unlock lid. When cool enough to handle, use two forks to shred pork off of bones. Discard bones.
3. Scatter chips on a serving platter. Using a slotted spoon, place rib meat over chips. Add cheese and tomatoes. Serve immediately.

Chicken & Noodle Soup

Servings: 2 | Cooking Time: 35 Minutes

Ingredients:
- 8 oz egg noodles
- 2 Carrots, sliced
- 1 tbsp Olive Oil
- 1 small onion, chopped
- 2 Celery Ribs, diced
- 1 Banana Pepper, minced
- 1 garlic clove, minced
- 1 small Bay Leaf
- 2 Chicken Breasts
- 3 cups Chicken Broth

Directions:
1. Warm olive oil in your Instant Pot on Sauté. Place the onion, celery, carrots, garlic, and banana pepper and cook for 4 minutes. Add in bay leaf, chicken, and broth. Seal the lid, select Manual, and cook for 15 minutes on High. When done, perform a quick pressure release. Transfer the chicken onto a cutting board and shred it. Put the chicken back in the pot with the egg noodles and cook for 7-8 minutes on Sauté. Serve.

Chorizo & Bean Soup

Servings: 6 | Cooking Time: 55 Minutes

Ingredients:
- 2 tbsp olive oil
- ¾ lb chorizo sausage, sliced
- 1 cup white beans, soaked
- 1 sweet pepper, sliced
- 14 oz can diced tomatoes
- 1 clove garlic, minced
- 1 onion, diced
- ½ tsp dried oregano
- 1 tsp chili powder
- 6 cups chicken broth

Directions:
1. Warm the olive oil in your Instant Pot on Sauté. Add in onion, garlic, chorizo, sweet pepper, chili powder, and oregano and cook for 4-5 minutes. Stir in chicken broth, tomatoes, and white bean and seal the lid. Select Manual and cook for 30 minutes. Once ready, perform a quick pressure release and let sit for 10 minutes. Serve warm.

Pea & Garbanzo Bean Soup

Servings: 4 | Cooking Time: 30 Minutes

Ingredients:
- 2 tbsp olive oil
- ½ cup shallots, sliced
- 14 oz can garbanzo beans
- ½ cup green peas
- 2 Roma chopped tomatoes
- 4 cups vegetable broth
- Salt and pepper to taste
- 1 lemon, zested and juiced

Directions:
1. Warm the olive oil in your Instant Pot on Sauté. Add in shallots and cook for 3 minutes until tender and fragrant. Pour in vegetable broth, tomatoes, lemon zest, and garbanzo beans and stir.
2. Seal the lid, select Manual, and cook for 10 minutes on High pressure. Once over, allow a natural release for 10 minutes, then perform a quick pressure release and unlock the lid. Stir in green peas and let it sit covered in the residual heat until warmed through. Season with salt and pepper and drizzle with lemon juice. Serve.

Dill Potatoes With Butter & Olives

Servings: 4 | Cooking Time: 40 Minutes

Ingredients:
- 1 lb potatoes, chopped
- 2 tbsp butter
- 2 tbsp dill, chopped
- 1 tsp sea salt flakes
- 3 tbsp sliced Kalamata olives

Directions:
1. Cover the potatoes with enough water in your Instant Pot and seal the lid. Select Manual and cook for 12 minutes on High pressure. Once over, allow a natural release for 10 minutes, then perform a quick pressure release, and unlock the lid. Drain potatoes and leave them to dry.
2. Press Sauté and melt the butter. Put the dried potatoes back and

cook for 3-4 minutes until lightly browned. Remove to a serving bowl and add in Kalamata olives; toss to combine. Sprinkle with dill and salt and serve.

Senate Bean Soup

Servings:4 | Cooking Time: 45 Minutes

Ingredients:
- ½ pound dried great northern beans, rinsed and drained
- 4 cups chicken broth
- 1 cup water
- 1 small yellow onion, peeled and diced
- 3 medium stalks celery, sliced
- ½ teaspoon garlic salt
- 1 smoked ham hock
- 2 tablespoons Italian seasoning

Directions:
1. Place all ingredients in the Instant Pot and stir to combine. Lock lid.
2. Press the Manual or Pressure Cook button and adjust time to 45 minutes. When timer beeps, let pressure release naturally until float valve drops. Unlock lid.
3. Using two forks, shred meat off of ham bone. Discard bone.
4. Ladle soup into bowls. Serve warm.

Mascarpone Mashed Turnips

Servings: 4 | Cooking Time: 32 Minutes

Ingredients:
- 1 lb turnips, cubed
- 1 onion, chopped
- ½ tsp ground nutmeg
- ½ cup chicken stock
- Salt and pepper to taste
- ¼ cup sour cream
- 2 tbsp mascarpone

Directions:
1. Place the turnips, onion, and chicken stock in your Instant Pot and seal the lid. Select Manual and cook for 12 minutes on High. Once over, allow a natural release for 10 minutes and unlock the lid. Add in sour cream, nutmeg, and mascarpone and mash it using a potato masher until smooth. Sprinkle with salt and pepper.

Saucy Carrots With Crispy Bacon

Servings: 4 | Cooking Time: 20 Minutes

Ingredients:
- 3 slices bacon, crumbled
- 2 lb carrots, chopped
- ½ cup orange juice
- ¼ cup olive oil
- 1 tsp honey
- 1 tsp salt
- 2 tsp cornstarch
- 1 tbsp cold water

Directions:
1. Fry the bacon on Sauté until crispy, about 5 minutes. Set aside. In a bowl, mix salt, olive oil, orange juice, and honey; add the mixture and carrots to the pot and mix well to coat. Seal the lid, and cook for 6 minutes on High Pressure. Release the pressure quickly. Transfer carrots to a serving dish. Press Cancel, then press Sauté. In a bowl, mix cold water and cornstarch until dissolved. Add to the liquid remaining in the cooker. Simmer sauce as you stir for 2 minutes to obtain a thick and smooth consistency. Spoon the sauce over the carrots and scatter over the bacon. Serve.

Celery-cauliflower Soup With Blue Cheese

Servings: 5 | Cooking Time: 20 Minutes

Ingredients:
- 2 tbsp butter
- ½ tbsp olive oil
- 1 onion, chopped
- 2 stalks celery, chopped
- 10 oz cauliflower florets
- 1 potato, finely diced
- 3 cups vegetable broth
- Salt and pepper to taste
- 2 cups milk
- 1 bay leaf
- 4 oz blue cheese, crumbled

Directions:
1. Warm oil and butter on Sauté. Add celery and onion and sauté for 3-5 minutes until fragrant. Stir in half the cauliflower and cook for 5 minutes until golden brown. Add in broth, bay leaf, potato, and the remaining cauliflower. Seal the lid. Cook on High Pressure for 5 minutes. Release the pressure quickly.
2. Remove the bay leaf. Puree the soup with an immersion blender until smooth. Stir in the milk. Adjust the seasoning. Top with blue cheese before serving.

Orange Glazed Carrots

Servings: 4 | Cooking Time: 25 Minutes

Ingredients:
- 1 tbsp butter
- 6 carrots, sliced diagonally
- ¼ tsp orange zest
- ½ cup orange juice
- 1 tbsp orange marmalade
- Salt and black pepper to taste

Directions:
1. Pour 1 cup of water into your Instant Pot and fit in a steamer basket. Place in the carrots and seal the lid. Select Manual and cook for 8 minutes on High. When done, perform a quick release. Remove carrots to a bowl.
2. Clean the pot and melt in the butter on Sauté. Add in orange zest, orange juice, orange marmalade, salt, and pepper and stir to combine. Add in carrots and cook until they are caramelized and sticky, 5-8 minutes. Serve.

Fall Vegetable Soup

Servings: 4 | Cooking Time: 35 Minutes

Ingredients:
- 2 tbsp olive oil
- 1 onion, chopped
- 2 carrots, chopped
- 1 cup celery, chopped
- 2 cloves garlic, minced
- 5 cups vegetable broth
- 2 turnips, chopped
- 28 oz canned tomatoes
- 15 oz can garbanzo beans
- 1 cup frozen green peas
- 2 bay leaves
- 1 sprig fresh sage
- Salt and pepper to taste
- ¼ cup Parmesan, grated

Directions:
1. On Sauté, warm oil, stir in celery, carrots, and onion, and cook for 4 minutes until soft. Add in garlic and cook for 30 seconds. Add in vegetable broth, turnips, garbanzo beans, bay leaves, tomatoes, pepper, salt, peas, and sage.
2. Seal the lid and cook on High Pressure for 12 minutes. Allow natural pressure release for 10 minutes. Carefully unlock the lid. Serve topped with Parmesan cheese.

Nutmeg Broccoli Soup With Cheddar

Servings: 4 | Cooking Time: 25 Minutes

Ingredients:
- 2 garlic cloves, minced
- 1 tbsp butter
- ½ lb broccoli florets
- ¼ tsp nutmeg
- ½ tsp garlic powder
- 1 cup vegetable broth
- ¼ cup grated cheddar
- ¼ cup chopped onion
- ¼ tsp paprika
- Salt and pepper to taste

Directions:
1. Melt butter in your Instant Pot on Sauté. Place the onion and garlic and cook until wilted and aromatic. Put in vegetable broth, broccoli, black pepper, paprika, salt, nutmeg, and garlic powder. Seal the lid, select Manual, and cook for 5 minutes on High pressure.
2. When done, allow a natural release for 10 minutes and unlock the lid. Using an immersion blender, pulse the soup until smooth. Divide between bowls and serve.

Chicken & Potato Soup

Servings: 4 | Cooking Time: 45 Minutes

Ingredients:
- 2 tbsp olive oil
- ½ lb chicken thighs
- 2 potatoes, cut into chunks
- 1 carrot, cut into chunks
- 1 yellow onion, diced
- 2 garlic cloves, minced
- 1 celery rib, chopped
- 4 cups chicken bone broth
- Salt and pepper to taste
- 2 tbsp parsley, chopped

Directions:
1. Heat oil in your Instant Pot on Sauté and cook onion, carrot, celery, and garlic for 3 minutes. Add in chicken and Sauté for 4-5 minutes. Pour in broth and potatoes and seal the lid. Select Manual and cook for 15 minutes on High. Once ready, allow a natural release for 10 minutes. Adjust the taste and top with parsley. Serve.

Frittata With Vegetables & Cheese

Servings: 4 | Cooking Time: 30 Minutes

Ingredients:
- 4 eggs
- 8 oz spinach, finely chopped
- ½ cup cheddar, shredded
- ½ cup ricotta, crumbled
- 3 cherry tomatoes, halved
- ¼ cup bell pepper, chopped
- 1 cup chopped broccoli
- 4 tbsp olive oil
- Salt and pepper to taste
- ¼ tsp dried oregano
- 2 tsp celery leaves, chopped

Directions:
1. Heat olive oil on Sauté. Add spinach and cook for 5 minutes, stirring occasionally. Add tomatoes, peppers, and broccoli and stir-fry for 3-4 more minutes. In a bowl, Whisk eggs, cheddar cheese, and ricotta cheese. Pour in the pot and cook for 5-7 minutes. Season with salt, black pepper, and oregano; press Cancel. Serve with celery.

Buttered Egg Noodles

Servings:6 | Cooking Time: 4 Minutes

Ingredients:
- 1 bag egg noodles
- 3 tablespoons butter
- ¼ cup grated Parmesan cheese
- ½ teaspoon sea salt
- ¼ teaspoon ground black pepper
- ¼ cup chopped fresh parsley

Directions:
1. Place noodles in an even layer in Instant Pot. Pour enough water to come about ¼" over pasta. Lock lid.
2. Press the Manual button and adjust time to 4 minutes. When timer beeps, unplug the Instant Pot and let pressure release naturally for 3 minutes. Quick-release any additional pressure until float valve drops and then unlock lid.
3. Drain any residual water. Toss pasta with butter, Parmesan cheese, salt, pepper, and parsley. Serve immediately.

Chipotle & Garlic Mashed Potatoes

Servings: 4 | Cooking Time: 25 Minutes

Ingredients:
- 1 lb potatoes, cubed
- 2 garlic cloves
- 1 tbsp chipotle paste
- 1 cup chicken broth
- ¼ cup milk
- 1 tbsp butter
- 1 tbsp chili oil
- Salt to taste

Directions:
1. Place the potatoes, garlic, and chicken broth in your Instant Pot and seal the lid. Select Manual and cook for 15 minutes on High pressure. When done, perform a quick pressure release and unlock the lid.
2. Drain potatoes and transfer to a bowl. Add in milk, chipotle paste, chili oil, and butter and mash them using a potato masher until smooth. Sprinkle with salt. Serve.

Cheesy Vegetable Medley

Servings: 4 | Cooking Time: 20 Minutes

Ingredients:
- 2 tbsp canola oil
- 1 red onion, sliced
- 1 cup broccoli florets
- 2 red bell peppers, sliced
- 2 green bell pepper, sliced
- 1 yellow bell peppers, sliced
- 2 tomatoes, chopped
- Salt and pepper to taste
- 2 garlic cloves, minced
- 2 tbsp parsley, chopped
- 3 tbsp mozzarella, shredded

Directions:
1. Warm the canola oil in your Instant Pot on Sauté. Place the onion and garlic and cook for 3 minutes until softened. Add in bell peppers and Sauté for 5 minutes.
2. Stir in tomatoes, broccoli, salt, and pepper and seal the lid. Select Manual and cook for 2 minutes on High pressure. When done, perform a quick pressure release and unlock the lid. Remove the vegetables to a bowl and top with mozzarella cheese and parsley. Serve immediately.

Creamy Chicken Soup

Servings:4 | Cooking Time: 25 Minutes

Ingredients:
- 1 pound bone-in chicken thighs, cut in ½" cubes (save bones)
- 1 teaspoon salt
- ½ teaspoon ground black pepper
- 2 tablespoons unsalted butter
- 1 small yellow onion, peeled and diced
- 1 large carrot, peeled and diced
- 4 cups chicken broth
- 1 tablespoon Italian seasoning
- ½ cup heavy cream

Directions:
1. Season chicken with salt and pepper.
2. Press the Sauté button on the Instant Pot. Add butter and heat until melted. Add chicken, onion, and carrot. Sauté 3–5 minutes until onions are translucent. Add broth, Italian seasoning, and chicken bones. Press the Cancel button. Lock lid.
3. Press the Soup button and adjust time to 20 minutes. When timer beeps, let pressure release naturally for 10 minutes. Quick-release any additional pressure until float valve drops. Unlock lid. Remove and discard chicken bones.
4. Stir in cream. Ladle soup into bowls. Serve warm.

Moroccan Lentil Soup

Servings: 4 | Cooking Time: 30 Minutes

Ingredients:
- 2 tsp olive oil
- 2 garlic cloves, minced
- 1 onion, chopped
- 1 cup red lentils
- 2 tbsp tomato purée
- 1 potato, chopped
- 1 carrot, chopped
- ½ cup celery
- ½ tsp ground coriander
- ½ tsp ground cumin
- ½ tsp cinnamon
- 1 red chili pepper, chopped
- 4 cups water
- Salt and pepper to taste
- 2 tbsp fresh mint, chopped

Directions:
1. Warm olive oil in your Instant Pot on Sauté. Add in garlic, celery, carrot, and onion and cook for 3 minutes. Stir in chili pepper, tomato puree, ground coriander, cumin, salt, pepper, and cinnamon and cook for 1 minute. Pour in lentils, potato, and 4 cups of water and stir.
2. Seal the lid, select Manual, and cook for 10 minutes on High pressure. When done, allow a natural release for 10 minutes and unlock the lid. Sprinkle with mint and serve.

Garlic Eggplants With Parmesan

Servings: 4 | Cooking Time: 20 Minutes

Ingredients:
- 2 tbsp olive oil
- 1 onion, chopped
- 3 garlic cloves, minced
- 1 lb eggplants, cubed
- Salt and pepper to taste
- 1 cup tomato sauce
- ½ tsp dried oregano
- ¼ cup Parmesan, grated

Directions:
1. Warm the olive oil in your Instant Pot on Sauté. Place the onion and garlic and cook for 3 minutes. Add in the eggplants, salt, pepper, tomato sauce, oregano, and ½ of water. Season with salt and pepper.
2. Seal the lid, select Manual, and cook for 8 minutes on High. Once ready, perform a quick pressure release and unlock the lid. Serve topped with Parmesan cheese.

Beef Layer Tart With Yogurt

Servings: 6 | Cooking Time: 30 Minutes

Ingredients:
- 2 lb lean ground beef
- 4 garlic cloves, minced
- Salt and pepper to taste
- 1 pack pie dough
- ½ tbsp butter, melted
- 1 tbsp sour cream
- 3 cups liquid yogurt

Directions:
1. In a bowl, mix beef, garlic, salt, and pepper until fully incorporated. Lay a sheet of dough on a flat surface and brush with melted butter. Line with the meat mixture and roll-up. Repeat the process until you have used all the ingredients. Grease a baking dish and carefully place the rolls inside. In your Instant Pot, pour in 1 ½ cups of water and place a trivet. Lay the baking dish on the trivet.
2. Seal the lid and cook on High Pressure for 15 minutes. When ready, do a quick pressure release. Transfer the pie to a serving plate. Mix sour cream and yogurt. Spread the mixture over the pie and serve cold.

Lamb Stew

Servings:4 | Cooking Time: 44 Minutes

Ingredients:
- ¼ cup all-purpose flour
- 1 pound cubed boneless lamb
- 2 tablespoons olive oil
- 1 medium yellow onion, peeled and diced
- 2 large carrots, sliced into ½" sections
- 4 cups beef broth
- 1 can fire-roasted diced tomatoes, including juice
- 2 large Yukon gold potatoes, peeled and cut into ¾" cubes
- 2 teaspoons Italian seasoning
- 1 teaspoon salt
- ½ teaspoon ground black pepper

Directions:
1. In a medium bowl, toss flour and lamb cubes until lamb is coated.
2. Press the Sauté button on the Instant Pot and heat oil. Add lamb cubes, searing on all sides for a total of 6 minutes. Set lamb aside. Add onion and carrots and stir-fry 2–3 minutes until onions are translucent.
3. Add broth and deglaze by scraping any bits from the bottom and sides of pot. Stir in remaining ingredients, including lamb. Press the Cancel button. Lock lid.
4. Press the Meat button and cook for the default time of 35 minutes. When timer beeps, let pressure release naturally until float valve drops. Unlock lid.
5. Ladle stew into individual bowls. Serve warm.

Hazelnut Brussels Sprouts With Parmesan

Servings: 4 | Cooking Time: 15 Minutes

Ingredients:
- 1 lb Brussels sprouts, halved
- 2 tbsp butter
- 2 garlic cloves, minced
- ¼ cup hazelnuts, chopped
- ½ tsp thyme
- ¼ cup grated Parmesan cheese
- Salt and pepper to taste

Directions:
1. Pour 1 cup of water into your Instant Pot and fit in a steamer basket. Place in the sprouts halves and seal the lid. Select Manual and cook for 3 minutes on High.
2. Once ready, perform a quick pressure release. Unlock the lid. Clean the pot and melt the butter on Sauté. Add in Brussels sprouts and garlic and Sauté for 2-3 minutes, stirring occasionally. Season with salt, pepper, and thyme and mix in hazelnuts. Serve topped with Parmesan cheese.

Mushroom & Spinach Chicken Stew

Servings: 4 | Cooking Time: 40 Minutes

Ingredients:
- 1 ¼ lb white Button mushrooms, halved
- 1 celery stalk, chopped
- 3 tbsp olive oil
- 4 chicken breasts, diced
- 1 onion, sliced
- 5 garlic cloves, minced
- Salt and pepper to taste
- 1 ¼ tsp arrowroot starch
- ½ cup spinach, chopped
- 1 bay leaf
- 1 ½ cup chicken stock
- 1 tsp Dijon mustard
- 1 ½ cup sour cream
- 3 tbsp chopped parsley

Directions:
1. Warm olive oil in your Instant Pot on Sauté. Place the onion and cook for 3 minutes. Stir in mushrooms, chicken, celery, garlic, bay leaf, salt, black pepper, Dijon mustard, and chicken broth. Seal the lid, select Meat/Stew, and cook for 15 minutes on High. When done, allow a natural release for 10 minutes and unlock the lid.
2. Discard bay leaf. In a bowl, combine some cooking liquid with arrowroot starch until any lump left. Pour it into the pot and stir until the sauce thickens. Add in sour cream and spinach and let sit for 4 minutes. Divide between bowls and sprinkle with parsley. Serve with squash mash.

Chickpea Hummus

Servings:10 | Cooking Time: 35 Minutes

Ingredients:
- 1 cup dried chickpeas
- 3 tablespoons olive oil, divided
- 2 cups water
- 2 cups vegetable broth
- ¼ cup tahini
- Juice of 1 lemon
- 1 teaspoon lemon zest
- 1 teaspoon salt
- 3 cloves garlic, minced
- 2 teaspoons smoked paprika

Directions:
1. Rinse and drain chickpeas.
2. Press the Sauté button on Instant Pot. Heat 1 tablespoon olive oil. Toss in chickpeas and sauté for 2 minutes. Add water and vegetable broth. Lock lid.
3. Press the Bean button and cook for the default time of 30 minutes. When timer beeps, let pressure release naturally for 10 minutes. Quick-release any additional pressure until the float valve drops and then unlock lid.
4. Using a slotted spoon, transfer pot ingredients to a food processor or blender. Pulse. Add tahini, lemon juice, lemon zest, salt, and garlic. Add some of the cooking liquid from the Instant Pot if hummus is too thick.
5. Transfer to a serving bowl and garnish with smoked paprika and remaining 2 tablespoons olive oil.

Yummy Vegetable Soup

Servings: 4 | Cooking Time: 25 Minutes

Ingredients:
- 2 tbsp olive oil
- 1 cup leeks, chopped
- 2 garlic cloves, minced
- 4 cups vegetable stock
- 1 carrot, diced
- 1 parsnip, diced
- 1 celery stalk, diced
- 1 cup mushrooms
- 1 cup broccoli florets
- 1 cup cauliflower florets
- ½ red bell pepper, diced
- ¼ head cabbage, chopped
- ½ cup green beans
- 2 tbsp nutritional yeast
- Salt and pepper to taste
- ½ cup parsley, chopped

Directions:
1. Heat oil on Sauté. Add in garlic and leeks and cook for 6 minutes until slightly browned. Add in stock, carrot, celery, broccoli, bell pepper, green beans, salt, nutritional yeast, cabbage, cauliflower, mushrooms, parsnip, and pepper. Seal the lid and cook on High Pressure for 6 minutes. Release pressure naturally. Stir in parsley to serve.

Green Bean & Feta Salad

Servings: 4 | Cooking Time: 25 Minutes

Ingredients:
- 1 cup feta cheese, crumbled
- 1 lb green beans, washed
- 2 tbsp olive oil
- 2 tbsp white wine vinegar
- 3 garlic cloves, sliced
- Salt and pepper to taste

Directions:
1. Place 1 cup of water in your Instant Pot and fit in a steamer basket. Put in green beans and seal the lid. Select Manual and cook for 2 minutes on High pressure. Whisk olive oil, vinegar, garlic, salt, and pepper in a bowl.
2. Once ready, perform a quick pressure release and unlock the lid. Remove the beans to a bowl and pour in the vinegar mixture. Mix it and let sit for 10 minutes. Discard garlic slices and scatter with feta cheese. Serve.

Cabbage & Pork Soup

Servings: 6 | Cooking Time: 20 Minutes

Ingredients:
- 1 lb ground pork
- 1 onion, diced
- 2 lb napa cabbage, chopped
- 1 potato, diced
- 6 button mushrooms, sliced
- 3 scallions, sliced
- 2 tbsp butter
- 4 cups vegetable broth
- Salt and pepper to taste

Directions:
1. Melt butter on Sauté and add the pork. Cook until it browned, breaking it with a spatula. Once browned, add onion and mushrooms and cook for another 4-5 minutes. Season with salt and pepper. Pour in vegetable broth and stir in cabbage, potato, and scallions. Seal the lid, cook on Pressure Cook for 6 minutes on High. Do a quick release. Carefully unlock the lid. Serve.

Homemade Winter Soup

Servings: 4 | Cooking Time: 40 Minutes

Ingredients:
- 3 sweet potatoes, chopped
- 1 tsp salt
- 2 fennel bulbs, chopped
- 16 oz pureed pumpkin
- 1 large onion, chopped
- 1 tbsp coconut oil
- 4 cups water
- 1 tbsp sour cream

Directions:
1. Heat the oil on Sauté, and add onion and fennel bulbs. Cook for 3-5 minutes until tender. Add sweet potatoes, salt, pumpkin puree, and water, and seal the lid. Cook on High Pressure for 25 minutes. Do a quick release. Carefully unlock the lid. Transfer the soup to a food processor and blend for 20 seconds until creamy. Top with sour cream and serve.

Red Soup With Cheesy Croutons

Servings: 4 | Cooking Time: 1 Hour

Ingredients:
- 2 tbsp olive oil
- 1 onion, chopped
- 2 garlic cloves, minced
- 1 carrot, chopped
- Salt and pepper to taste
- 1 cup vegetable stock
- 28 oz canned tomatoes
- 1 cup heavy cream
- 2 Monterey Jack slices
- 4 bread slices
- 2 gouda cheese slices
- 2 tbsp butter, softened

Directions:
1. Warm oil on Sauté. Stir-fry onion, garlic, carrot, pepper, and salt for 6 minutes until soft. Add in vegetable stock to deglaze. Scrape any brown bits from the pot. Mix the stock with tomatoes. Seal the lid and cook on High Pressure for 30 minutes. Allow for a natural release for 10 minutes. Transfer soup to a blender and process until smooth. Add in heavy cream and stir.
2. Place 1 slice Monterey Jack cheese on 1 bread slice and cover with 1 Gouda cheese slice and the second slice of bread. Brush the bread with butter. Do the same with the rest of the ingredients. Heat a skillet over medium heat. Place the sandwiches on the skillet. Cook each side for 3 to 5 minutes until browned and all cheese melts. Transfer sandwiches to a cutting board and chop them into bite-sized pieces. Divide the soup into serving plates and top with cheese croutons before serving.

Aioli Deviled Eggs

Servings: 4 | Cooking Time: 20 Minutes

Ingredients:
- 1 tbsp aioli
- 8 eggs
- ¼ cup heavy cream
- 1 tbsp Dijon mustard
- Salt and pepper to taste
- 2 tbsp dill, chopped

Directions:
1. Pour 1 cup of water into your Instant Pot and fit in a trivet. Place eggs on the trivet and seal the lid. Select Manual and cook for 5 minutes on High pressure. Once ready, perform a quick pressure release. Remove the eggs and transfer to a bowl with cold water for 2-3 minutes.
2. Peel the eggs, slice them in half lengthwise, and remove the yolks to a bowl. Using a fork, mash the yolks into a fine crumble and combine with heavy cream, aioli, mustard, salt, and pepper. Pour into a pastry bag. Stuff each egg white with the mixture and top with dill.

Egg Bites With Mushrooms & Arugula

Servings: 4 | Cooking Time: 15 Minutes

Ingredients:
- 12 oz button mushrooms, sliced
- 4 oz asiago cheese, shredded
- 8 oz arugula
- 4 eggs
- 2 tbsp butter, melted
- ½ red chili flakes

Directions:
1. Place a trivet in the Instant Pot and pour in 1 cup water. Grease 4 heatproof cups with the butter. In a bowl, whisk the eggs and stir in the mushrooms and arugula. Pour the mixture into the cups. Top with the cheese and chili flakes. Arrange the cups on the trivet. Seal the lid and cook on Manual for 7 minutes. Do a quick release. Serve chilled.

Happy Dip

Servings:8 | Cooking Time: 3 Minutes

Ingredients:
- 8 ounces cream cheese, softened
- 1 tablespoon Italian seasoning
- 6 slices bacon, cooked and crumbled
- 2 cups shredded sharp Cheddar cheese
- 16 ounces sour cream
- 1 medium green onion, sliced (whites and greens separated)
- 1 cup water

Directions:
1. In a medium bowl, combine cream cheese, Italian seasoning, bacon, Cheddar cheese, sour cream, and onion whites. Transfer mixture to a 7-cup glass bowl.
2. Add water to the Instant Pot and insert steam rack. Place glass bowl on steam rack. Lock lid.
3. Press the Manual or Pressure Cook button and adjust time to 3 minutes. When timer beeps, quick-release pressure until float valve drops. Unlock lid.
4. Remove glass baking dish from pot. Garnish with onion greens. Serve warm.

Cheesy & Creamy Broccoli Soup

Servings: 4 | Cooking Time: 25 Minutes

Ingredients:
- 1 ½ cups grated Cheddar Cheese + extra for topping
- 2 tbsp cilantro, chopped
- 1 lb chopped Broccoli
- 3 cups Heavy Cream
- 3 cups Chicken Broth
- 4 tbsp Butter
- 4 tbsp Almond flour
- 1 red onion, chopped
- 3 garlic cloves, minced
- 1 tsp Italian Seasoning
- Salt and pepper to taste
- 4 oz Cream Cheese

Directions:
1. Melt butter in your Instant Pot on Sauté. Place the almond flour and stir until it clumps up. Slowly pour in heavy cream and stir until it gets a sauce. Remove to a bowl. Put the onions, garlic,

chicken broth, broccoli, Italian seasoning, and cream cheese in the pot and stir.

2. Seal the lid, select Soup, and cook for 15 minutes on High pressure. When done, perform a quick pressure release and unlock the lid. Mix in butter sauce and cheddar cheese until the cheese melts. Divide between bowls and top with cheddar cheese. Serve topped with cilantro.

Green Vegetables With Tomatoes

Servings: 6 | Cooking Time: 15 Minutes

Ingredients:
- 1 tsp olive oil
- 1 clove garlic, minced
- 2 cups chopped tomatoes
- ½ cup vegetable stock
- ½ lb green beans, trimmed
- ½ cup green peas
- ½ lb asparagus, trimmed
- Salt and pepper to taste

Directions:
1. Warm the olive oil in your Instant Pot on Sauté. Place in garlic and cook for 30 seconds until fragrant. Stir in tomatoes. Pour in vegetable stock, green beans, green peas, and asparagus; season with salt, and pepper. Seal the lid, select Manual, and cook for 5 minutes on High pressure. When done, perform a quick pressure release.

Brussel Sprout & Pork Soup

Servings: 4 | Cooking Time: 40 Minutes

Ingredients:
- ½ lb Brussels sprouts, shredded
- 1 cup carrot, shredded
- ½ tsp ground ginger
- 1 small onion, chopped
- ½ lb ground pork
- 4 cups chicken broth
- 1 tbsp soy sauce
- 2 tbsp olive oil
- Salt and pepper to taste

Directions:
1. Place the olive oil and ground pork in your Instant Pot and cook for 4-5 minutes until browned on Sauté. Stir in carrot, Brussels sprouts, ginger, onion, chicken broth, soy sauce, salt, and black pepper. Seal the lid, select Manual, and cook for 25 minutes on High pressure. When done, perform a quick pressure release. Serve and enjoy!

Savoy Cabbage Rolls

Servings:20 | Cooking Time: 20 Minutes

Ingredients:
- 1 medium head savoy cabbage
- 3 cups water, divided
- ½ pound ground beef
- 1 cup long-grain rice
- 1 small red bell pepper, seeded and minced
- 1 medium onion, peeled and diced
- 1 cup beef broth
- 1 tablespoon olive oil
- 2 tablespoons minced fresh mint
- 1 teaspoon dried tarragon
- 1 teaspoon salt
- ½ teaspoon ground black pepper
- 2 tablespoons lemon juice

Directions:
1. Wash the cabbage. Remove the large outer leaves and set aside. Remove remaining cabbage leaves and place them in the Instant Pot. Pour in 1 cup water. Lock lid.
2. Press the Steam button and adjust time to 1 minute. Press the Pressure button to change the pressure to Low. When the timer beeps, quick-release the pressure until float valve drops and then unlock lid. Drain the cabbage leaves in a colander and then move them to a cotton towel.
3. In a medium mixing bowl, add the ground beef, rice, bell pepper, onion, broth, olive oil, mint, tarragon, salt, and pepper. Stir to combine.
4. Place the reserved (uncooked) cabbage leaves on the bottom of the Instant Pot.
5. Remove the stem running down the center of each steamed cabbage leaf and tear each leaf in half lengthwise. Place 1 tablespoon of the ground beef mixture in the center of each cabbage piece. Loosely fold the sides of the leaf over the filling and then fold the top and bottom of the leaf over the folded sides. As you complete them, place each stuffed cabbage leaf in the Instant Pot.
6. Pour 2 cups water and the lemon juice over the stuffed cabbage rolls. Lock lid.
7. Press the Manual button and adjust time to 15 minutes. When timer beeps, let pressure release naturally for 10 minutes. Quick-release any additional pressure until float valve drops and then unlock lid.
8. Carefully move the stuffed cabbage rolls to a serving platter. Serve warm.

Chicken Wings With Teriyaki Sauce

Servings: 6 | Cooking Time: 25 Minutes

Ingredients:
- 1 tbsp honey
- 1 cup teriyaki sauce
- 1 tsp black pepper
- 2 lb chicken wings
- 2 tbsp cornstarch
- 1 tsp sesame seeds

Directions:
1. In the pot, combine honey, teriyaki sauce, and black pepper until the honey dissolves. Toss in chicken wings to coat. Seal the lid, press Manual, and cook for 10 minutes on High. Release the pressure quickly. Transfer chicken wings to a platter. Mix 2 tbsp of water with the cornstarch. Press Sauté and stir the slurry into

the sauce. Cook for 4 minutes until thickened. Top the chicken wings with the thickened sauce. Add a garnish of sesame seeds and serve.

Bbq Cocktail Weenies

Servings:8 | Cooking Time: 15 Minutes

Ingredients:
- 1 ½ cups barbecue sauce
- 1 cup Dr Pepper
- 1 tablespoon Dijon mustard
- 1 package beef little smokies

Directions:
1. In a medium bowl, whisk together barbecue sauce, Dr Pepper, and mustard.
2. Add smokies to the Instant Pot. Pour in barbecue sauce mixture. Lock lid.
3. Press the Manual or Pressure Cook button and adjust time to 15 minutes. When timer beeps, quick-release pressure until float valve drops. Unlock lid.
4. Serve warm with toothpicks.

Creamy Creamed Corn

Servings:6 | Cooking Time: 7 Minutes

Ingredients:
- 6 large ears of corn or 8 medium, husked
- ½ cup water
- ½ teaspoon sea salt
- ½ teaspoon ground black pepper
- 4 ounces cream cheese, cubed and room temperature
- 4 tablespoons ghee, cubed and room temperature
- 1 teaspoon sugar
- 1 cup heavy cream
- 1 tablespoon flour

Directions:
1. Cut off the corn kernels from the cob, really scraping the cobs to release that milky substance. Place the kernels, water, salt, pepper, cream cheese, ghee, and sugar in the Instant Pot. Lock lid.
2. Press the Manual button and adjust time to 2 minutes.
3. In a small bowl, whisk together the heavy cream and flour to create a slurry.
4. When timer beeps, quick-release the pressure until the float valve drops and then unlock lid. Add the slurry to the corn in the Instant Pot and stir. Press the Keep Warm button and warm unlidded for 5 minutes to thicken.
5. Transfer to a medium bowl and serve warm.

Chili Corn On The Cob

Servings: 4 | Cooking Time: 10 Minutes

Ingredients:
- 4 ears corn on the cob, husked
- 1 Poblano chili pepper, chopped
- 4 tbsp butter, softened
- 2 tbsp parsley, chopped

Directions:
1. Pour 1 cup of water into your Instant Pot and fit in a trivet. Mix the chili pepper, parsley, and butter in a blender until smooth. Rub the mixture all over the corn and place on the trivet. Seal

the lid, select Manual, and cook for 2 minutes on High pressure. Serve right away.

Potato & Salmon Salad

Servings: 6 | Cooking Time: 20 Minutes

Ingredients:
- ½ lb smoked salmon, chopped
- 6 eggs
- 3 lb red potatoes, cubed
- 2 cups mayonnaise
- 2 tbsp capers
- 1 tbsp chives, chopped
- Salt and pepper to taste

Directions:
1. Pour 1 cup of water into your Instant Pot and fit in a steamer basket. Place in the eggs and potatoes and seal the lid. Select Manual and cook for 5 minutes on High.
2. Once ready, perform a quick pressure release and unlock the lid. Remove the egg to a bowl with iced water and let cool for a few minutes.
3. In another bowl, mix cooked potatoes, mayonnaise, smoked salmon, and capers. Peel and chop the eggs and mix them in the salad bowl. Sprinkle with salt and pepper. Serve topped with chives.

Scallion Chicken & Lentil Soup

Servings: 4 | Cooking Time: 45 Minutes

Ingredients:
- 4 garlic cloves, sliced
- 6 oz skinless chicken thighs
- ½ lb dried lentils
- ½ chopped onion
- 4 cups water
- ¼ tsp paprika
- ½ tsp garlic powder
- 1 diced tomato
- 2 tbsp chopped cilantro
- ¼ tsp oregano
- ½ tsp cumin
- 1 chopped scallion
- ¼ tsp salt

Directions:
1. Place the chicken thighs, dried lentils, onion, water, paprika, garlic powder, sliced garlic, tomato, cilantro, oregano, cumin, scallion, and salt in your Instant Pot. Seal the lid, select Soup, and cook for 30 minutes. When done, allow a natural release for 10 minutes and unlock the lid. Using a fork, shred the chicken before serving.

Easy Veggie Soup

Servings: 4 | Cooking Time: 35 Minutes

Ingredients:
- 1 cup okra, trimmed
- 1 Carrot, sliced
- 1 cup Broccoli florets
- 1 green Bell Pepper, sliced
- 1 red Bell Pepper, sliced
- 1 Onion, sliced
- 2 cups vegetable broth
- 1 tbsp Lemon juice
- 4 Garlic cloves, minced
- Salt and pepper to taste
- 2 tbsp Olive oil

Directions:
1. Warm olive oil in your Instant Pot on Sauté. Place the onion and garlic and cook for 1 minute. Add in carrot, okra, broccoli florets, green bell pepper, and red bell pepper and cook for 5-10 minutes.
2. Stir in vegetable broth, salt, and black pepper and seal the lid. Select Meat/Stew and cook for 15 minutes on High pressure. When done, perform a quick pressure release and unlock the lid. Sprinkle with lemon juice and divide between bowls before serving.

Broccoli & Cherry Tomato Salad

Servings: 4 | Cooking Time: 20 Minutes

Ingredients:
- 2 tbsp olive oil
- 1 cup mushrooms, sliced
- 1 tbsp soy sauce
- 10 oz broccoli florets
- 1 cup cherry tomatoes, halved
- 1 cup vegetable broth

Directions:
1. Warm the olive oil in your Instant Pot on Sauté. Place the mushrooms and cook for 5 minutes. Add in soy sauce and broccoli and Sauté for 1 more minute.
2. Stir in vegetable broth and seal the lid. Select Manual and cook for 2 minutes on High. Once ready, perform a quick pressure release and unlock the lid. Let cool for a few minutes, top with cherry tomatoes, and serve.

Bbq Pork Sliders

Servings:10 | Cooking Time: 60 Minutes

Ingredients:
- 1 pork shoulder
- 2 teaspoons salt
- 2 teaspoons ground black pepper
- 2 tablespoons olive oil
- 1 cup barbecue sauce
- 20 slider buns

Directions:
1. Season pork shoulder with salt and pepper.
2. Press the Sauté button on the Instant Pot and heat oil. Sear pork shoulder on all sides, ensuring they are browned, a total of 8–10 minutes. Add enough water to almost cover meat. Press the Cancel button. Lock lid.

3. Press the Manual or Pressure Cook button and adjust time to 45 minutes. When timer beeps, let pressure release naturally for 10 minutes. Quick-release any additional pressure until float valve drops. Press the Cancel button. Unlock lid.
4. Transfer pork to a platter. Using two forks, shred meat. Discard all but 2 tablespoons cooking liquid. Add pork, 2 tablespoons cooking liquid, and barbecue sauce back into the Instant Pot. Press the Sauté button and stir-fry meat 4–5 minutes, creating some crispy edges.
5. Serve warm on buns.

Twice-baked Potatoes

Servings:4 | Cooking Time: 13 Minutes

Ingredients:
- 1 cup water
- 2 medium russet potatoes
- 2 slices bacon, cooked and crumbled
- ¼ cup whole milk
- 4 tablespoons unsalted butter
- ½ cup shredded Cheddar cheese, divided
- ½ teaspoon salt
- ¼ teaspoon ground black pepper

Directions:
1. Add water to the Instant Pot and insert steamer basket. Pierce potatoes with a fork and add to basket. Lock lid.
2. Press the Manual or Pressure Cook button and adjust time to 10 minutes. When timer beeps, let pressure release naturally until float valve drops. Press the Cancel button. Unlock lid.
3. Transfer potatoes to a cutting board and let cool enough to handle.
4. In a medium mixing bowl, add bacon, milk, butter, ¼ cup cheese, salt and pepper.
5. Slice potatoes in half lengthwise. Scoop out potato flesh, leaving a bowl-like shell.
6. Add scooped potatoes to bowl with remaining ingredients. Using a potato masher or the back of a fork, work ingredients together. Distribute mixture evenly among the bowl-like shells. Sprinkle with remaining cheese. Place potatoes in basket and insert in the Instant Pot. Lock lid.
7. Press the Manual or Pressure Cook button and adjust time to 3 minutes. When timer beeps, let pressure release naturally until float valve drops. Unlock lid. Serve.

Warm Spinach Salad With Eggs & Nuts

Servings: 4 | Cooking Time: 20 Minutes

Ingredients:
- 1 lb spinach, chopped
- 3 tbsp olive oil
- 1 tbsp butter
- 1 tbsp almonds, crushed
- 1 tbsp peanuts, crushed
- 4 eggs
- ½ tsp chili flakes
- ½ tsp salt

Directions:
1. Pour 1 ½ cups of water into the inner pot and insert a steamer basket. Place the eggs onto the basket. Seal the lid and cook on High Pressure for 5 minutes. Do a quick release. Unlock the lid. Remove the eggs to an ice bath.
2. Wipe the pot clean, and heat oil on Sauté. Add spinach and cook for 2-3 minutes, stirring occasionally. Stir in 1 tbsp of butter and season with salt and chili flakes. Mix well and cook for 1 more minute. Sprinkle with nuts. Peel and slice each egg in half, lengthwise. Transfer to a serving plate and pour over spinach mixture. Enjoy!

Italian-style Brussels Sprouts

Servings: 4 | Cooking Time: 15 Minutes

Ingredients:
- 1 lb Brussels sprouts, halved
- 2 garlic cloves, minced
- 1 tbsp mustard seeds
- 1 cup vegetable broth
- Salt and pepper to taste
- 1 tsp olive oil
- 2 tbsp rosemary, chopped

Directions:
1. Heat the olive oil in your Instant Pot and on Sauté. Cook Brussels sprouts, garlic, and mustard seeds for 2 minutes, stirring often. Pour in vegetable broth, salt, and pepper and seal the lid. Select Manual and cook for 4 minutes on High pressure. When done, perform a quick pressure release and unlock the lid. Serve topped with rosemary.

Homemade Vichyssoise Soup With Chives

Servings: 4 | Cooking Time: 30 Minutes

Ingredients:
- 2 tbsp butter
- 3 leeks, chopped
- 2 cloves garlic, minced
- 4 cups vegetable broth
- 3 potatoes, peeled, cubed
- ½ cup sour cream
- 2 tbsp rosemary
- Salt and pepper to taste
- 2 tbsp chives, chopped

Directions:
1. Melt butter on Sauté. Stir in garlic and leeks and cook for 3-4 minutes until soft. Stir in potatoes, rosemary, and broth. Seal the lid and cook on High Pressure for 15 minutes. Release pressure quickly. Transfer soup to a food processor and puree to obtain a smooth consistency. Season with salt and pepper. Top with fresh chives and sour cream. Serve

Chapter 5 : Beans, Rice, & Grains Recipes

Chapter 5 : Beans, Rice, & Grains Recipes

Chorizo & Lentil Stew

Servings: 4 | Cooking Time: 60 Minutes

Ingredients:
- 1 cups lentils
- 4 oz chorizo, chopped
- 1 onion, diced
- 2 garlic cloves, minced
- 2 cups tomato sauce
- 2 cups vegetable broth
- ½ cup mustard
- ½ cup cider vinegar
- 3 tbsp Worcestershire sauce
- 2 tbsp maple syrup
- 2 tbsp liquid smoke
- 1 tbsp lime juice
- 2 cups brown sugar
- Salt and pepper to taste
- 1 tsp chili powder
- 1 tsp paprika
- ¼ tsp cayenne pepper

Directions:
1. Set to Sauté the Instant Pot. Add in chorizo and cook for 3 minutes as you stir until crisp. Add garlic and onion and cook for 2 minutes. Mix in tomato sauce, cider vinegar, liquid smoke, Worcestershire sauce, lime juice, mustard, and maple syrup and cook for 2 minutes.
2. Stir in broth and scrape the bottom to do away with any browned bits of food. Add pepper, chili, sugar, paprika, salt, and cayenne into the sauce as you stir to mix.
3. Stir in lentils to coat. Seal the lid and cook on High Pressure for 30 minutes. Release pressure naturally for 10 minutes and unlock the lid. Serve warm.

Wild Rice Pilaf

Servings: 4 | Cooking Time: 20 Minutes

Ingredients:
- 1 cup wild rice
- 2 tbsp butter
- Salt and pepper to taste
- 2 tbsp chives, chopped

Directions:
1. Stir the rice, butter, 2 cups of water, salt, and pepper in your Instant Pot. Seal the lid, select Manual, and cook for 5 minutes on High pressure. When ready, allow a natural release for 10 minutes and unlock the lid. Using a fork, fluff the rice. Top with chives and serve.

Kiwi Steel Cut Oatmeal

Servings: 4 | Cooking Time: 25 Minutes

Ingredients:
- 2 kiwi, mashed
- 2 cups steel cut oatmeal
- ¼ tsp nutmeg
- 1 tsp cinnamon
- 1 tsp vanilla
- ¼ tsp salt
- ½ cup hazelnuts, chopped
- ¼ cup honey

Directions:
1. Place the kiwi, oats, 3 cups water, nutmeg, cinnamon, vanilla, and salt in your Instant Pot and stir to combine. Seal the lid and cook on Manual for 10 minutes on High. When done, allow a natural release for 10 minutes and unlock the lid. Mix in hazelnuts and honey and let chill.

Pancetta With Garbanzo Beans

Servings: 6 | Cooking Time: 60 Minutes

Ingredients:
- 3 strips pancetta
- 1 onion, diced
- 15 oz can garbanzo beans
- 1 cup apple cider
- 2 garlic cloves, minced
- ½ cup ketchup
- 1 tbsp mustard powder
- Salt and pepper to taste

Directions:
1. Cook pancetta for 5 minutes until crispy on Sauté. Add onion and garlic, and cook for 3 minutes until soft. Mix in garbanzo beans, ketchup, salt, apple cider, mustard powder, 2 cups water, and black pepper. Seal the lid, press Bean/Chili, and cook on High Pressure for 30 minutes. Release pressure naturally for 10 minutes. Serve.

Barley & Smoked Salmon Salad

Servings: 4 | Cooking Time: 30 Minutes

Ingredients:
- 4 smoked salmon fillets, flaked
- 1 cup pearl barley
- Salt and pepper to taste
- 1 cup arugula
- 1 green apple, chopped

Directions:
1. Place the barley, 2 cups of water, salt, and pepper in your Instant Pot. Seal the lid, select Manual, and cook for 20 minutes on High pressure.
2. Once ready, perform a quick pressure release and unlock the

lid. Remove barley to a serving bowl. Mix in apple and salmon. Top with arugula.

Broccoli & Pancetta Carbonara

Servings: 4 | Cooking Time: 30 Minutes

Ingredients:
- 1 lb pasta rigatoni
- 12 oz broccoli florets
- ½ fennel bulb, sliced
- 4 large eggs, beaten
- ½ cup Grana Padano, grated
- Salt and pepper to taste
- 8 oz pancetta, chopped
- ¼ cup heavy cream

Directions:
1. Cover the pasta with salted water in your Instant Pot and seal the lid. Select Manual and cook for 4 minutes on High. Drain and set aside, reserving 1 cup of cooking liquid. Beat the eggs in a bowl, add the cheese, and mix to combine. Clean the pot and select Sauté. Cook the pancetta for 4 minutes then add in the fennel; cook for 2-3 more minutes. Pour in the broccoli and pasta liquid and cook for 4-5 minutes. Stir in the egg mixture and heavy cream for 2-3 minutes. Adjust the seasoning. Add the pasta and let sit for 5 minutes before serving.

Salmon & Tomato Farfalle

Servings: 4 | Cooking Time: 15 Minutes

Ingredients:
- 16 oz farfalle pasta
- 2 tbsp olive oil
- 2 garlic cloves, sliced
- 2 cups tomatoes, diced
- ¼ tsp chili pepper
- ¼ tsp oregano
- ¾ cup red wine
- 4 oz smoked salmon, flaked
- 10 green olives, sliced
- ½ cup Parmesan, grated

Directions:
1. Warm olive oil in your Instant Pot on Sauté. Add in garlic and cook for 1 minute. Stir in tomatoes, farfalle, chili pepper, 4 cups water, red wine, and oregano. Seal the lid.
2. Select Manual, and cook for 5 minutes on High. Once ready, perform a quick pressure release. Mix in salmon and green olives. Serve sprinkled with Parmesan cheese.

Mexican Frijoles Chili

Servings: 4 | Cooking Time: 55 Minutes

Ingredients:
- ¼ cup Cotija cheese, crumbled
- 1 tsp olive oil
- 1 onion, chopped
- 3 cloves garlic, minced
- 6 cups vegetable broth
- 1 cup black beans, soaked
- 1 jalapeño pepper, diced
- 1 tsp dried oregano
- 1 tsp dried chili flakes
- Salt to taste
- 2 tbsp cilantro, chopped

Directions:
1. Warm oil on Sauté. Add in garlic and onion and cook for 3 to 4 minutes until fragrant. Add beans, vegetable broth, oregano, chili flakes, salt, and jalapeño pepper. Seal the lid and cook for 35 minutes on High Pressure. Quick-release the pressure. Divide into serving plates. Top with cilantro and Cotija cheese and serve.

Broccoli Couscous

Servings: 4 | Cooking Time: 15 Minutes

Ingredients:
- 10 oz broccoli florets
- 2 tbsp butter, melted
- 1 cup couscous
- Salt and pepper to taste
- 2 tbsp parsley, chopped
- 1 ¼ cups of boiling water

Directions:
1. Pour 1 cup of water into the Instant Pot and add a steamer basket. Place the broccoli in the basket and seal the lid. Select Steam and cook for 3 minutes on High. Once pressure cooking is complete, use a quick release.
2. In a bowl cover couscous with salted boiled water. Let it stand for 2-3 minutes until the water has absorbed. Fluff with a fork and stir in broccoli and butter and adjust the seasoning with salt and pepper. Top with parsley and serve.

Salsa Rice

Servings:6 | Cooking Time: 15 Minutes

Ingredients:
- 1 cup basmati rice
- 1 cup chicken broth
- 1 jar chunky salsa
- 1 teaspoon salt
- ½ teaspoon ground black pepper

Directions:
1. Place all ingredients in the Instant Pot. Lock lid.
2. Press the Rice button. When timer beeps, let pressure release naturally for 10 minutes. Quick-release any additional pressure until float valve drops. Unlock lid.
3. Transfer rice to a dish. Serve warm.

Tomato & Feta Pearl Barley

Servings: 4 | Cooking Time: 30 Minutes

Ingredients:
- ½ cup sundried tomatoes in oil, chopped
- ½ cup feta, crumbled
- 1 cup pearl barley
- 2 cups chicken broth
- Salt to taste
- 2 tbsp butter, melted

Directions:
1. Place barley, chicken broth, and salt in your Instant Pot. Seal the lid, select Manual, and cook for 25 minutes on High pressure. When done, allow a natural release for 15 minutes and unlock the lid. Mix in tomatoes and top with feta and butter to serve.

Black Beans With Jalapeño Salsa

Servings: 4 | Cooking Time: 50 Minutes

Ingredients:
- 2 tbsp olive oil
- 1 cup black beans, soaked
- 3 cups veggie broth
- 1 onion, quartered
- 1 tsp cumin
- Salt and pepper to taste
- ½ cup Jalapeno-cilantro salsa

Directions:
1. Warm the olive oil in your Instant Pot. Place in onion and cook for 3 minutes. Stir in black beans, veggie broth, cumin, salt, and pepper. Seal the lid, select Manual, and cook for 25 minutes on High pressure. When ready, allow a natural release for 10 minutes and unlock the lid. Drizzle with Jalapeño-Cilantro Salsa and serve.

Bean Pasta With Vegetables

Servings: 4 | Cooking Time: 30 Minutes

Ingredients:
- 1 cup butternut squash, shredded
- 1 lb penne pasta
- 1 cup pasta sauce
- 1 cup canned white beans
- ½ cup frozen lima beans
- ½ cup black olives, sliced
- 1 cup baby spinach
- ½ zucchini, sliced
- ½ tsp garlic powder
- ½ tsp onion powder
- ½ tsp ground nutmeg
- ½ tsp oregano
- ½ tbsp Italian seasoning

Directions:
1. Place pasta, 3 cups of water, butternut squash, and pasta sauce in your Instant Pot. Seal the lid, select Manual, and cook for 4 minutes on High. When done, allow a natural release for 10 minutes and unlock the lid. Stir in white beans, lima beans, olives, spinach, zucchini, garlic powder, onion powder, nutmeg, oregano, and Italian seasoning and press Sauté. Cook for 5-6 minutes and adjust the seasoning. Serve right away.

Millet Tabouleh

Servings:4 | Cooking Time: 10 Minutes

Ingredients:
- 1½ cups chopped fresh parsley
- ¼ cup chopped fresh mint leaves
- 1 cup peeled and diced red onion
- ¼ cup small-diced zucchini
- ½ cup peeled, seeded, and small-diced cucumber
- 4 small Roma tomatoes, seeded and diced
- ¼ cup plus 2 teaspoons olive oil, divided
- ¼ cup lemon juice
- 1 teaspoon lemon zest
- 1½ teaspoons sea salt, divided
- ¼ teaspoon ground black pepper
- 1 cup millet

- 2 cups vegetable broth

Directions:
1. In a medium bowl, combine parsley, mint, onion, zucchini, cucumber, tomatoes, ¼ cup olive oil, lemon juice, lemon zest, 1 teaspoon salt, and pepper. Cover and refrigerate for 30 minutes up to overnight.
2. Drizzle 2 teaspoons olive oil in Instant Pot. Add millet to Instant Pot in an even layer. Add broth and remaining ½ teaspoon salt. Lock lid.
3. Press the Rice button. When the timer beeps, let pressure release naturally for 5 minutes. Quick-release any additional pressure until float valve drops and then unlock lid.
4. Transfer millet to a serving bowl and set aside to cool. When cooled, add to refrigerated mixture and stir. Serve.

Bresaola & Black Eyed Peas

Servings: 4 | Cooking Time: 60 Minutes

Ingredients:
- ½ lb dried black-eyed peas
- 3 ½ cups chicken stock
- 3 oz bresaola, chopped
- Salt and pepper to taste

Directions:
1. Place the black-eyed peas and chicken stock in your Instant Pot. Seal the lid, select Manual, and cook for 30 minutes on High pressure. Once ready, allow a natural release for 20 minutes and unlock the lid. Sprinkle with salt and pepper to taste. Serve topped with bresaola.

Gluten-free Porridge

Servings: 4 | Cooking Time: 25 Minutes

Ingredients:
- 1 cup buckwheat groats
- 2 cups rice milk
- 1 banana, sliced
- ¼ cup raisins
- 1 tsp ground cardamom
- ½ tsp vanilla
- 2 tbsp pistachios, chopped

Directions:
1. Place buckwheat, milk, raisins, cardamom, and vanilla in your Instant Pot. Seal the lid, select Manual, and cook for 6 minutes on High pressure. When done, allow a natural release for 10 minutes and unlock the lid. Serve topped with banana and pistachios.

Saffron Quinoa Pilaf

Servings: 4 | Cooking Time: 30 Minutes

Ingredients:
- 1 shallot, chopped
- 2 tbsp olive oil
- 2 cloves garlic, minced
- 1 cup quinoa
- Pinch of saffron
- Salt to taste
- 2 tbsp parsley, chopped

Directions:
1. Submerge saffron in ½ cup of hot water and let soak for 10

minutes. Set your Instant Pot to Sauté. Heat the olive oil and add the garlic and shallot; sauté for 3 minutes. Stir in quinoa, saffron with the liquid, salt, and 2 cups of water. Seal the lid, select Manual, and cook for 1 minute on High pressure. Once over, allow a natural release for 10 minutes. Using a fork, fluff the quinoa. Adjust the seasoning with salt. Serve topped with parsley.

Garlic Mushroom Polenta

Servings: 4 | Cooking Time: 35 Minutes

Ingredients:
- 1 cup mixed mushrooms, sliced
- 2 tsp olive oil
- 4 green onions, chopped
- 2 garlic cloves, sliced
- 2 tbsp cilantro, minced
- 1 tbsp chili powder
- ½ tsp cumin
- Salt and pepper to taste
- ¼ tsp cayenne pepper
- 2 cups veggie stock
- 1 cup polenta

Directions:
1. Warm olive oil in your Instant Pot on Sauté and add mushrooms, garlic, and green onions. Cook for 4 minutes. Stir in chili powder, cumin, salt, pepper, cayenne, and stock. Combine polenta with 1 ½ cups of hot water in a bowl and transfer to the Instant Pot. Seal the lid, select Manual, and cook for 10 minutes on High pressure. Once done, allow a natural release for 10 minutes and unlock the lid. Top with cilantro and serve.

Bulgur Pilaf With Roasted Bell Peppers

Servings: 4 | Cooking Time: 25 Minutes

Ingredients:
- 2 tbsp olive oil
- 1 garlic clove, minced
- 1 onion, chopped
- 2 cups vegetable stock
- ¼ cup lemon juice
- 1 tsp grated lemon zest
- 1 cup bulgur
- Salt and pepper to taste
- 6 oz roasted bell peppers

Directions:
1. In a bowl, toss bell peppers with some oil, salt, and pepper. Warm the remaining oil on Sauté and cook onion and garlic until soft, about 3 minutes. Stir in stock, lemon juice, lemon zest, and bulgur. Seal the lid and cook on High Pressure for 5 minutes. Do a natural pressure release for 10 minutes. Carefully unlock the lid. Fluff the rice with a fork. Top with roasted peppers to serve.

Spicy Three-bean Vegetable Chili

Servings: 6 | Cooking Time: 40 Minutes

Ingredients:
- 1 tbsp canola oil
- 1 onion, chopped
- 3 stalks of celery, chopped
- 1 cup green peas
- 10 oz broccoli florets
- 2 tbsp minced garlic
- 2 tbsp chili powder
- 2 tsp ground cumin
- 4 cups vegetable broth
- 28-oz can tomatoes, diced
- ½ cup pinto beans, soaked
- ½ cup black beans, soaked
- ½ cup cannellini beans
- Salt to taste
- 2 tbsp parsley, chopped

Directions:
1. Warm oil on Sauté. Add in onion, broccoli, and celery and cook for 5 minutes until softened. Mix in cumin, chili powder, and garlic and cook for another 1 minute. Pour in vegetable broth, tomatoes, green peas, black beans, salt, cannellini beans, and pinto beans and stir. Seal the lid and cook for 25 minutes on High Pressure. Do a quick pressure release. Dispose of the bay leaf. Adjust the seasonings. Sprinkle with parsley and serve.

Spanish Rice

Servings:6 | Cooking Time: 15 Minutes

Ingredients:
- 1 tablespoon olive oil
- 1 medium onion, peeled and diced
- 1 medium yellow bell pepper, seeded and diced small
- 3 cloves garlic, minced
- 1 cup basmati rice
- 1 cup chicken broth
- 1 can diced tomatoes, including juice
- 1 small jalapeño pepper, seeded and diced
- ¼ teaspoon saffron threads
- ½ teaspoon ground cumin
- ⅛ teaspoon cayenne pepper
- 1 teaspoon sea salt
- ½ teaspoon ground black pepper

Directions:
1. Press the Sauté button on Instant Pot. Heat olive oil and add onion and bell pepper. Stir-fry for 3–5 minutes until onions are translucent. Add garlic. Cook for an additional minute. Add basmati rice and toss to combine. Add chicken broth to the Instant Pot and deglaze by scraping the bottom and sides of the Instant Pot.
2. Add remaining ingredients to Instant Pot. Lock lid.
3. Press the Rice button. When the timer beeps, let pressure release naturally for 10 minutes. Quick-release any additional pressure until float valve drops and then unlock lid.
4. Transfer to a dish and serve warm.

Down South Savory Porridge

Servings:4 | Cooking Time: 25 Minutes

Ingredients:
- 1 tablespoon bacon grease
- 1 large Vidalia onion, peeled and diced
- 1 cup sliced cooked sausage
- 1 cup jasmine rice
- 1 cup water
- 1 cup vegetable broth
- 1 cup shredded Cheddar cheese

Directions:
1. Press the Sauté button on the Instant Pot and heat bacon grease. Add onion and sausage and cook 3–5 minutes until onions are translucent.
2. Add a level layer of rice. Slowly pour in water and broth. Lock lid.
3. Press the Porridge button and cook for the default time of 20 minutes. When timer beeps, let pressure release naturally for 10 minutes. Quick-release any additional pressure until float valve drops and then unlock lid.

Dried Cherry And Pistachio Quinoa Salad

Servings:4 | Cooking Time: 20 Minutes

Ingredients:
- 1 cup quinoa
- 1 ¾ cups water
- Juice and zest from 1 medium lime, separated
- 2 tablespoons olive oil
- ¼ cup chopped dried cherries
- ¼ cup chopped pistachios
- 1 teaspoon ground cumin
- ½ teaspoon salt

Directions:
1. Add quinoa, water, and lime juice to the Instant Pot. Stir well. Lock lid.
2. Press the Porridge button and cook for the default time of 20 minutes. When timer beeps, quick-release pressure until float valve drops. Unlock lid.
3. Transfer quinoa to a serving dish and fluff with a fork. Toss in lime zest and remaining ingredients. Serve chilled.

Cranberry Millet Pilaf

Servings: 4 | Cooking Time: 20 Minutes

Ingredients:
- ½ cup dried cranberries. chopped
- 2 tbsp olive oil
- 1 garlic clove, minced
- 1 shallot, chopped
- 1 cup long-grain white rice
- 1 cup millet
- Salt and pepper to taste

Directions:
1. Warm olive oil in your Instant Pot on Sauté. Add in shallot and garlic and cook for 3 minutes. Stir in rice, millet, 3 cups water, cranberries, salt, and pepper.
2. Seal the lid and for 10 minutes on Rice. When ready, perform a quick pressure release and unlock the lid. Using a fork, fluff the pilaf. Serve immediately.

Spring Risotto

Servings: 6 | Cooking Time: 40 Minutes

Ingredients:
- 3 tbsp Pecorino Romano cheese, shredded
- ½ cup green peas
- 1 cup baby spinach
- 2 tbsp olive oil
- 2 spring onions, chopped
- 1 ½ cups arborio rice
- 3 ½ cups chicken stock
- Salt and pepper to taste

Directions:
1. Warm olive oil in your Instant Pot on Sauté. Add spring onions and cook for 3 minutes. Pour in rice and stock. Seal the lid and cook for 15 minutes on Manual.
2. Once done, allow a natural release for 10 minutes and unlock the lid. Adjust the seasoning with salt and pepper. Mix in green peas and spinach and cover with the lid. Let sit for 5 minutes until everything is heated through. Top with Pecorino Romano cheese and serve.

Chickpea & Lentil Soup

Servings: 6 | Cooking Time: 40 Minutes

Ingredients:
- 2 tbsp olive oil
- 1 onion, chopped
- 3 garlic cloves, minced
- 2 carrots, sliced
- 1 cup canned chickpeas
- 1 sweet pepper, chopped
- ½ banana pepper, chopped
- 1 cup canned diced tomatoes
- 1 celery stalk, diced
- 1 tsp sweet paprika
- 1 tsp cumin
- 1 cup brown lentils, rinsed
- 2 cups spinach, chopped
- Salt and pepper to taste

Directions:
1. Warm the olive oil in your Instant Pot on Sauté. Add in onion, garlic, carrot, banana pepper, sweet pepper, celery, paprika, and cumin and cook for 5 minutes.
2. Stir in lentils, chickpeas, tomatoes, salt, pepper, and 6 cups of water and seal the lid. Select Manual and cook for 10 minutes on High pressure. Once done, allow a natural release for 10 minutes and unlock the lid. Mix in the spinach and adjust the seasoning. Serve warm.

Colorful Turkey Fajitas With Rotini Pasta

Servings: 6 | Cooking Time: 15 Minutes

Ingredients:
- 1 ½ lb turkey breast, cut into strips
- 3 mixed bell peppers, cut diagonally
- 2 tsp chili powder
- 1 tsp salt
- 1 tsp cumin
- 1 tsp onion powder
- 1 tsp garlic powder
- ½ tsp thyme
- 1 tbsp olive oil
- 1 red onion, cut into wedges
- 4 garlic cloves, minced
- 3 cups chicken broth
- 1 cup pasta sauce
- 16 oz rotini pasta
- 1 cup grated Gouda cheese
- ½ cup sour cream
- ½ cup chopped parsley

Directions:
1. In a bowl, mix chili powder, cumin, garlic powder, onion powder, salt, and thyme. Reserve 1 tbsp of the seasoning. Coat turkey with the remaining seasoning.
2. Warm oil on Sauté. Add in turkey strips and sauté for 5 minutes until browned. Place the turkey in a bowl. Sauté the red onion and minced garlic for 1 minute in the cooker until soft. Mix in salsa and broth and scrape the bottom of any brown bits. Stir in rotini pasta and cover with bell peppers and turkey. Seal the lid and cook for 5 minutes on High Pressure. Do a quick pressure release. Open the lid, sprinkle with shredded gouda cheese and reserved seasoning, and stir well. Divide into plates and top with sour cream. Top with parsley and serve.

Southern Cheese Grits

Servings: 6 | Cooking Time: 35 Minutes

Ingredients:
- 2 tbsp olive oil
- 1 cup stone-ground grits
- 2 cups vegetable broth
- 1 cup milk
- 4 oz cheddar, shredded
- 3 tbsp butter
- Salt to taste

Directions:
1. Set your Instant Pot to Sauté. Warm the olive oil, place in grits and cook for 3 minutes until fragrant. Stir in broth, milk, cheese, butter, and salt. Seal the lid, select Manual, and cook for 10 minutes on High. Once ready, allow a natural release for 15 minutes and unlock the lid. Serve.

Arroz Con Pollo

Servings: 4 | Cooking Time: 40 Minutes

Ingredients:
- 2 tbsp olive oil
- 1 sweet onion, diced
- 2 garlic cloves, minced
- 1 lb boneless chicken thighs
- Salt and pepper to taste
- ½ tsp chili powder
- 2 carrots, diced
- 1 cup white jasmine rice
- 1 ½ cups chicken stock
- ½ tsp Mexican oregano

Directions:
1. Warm olive oil in your Instant Pot on Sauté. Add in onion and garlic and cook until fragrant, about 3 minutes. Stir in chicken, salt, and pepper and cook for 5 minutes more. Mix in carrots, rice, chili powder, chicken stock, and oregano. Seal the lid, select Manual, and cook for 10 minutes on High pressure. Once done, allow a natural release for 10 minutes and unlock the lid. Fluff the rice.

Spicy Rice Noodles With Tofu & Chives

Servings: 6 | Cooking Time: 15 Minutes

Ingredients:
- ½ cup soy sauce
- 2 tbsp brown sugar
- 2 tbsp rice vinegar
- 1 tbsp sweet chili sauce
- 1 tbsp sesame oil
- 1 tsp fresh minced garlic
- 20 oz tofu, cubed
- 8 oz rice noodles
- ¼ cup chopped chives

Directions:
1. Heat the oil on Sauté. Fry the tofu for 5 minutes until golden brown; reserve. To the pot, add 2 cups water, garlic, vinegar, sugar, soy sauce, and chili sauce and mix until smooth. Stir in rice noodles. Seal the lid and cook on High Pressure for 3 minutes. Divide noodles between bowls. Top with tofu and sprinkle with chives and serve.

Asparagus Pasta With Pesto Sauce

Servings: 4 | Cooking Time: 15 Minutes

Ingredients:
- 1 cup cherry tomatoes, quartered
- 1 lb farfalle
- 1 lb asparagus, chopped
- ¾ cup pesto sauce
- ½ cup Parmesan, grated

Directions:
1. Place the farfalle and 4 cups of salted water in your Instant Pot and fit in a trivet. Arrange the asparagus on the trivet and seal the lid. Select Manual and cook for 4 minutes on High. Once done, perform a quick pressure release. Drain the pasta and put it back in the pot. Add in the pesto sauce, asparagus, and cherry tomatoes and stir. Sprinkle with Parmesan cheese and serve.

Homemade Veggie Quinoa

Servings: 6 | Cooking Time: 30 Minutes

Ingredients:
- 1 cup quinoa, rinsed
- 2 carrots, cut into sticks
- 1 large onion, chopped
- 2 tbsp olive oil
- Salt to taste
- 2 tbsp cilantro, chopped

Directions:
1. Heat olive oil in the Instant Pot on Sauté. Add in onion and carrots and stir-fry for about 10 minutes until tender and crispy. Remove to a plate and set aside. Add 2 cups of water, salt, and quinoa to the pot. Seal the lid and cook on High Pressure for 10 minutes. Do a quick release. Transfer to a serving plate and top with the carrots and onion. Serve scattered with cilantro.

Wild Rice With Hazelnuts And Dried Apricots

Servings:8 | Cooking Time: 30 Minutes

Ingredients:
- 2 cups wild rice, rinsed
- 3 cups vegetable broth
- 2½ cups water
- 2 teaspoons sea salt
- 1 tablespoon butter
- ½ cup chopped hazelnuts
- ½ cup chopped dried apricots

Directions:
1. Place all ingredients into Instant Pot. Lock lid.
2. Press the Manual button and adjust time to 30 minutes. When timer beeps, let pressure release naturally for 5 minutes. Quick-release any additional pressure until float valve drops and then unlock lid.
3. Transfer to a dish and serve warm.

Tomato & Spinach Sausage Spaghetti

Servings: 4 | Cooking Time: 25 Minutes

Ingredients:
- 2 tbsp olive oil
- ½ cup onion, chopped
- 1 garlic clove, minced
- 1 lb pork sausage meat
- 14-oz can diced tomatoes
- ½ cup sun-dried tomatoes
- 1 tbsp dried oregano
- 1 tbsp Italian seasoning
- 1 jalapeño pepper, minced
- 1 tbsp salt
- 8 oz spaghetti, halved
- 1 cup spinach

Directions:
1. Warm olive oil on Sauté. Add in onion and garlic and cook for 2 minutes. Stir in sausage meat and cook for 5 minutes. Stir in jalapeño pepper, 4 cups water, sun-dried tomatoes, Italian seasoning, oregano, diced tomatoes, and salt. Mix spaghetti and press to submerge into the sauce. Seal the lid and cook on High Pressure for 5 minutes. Release the pressure quickly. Stir in spinach simmer on Sauté for 3 minutes until spinach is wilted. Serve warm.

Coconut Rice Breakfast

Servings: 4 | Cooking Time: 25 Minutes

Ingredients:
- 1 cup brown rice
- 1 cup water
- 1 cup coconut milk
- ½ cup coconut chips
- ¼ cup walnuts, chopped
- ¼ cup raisins
- ¼ tsp cinnamon powder
- ½ cup maple syrup

Directions:
1. Place the rice and water in your Instant Pot. Seal the lid, select Manual, and cook for 15 minutes on High. When ready, perform a quick pressure release and unlock the lid. Stir in coconut milk, coconut chips, raisins, cinnamon, and maple syrup. Seal the lid, select Manual, and cook for another 5 minutes on High pressure. When over, perform a quick pressure release. Top with walnuts.

Vegetable Paella

Servings: 4 | Cooking Time: 37 Minutes

Ingredients:
- 2 tbsp butter
- 1 cup long-grain rice
- 1 ½ cups vegetable stock
- A pinch of saffron
- 1 red bell pepper, chopped
- ½ cup green peas
- 1 cup tomato sauce
- 1 tsp cumin
- 1 tsp chili powder
- ½ tsp garlic powder
- ½ tsp onion powder
- 1 lemon, cut into wedges

Directions:
1. Melt butter in your Instant Pot to Sauté. Add in rice and bell pepper and cook for 2 minutes. Mix in vegetable stock, tomato sauce, cumin, saffron, chili powder, garlic powder, and onion powder. Seal the lid, select Manual, and cook for 10 minutes on High pressure. Once ready, allow a natural release for 10 minutes and unlock the lid. Stir in green peas and cook for 4-5 minutes more on Sauté. Serve with lemon wedges.

Lime Brown Rice

Servings: 6 | Cooking Time: 45 Minutes

Ingredients:
- ½ bunch spring onions, chopped diagonally
- 2 cups brown rice, rinsed
- 2 small bay leaves
- 2 tbsp olive oil
- 1 lime, juiced
- Salt to taste

Directions:
1. Place the rice, 2 ¾ cups of water, salt, and bay leaves in your

Instant Pot. Seal the lid and cook on Manual for 22 minutes on High. When done, allow a natural release for 10 minutes and unlock the lid. Drizzle with olive oil and lime juice and top with spring onions to serve.

Cilantro & Spring Onion Quinoa

Servings: 4 | Cooking Time: 15 Minutes

Ingredients:
- 1 cup quinoa
- 2 cups vegetable broth
- Juice of 1 lemon
- ½ tsp salt
- 2 spring onions, sliced
- 2 tbsp cilantro, chopped

Directions:
1. Place the quinoa, broth, and salt in your Instant Pot. Seal the lid, select Manual, and cook for 1 minute on High.
2. Once ready, allow a natural release for 10 minutes and unlock the lid. Using a fork, fluff the quinoa. Sprinkle lemon juice, cilantro, and spring onions and serve.

Mustard Macaroni & Cheese

Servings: 4 | Cooking Time: 20 Minutes

Ingredients:
- 16 oz elbow macaroni
- 1 cup heavy cream
- Salt and pepper to taste
- 1 tbsp butter
- 1 tsp mustard powder
- 3 cups cheddar, shredded
- ½ cup Parmesan, grated

Directions:
1. Place macaroni and 4 cups of water in your Instant Pot. Sprinkle with salt and pepper and seal the lid. Select Manual and cook for 4 minutes on High. Once done, perform a quick pressure release. Mix in heavy cream, butter, mustard powder, and cheddar and let sit for 5 minutes. Sprinkle with Parmesan cheese and serve.

Coconut Cherry Steel Cut Oats

Servings: 4 | Cooking Time: 20 Minutes

Ingredients:
- 1 cup cherries, pitted and halved
- 1 cup steel-cut oats
- 1 cup coconut milk
- 2 cups water
- ½ tsp vanilla extract

Directions:
1. Place cherries, oats, milk, water, and vanilla extract in your Instant Pot. Seal the lid, select Manual, and cook for 3 minutes on High pressure. Once ready, allow a natural release for 10 minutes and unlock the lid. Serve.

Rice & Red Bean Pot

Servings: 4 | Cooking Time: 55 Minutes

Ingredients:
- 1 cup red beans, soaked
- 2 tbsp vegetable oil
- ½ cup rice
- ½ tbsp cayenne pepper
- 1 ½ cups vegetable broth
- 1 onion, diced
- 1 garlic clove, minced
- 1 red bell pepper, diced
- 1 stalk celery, diced
- Salt and pepper to taste

Directions:
1. Place beans in your Instant Pot with enough water to cover them by a couple of fingers. Seal the lid and cook for 25 minutes on High Pressure. Release the pressure quickly. Drain the beans and set aside.
2. Rinse and pat dry the inner pot. Add in oil and press Sauté. Add in onion and garlic and sauté for 3 minutes until soft. Add celery and bell pepper and cook for 2 minutes.
3. Add in the rice, reserved beans, vegetable broth. Stir in pepper, cayenne pepper, and salt. Seal the lid and cook for 15 minutes on High Pressure. Release the pressure quickly. Carefully unlock the lid. Serve warm.

Honey Oat & Pumpkin Granola

Servings: 4 | Cooking Time: 45 Minutes

Ingredients:
- 1 tbsp soft butter
- 1 cup steel-cut oats
- 1 cup pumpkin puree
- 3 cups water
- 2 tsp cinnamon
- A pinch of salt
- ¼ cup clear honey
- 1 tsp pumpkin pie spice

Directions:
1. Set your Instant Pot to Sauté and melt in the butter. Stir in oats and cook for 3 minutes. Add in pumpkin puree, water, cinnamon, salt, honey, and pumpkin spice and stir. Seal the lid, select Manual, and cook for 10 minutes on High. Once ready, allow a natural release for 10 minutes. Stir the granola and let sit for 10 minutes. Serve.

Tomato & Mushroom Rotini

Servings: 4 | Cooking Time: 35 Minutes

Ingredients:
- 1 lb rotini pasta
- 2 tbsp olive oil
- ½ yellow onion, diced
- 2 garlic cloves, minced
- 16 oz crushed tomatoes
- 1 cup Mushrooms, sliced
- ½ tbsp grated nutmeg
- ¼ cup basil, chopped
- Salt and pepper to taste

Directions:

1. Cover rotini pasta with salted water in your Instant Pot and seal the lid. Select Manual and cook for 4 minutes on High. When done, allow a natural release for 10 minutes, then perform a quick pressure release, and unlock the lid. Drain the pasta and transfer to a bowl.
2. Heat the olive oil on Sauté and cook the onion, mushrooms, and garlic for 3-4 minutes. Stir in tomatoes and nutmeg and simmer for 5-6 minutes. Stir in basil and cooked pasta; adjust the seasoning. Serve.

One-pot Mexican Rice

Servings: 4 | Cooking Time: 35 Minutes

Ingredients:
- 2 tbsp olive oil
- 1 onion, diced
- 2 garlic cloves, sliced
- 1 cup long-grain white rice
- 2 cups chicken stock
- 1 tbsp chipotle chili paste
- 2 mixed peppers, sliced
- 1 cup salsa
- Salt and pepper to taste
- 2 tbsp cilantro, chopped

Directions:
1. Warm olive oil in your Instant Pot on Sauté and add in onion, garlic, and mixed peppers; cook for 2-3 minutes.
2. Add in rice and cook for another 1-2 minutes. Mix in stock, salsa, salt, and pepper. Seal the lid, select Manual, and cook for 10 minutes on High pressure.
3. When over, allow a natural release for 10 minutes and unlock the lid. Stir in the chipotle paste. Serve topped with cilantro. Enjoy!

Spinach & Cheese Filled Conchiglie Shells

Servings: 6 | Cooking Time: 45 Minutes

Ingredients:
- ¾ cup grated Pecorino Romano cheese
- 2 cups onions, chopped
- 1 cup carrots, chopped
- 3 garlic cloves, minced
- 3 ½ tbsp olive oil
- 28-oz can tomatoes, diced
- 12 oz conchiglie pasta
- 1 tbsp olive oil for greasing
- 2 cups ricotta, crumbled
- 1 ½ cups feta, crumbled
- 2 cups spinach, chopped
- 2 tbsp chopped fresh chives
- 1 tbsp chopped fresh dill
- Salt and pepper to taste
- 1 cup shredded cheddar

Directions:
1. Warm olive oil on Sauté. Add in onions, carrots, and garlic and cook for 5 minutes until tender. Stir in tomatoes and cook for another 10 minutes. Remove to a bowl. Wipe the pot with a damp cloth, add pasta, and cover with enough water. Seal the lid and cook for 5 minutes on High Pressure. Do a quick release and drain the pasta. Lightly grease olive oil on a baking sheet.

2. In a bowl, combine feta and ricotta cheese. Add in spinach, Pecorino Romano cheese, dill, chives, salt, and pepper and stir. Using a spoon, fill the conchiglie shells with the mixture. Spread 4 cups of the tomato sauce on a baking sheet. Place the stuffed shells over with seam-sides down and sprinkle cheddar cheese on the top. Cover with aluminum foil.
3. Pour 1 cup of water into the cooker and insert a trivet. Lower the baking dish onto the trivet. Seal the lid and cook for 15 minutes on High Pressure. Do a quick release. Take away the foil. Top with the remaining tomato sauce before serving.

Hawaiian Rice

Servings: 4 | Cooking Time: 30 Minutes

Ingredients:
- 2 tsp olive oil
- 1 ½ cups coconut water
- 1 cup jasmine rice
- 2 green onions, sliced
- ½ pineapple, and chopped
- Salt to taste
- ¼ tsp red pepper flakes

Directions:
1. Stir olive oil, water, rice, pineapple, and salt in your Instant Pot. Seal the lid, select Manual, and cook for 10 minutes on low pressure. Once over, allow a natural release for 10 minutes, then a quick pressure release. Carefully unlock the lid. Using a fork, fluff the rice. Scatter with green onions and red pepper flakes and serve.

Bean & Rice Stuffed Zucchini Boats

Servings: 4 | Cooking Time: 25 Minutes

Ingredients:
- 2 small zucchinis, halved lengthwise
- ½ cup chopped toasted cashew nuts
- ½ cup cooked rice
- ½ cup canned white beans
- ½ cup chopped tomatoes
- ½ cup grated Parmesan
- 2 tbsp melted butter
- Salt and pepper to taste

Directions:
1. Pour 1 cup of water into the Instant Pot and insert a trivet. Scoop out the pulp of zucchinis and chop roughly. In a bowl, mix the zucchini pulp, rice, tomatoes, cashew nuts, beans, Parmesan, melted butter, salt, and pepper.
2. Fill the zucchini boats with the mixture, and arrange the stuffed boats in a single layer on the trivet. Seal the lid and cook for 15 minutes on Steam on High. Do a quick release. Carefully unlock the lid. Serve immediately.

Pasta Tortiglioni With Beef & Black Beans

Servings: 4 | Cooking Time: 25 Minutes

Ingredients:
- 2 tbsp olive oil
- 1 lb ground beef
- 16 oz tortiglioni pasta
- 15 oz tomato sauce
- 15-oz canned black beans
- 15-oz canned corn, drained
- 10 oz red enchilada sauce
- 4 oz diced green chiles
- 1 cup shredded mozzarella
- Salt and pepper to taste
- 2 tbsp Parmesan, grated
- 2 tbsp chopped parsley

Directions:
1. Heat oil on Sauté. Add ground beef and cook for 7 minutes. Mix in pasta, tomato sauce, enchilada sauce, black beans, 2 cups water, corn, and green chiles and stir. Seal the lid and cook on High Pressure for 10 minutes. Do a quick pressure release. Mix in mozzarella until melted and add pepper and salt. Garnish with parsley and Parmesan cheese and serve.

Red Pepper & Chicken Fusilli

Servings: 2 | Cooking Time: 15 Minutes

Ingredients:
- 8 oz fusilli pasta
- 1 cup tomato pasta sauce
- 1 tbsp paprika
- 1 red bell pepper, sliced
- 2 chicken breasts, sliced
- 2 garlic cloves, chopped
- ½ tsp Italian seasoning
- Salt and red pepper to taste
- 1 tbsp butter
- 1 cup Parmesan, grated

Directions:
1. Stir 1 cup of water, fusilli, and pasta sauce in your Instant Pot. Add in chicken breasts, garlic, red pepper, Italian seasoning, paprika, salt, and pepper and seal the lid. Select Manual and cook for 5 minutes on High. Once over, perform a quick pressure release and unlock the lid. Stir in butter and top with Parmesan cheese to serve.

Lentil & Chorizo Chili

Servings: 4 | Cooking Time: 40 Minutes

Ingredients:
- ½ lb chorizo sausage, sliced
- 2 tbsp olive oil
- 1 onion, diced
- 1 cup canned diced tomatoes
- 1 cup lentils
- 3 cups vegetable broth

Directions:
1. Warm the olive oil in your Instant Pot on Sauté. Place in onion and chorizo and sauté for 5 minutes. Add in tomatoes and cook for 1 more minute. Stir in lentils and vegetable broth. Seal the lid, select Manual, and cook for 15 minutes on High pressure. When ready, allow a natural release for 10 minutes and unlock the lid. Serve.

Basic Risotto

Servings: 4 | Cooking Time: 19 Minutes

Ingredients:
- 4 tablespoons unsalted butter
- 1 small yellow onion, peeled and finely diced
- 2 cloves garlic, peeled and minced
- 1 ½ cups Arborio rice
- 4 cups chicken broth, divided
- 3 tablespoons grated Parmesan cheese
- ½ teaspoon salt
- ¼ teaspoon ground black pepper

Directions:
1. Press the Sauté button on the Instant Pot. Add butter and heat until melted. Add onion and stir-fry 3–5 minutes until onions are translucent. Add garlic and rice and cook an additional 1 minute.
2. Add 1 cup broth and stir 2–3 minutes until it is absorbed by rice.
3. Add remaining 3 cups broth, cheese, salt, and pepper. Press the Cancel button. Lock lid.
4. Press the Manual or Pressure Cook button and adjust time to 10 minutes. When timer beeps, let pressure release naturally for 10 minutes. Quick-release any additional pressure until float valve drops. Unlock lid.
5. Ladle risotto into bowls. Serve warm.

Butternut Squash With Rice & Feta

Servings: 4 | Cooking Time: 30 Minutes

Ingredients:
- 2 cups vegetable broth
- 1 lb butternut squash, sliced
- 2 tbsp melted butter
- Salt and pepper to taste
- 1 cup feta cheese, cubed
- 1 tbsp coconut aminos
- 2 tsp arrowroot starch
- 1 cup jasmine rice, cooked

Directions:
1. Pour the rice and broth into the pot and stir to combine. In a bowl, toss butternut squash with 1 tbsp of melted butter and season with salt and black pepper. Mix in the pot with the rice. In another bowl, mix the remaining butter, water, and coconut aminos. Toss feta in the mixture, add the arrowroot starch, and toss again to combine well. Transfer to a greased baking dish.
2. Lay a trivet over the rice butternut squash and place the baking dish on the trivet. Seal the lid and cook on High for 15 minutes. Do a quick pressure release. Fluff the rice with a fork and serve with feta cheese.

Harissa Chicken With Fruity Farro

Servings: 4 | Cooking Time: 45 Minutes

Ingredients:
- 2 tbsp dried cherries, chopped
- 1 lb chicken breasts, sliced
- 1 tbsp harissa paste
- 1 cup whole-grain farro
- Salt to taste
- 3 tbsp olive oil
- 1 tbsp apple cider vinegar
- 4 green onions, chopped
- 10 mint leaves, chopped

Directions:
1. In a bowl, place chicken, apple cider vinegar, 1 tbsp of olive oil, and harissa paste and combine everything thoroughly. Allow marinating covered for 15 minutes.
2. Heat the remaining olive oil on Sauté and cook green onion for 3 minutes. Stir in farro and salt and pour 2 cups of water. Insert a trivet over the farro and place the chicken on the trivet. Seal the lid, select Manual, and cook for 20 minutes on High. When ready, do a quick pressure release. Open the lid, remove the chicken and the trivet. Add dried cherries and mint to the farro. Stir and transfer to a plate. Top with chicken and serve.

Creamy Fettuccine With Ground Beef

Servings: 6 | Cooking Time: 20 Minutes

Ingredients:
- 10 oz ground beef
- 1 lb fettuccine pasta
- 1 cup cheddar, shredded
- 1 cup fresh spinach, torn
- 1 medium onion, chopped
- 2 cups tomatoes, diced
- 1 tbsp butter
- Salt and pepper to taste

Directions:
1. Melt butter on Sauté. Stir-fry the beef and onion for 5 minutes. Add the pasta. Pour water enough to cover and season with salt and pepper. Cook on High Pressure for 5 minutes. Do a quick release. Press Sauté and stir in the tomatoes and spinach. Cook for 5 minutes. Top with shredded cheddar and serve.

Date & Apple Risotto

Servings: 4 | Cooking Time: 30 Minutes

Ingredients:
- 1 tbsp butter
- 1 ½ cups Arborio rice
- 1/3 cup brown sugar
- 2 apples, cored and sliced
- 1 cup apple juice
- 2 cups milk
- 1 ½ tsp cinnamon powder
- ½ cup dates, pitted

Directions:
1. Melt butter in your Instant Pot on Sauté and place in rice; cook for 1-2 minutes. Stir in brown sugar, apples, apple juice, milk, and cinnamon. Seal the lid, select Manual, and cook for 6 minutes on High pressure. Once done, allow a natural release for 6 minutes and unlock the lid. Mix in dates and cover with the lid. Let sit for 5 minutes.

Boston Baked Beans

Servings:10 | Cooking Time: 45 Minutes

Ingredients:
- 1 tablespoon olive oil
- 5 slices bacon, diced
- 1 large sweet onion, peeled and diced
- 4 cloves garlic, minced
- 2 cups dried navy beans
- 4 cups chicken broth
- 2 teaspoons ground mustard
- 1 teaspoon sea salt
- ¼ teaspoon ground black pepper
- ¼ cup molasses
- ½ cup ketchup
- ¼ cup packed dark brown sugar
- 1 teaspoon smoked paprika
- 1 teaspoon Worcestershire sauce
- 1 teaspoon apple cider vinegar

Directions:
1. Press Sauté button on Instant Pot. Heat olive oil. Add bacon and onions. Stir-fry for 3–5 minutes until onions are translucent. Add garlic. Cook for an additional minute. Add beans. Toss to combine.
2. Add broth, mustard, salt, and pepper. Lock lid.
3. Press the Bean button and cook for the default time of 30 minutes. When timer beeps, let pressure release naturally for 10 minutes. Quick-release any additional pressure until float valve drops and then unlock lid.
4. Stir in the molasses, ketchup, brown sugar, smoked paprika, Worcestershire sauce, and vinegar. Press the Sauté button on the Instant Pot, press the Adjust button to change the heat to Less, and simmer uncovered for 10 minutes to thicken the sauce; then transfer to a serving dish and serve warm.

Spinach & Kidney Beans

Servings: 4 | Cooking Time: 55 Minutes

Ingredients:
- 1 cup kidney beans, soaked
- 2 tomatoes, chopped
- Salt and pepper to taste
- 2 tbsp olive oil
- 1 carrot, diced
- 1 celery stick, chopped
- 1 onion, finely chopped
- 3 cups chicken stock
- 1 cup baby spinach
- 2 tbsp parsley, chopped

Directions:
1. Heat olive oil on Sauté and stir-fry onion, carrot, celery, salt, and black pepper for 3 minutes. Pour in tomatoes, chicken stock, and beans. Seal the lid, select Manual, and cook for 25 minutes on High pressure.
2. Once ready, allow a naturally pressure release for 10 minutes. Stir in baby spinach, press Sauté and cook for 5 minutes until the spinach wilts. Top with parsley.

Stuffed Mushrooms With Rice & Cheese

Servings: 4 | Cooking Time: 25 Minutes

Ingredients:
- 4 portobello mushrooms, stems and gills removed
- 2 tbsp melted butter
- ½ cup brown rice, cooked
- 1 tomato, chopped
- ¼ cup black olives, chopped
- 1 green bell pepper, diced
- ½ cup feta, crumbled
- Salt and pepper to taste
- 2 tbsp cilantro, chopped
- 1 cup vegetable broth

Directions:
1. Brush the mushrooms with butter. Arrange them in a single layer on a greased baking pan. In a bowl, mix the rice, tomato, olives, bell pepper, feta cheese, salt, and black pepper. Spoon the rice mixture into the mushrooms. Pour in the broth.
2. Pour 1 cup of water into the Instant Pot and insert a trivet. Place the baking dish on the trivet. Seal the lid and cook on High Pressure for 10 minutes. Do a quick release. Garnish with fresh cilantro and serve immediately.

Chicken & Broccoli Fettuccine Alfredo

Servings: 2 | Cooking Time: 15 Minutes

Ingredients:
- 1 cup cooked chicken breasts, chopped
- 1 cup broccoli florets
- 8 oz fettuccine, halved
- 1 tsp chicken seasoning
- 1 jar Alfredo sauce
- Salt and pepper to taste
- 1 tbsp parsley, chopped
- 1 tbsp Parmesan, grated

Directions:
1. Add 2 cups of water, fettuccine, and chicken seasoning to your Instant Pot. Place a steamer basket on top and add in the broccoli. Seal the lid, select Manual, and cook for 3 minutes on High. Once over, perform a quick pressure release. Drain the pasta and set aside. In a bowl, place Alfredo sauce, broccoli, parsley, and cooked chicken. Add in the pasta and mix to combine. Season with salt and pepper. Serve topped with Parmesan cheese.

Sausage & Red Bean Stew

Servings: 4 | Cooking Time: 50 Minutes

Ingredients:
- 1 cup red beans, soaked
- 4 sausages, sliced
- 6 cups water
- 2 carrots, chopped
- Salt and pepper to taste
- 2 tbsp vegetable oil
- 1 yellow onion, diced
- 1 tomato, chopped
- 2 green onions, chopped
- 2 tbsp cilantro, chopped

Directions:
1. Place red beans and water in your Instant Pot. Seal the lid, select Manual, and cook for 10 minutes on High pressure. Once ready, allow a natural release for 10 minutes and unlock the lid. Drain the beans and set aside. Warm the vegetable oil in the pot on Sauté.
2. Add in sausage, carrots, yellow onion, salt, and pepper and cook for 5 minutes. Stir in tomatoes, green onions, cooked beans, and 1 cup of water. Seal the lid, select Manual, and cook for 15 minutes on High pressure. Once done, perform a quick pressure release and unlock the lid. Scatter with cilantro and serve.

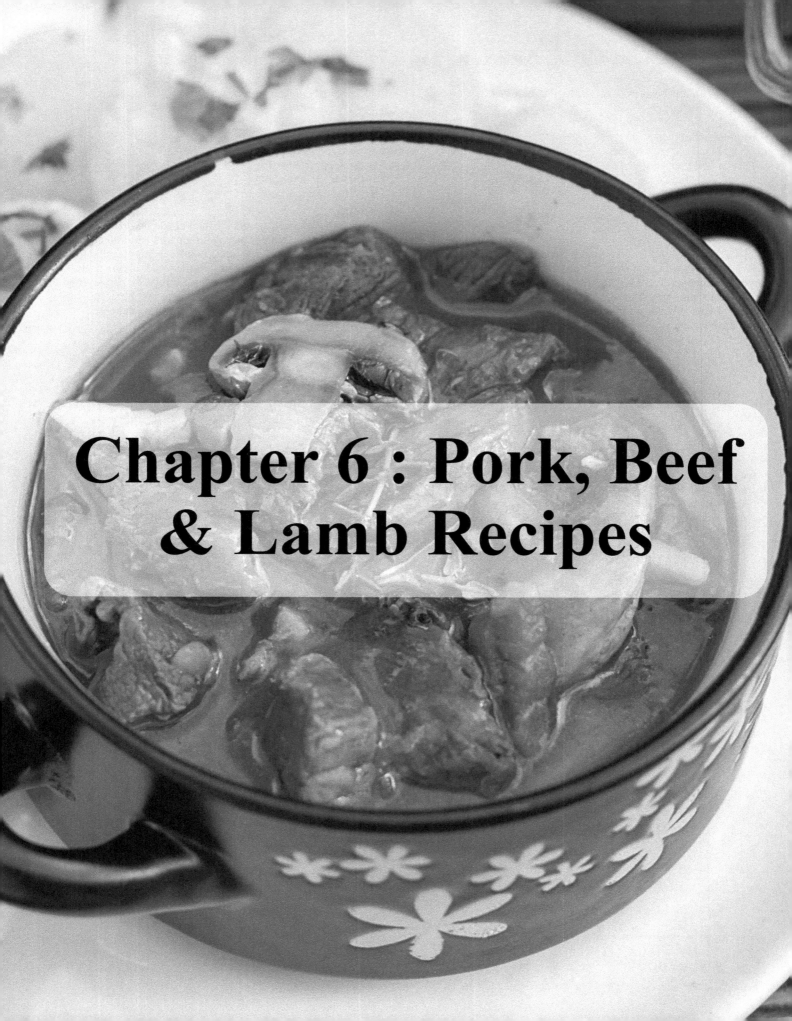

Chapter 6 : Pork, Beef & Lamb Recipes

Chapter 6 : Pork, Beef & Lamb Recipes

Seasoned Flank Steak

Servings:8 | Cooking Time: 20 Minutes

Ingredients:
- ⅓ cup fresh-squeezed orange juice
- 2 tablespoons honey
- 2 teaspoons ground cumin
- 1 teaspoon salt
- 1 tablespoon sriracha
- 3 tablespoons olive oil, divided
- 2 pounds flank steak
- 1 ½ cups beef broth

Directions:
1. In a small bowl, combine orange juice, honey, cumin, salt, sriracha, and 2 tablespoons oil. Place mixture and flank steak in a large sealable plastic bag. Seal, then massage mixture into meat through the bag. Refrigerate 1 hour.
2. Press the Sauté button on the Instant Pot and heat remaining 1 tablespoon oil. Sear meat on all sides, approximately 4–5 minutes. Add broth to deglaze pot, scraping any bits from the bottom and sides of pot. Press the Cancel button. Lock lid.
3. Press the Manual or Pressure Cook button and adjust time to 15 minutes. When timer beeps, let pressure release naturally for 10 minutes. Quick-release any additional pressure until float valve drops. Unlock lid.
4. Transfer meat to a serving platter. Thinly slice and serve.

Spring Onion & Pork Egg Casserole

Servings: 4 | Cooking Time: 35 Minutes

Ingredients:
- 1 tbsp butter, melted
- 4 spring onions, chopped
- 1 lb ground pork, chopped
- 6 eggs
- Salt and pepper to taste
- 1 cup water

Directions:
1. In a bowl, break the eggs and whisk until frothy. Mix in the onions and ground meat and season with salt and pepper. Grease a casserole dish with melted butter. Pour the egg mixture into the dish. Place a trivet in the pressure cooker and add water. Select Manual and cook for 25 minutes on High. Do a quick pressure release.

Beef Shawarma Bowls

Servings:4 | Cooking Time: 3 Minutes

Ingredients:
- 1 boneless sirloin, trimmed and sliced into 3" strips
- 2 tablespoons shawarma seasoning mix
- 1 tablespoon olive oil
- 1 cup water
- 3 medium Roma tomatoes, diced
- 1 small red onion, peeled and sliced
- 1 cup hummus

Directions:
1. In a medium bowl, combine sirloin and shawarma seasoning mix. Refrigerate covered 30 minutes.
2. Press the Sauté button on the Instant Pot and heat oil. Place sirloin in pot and stir-fry 2 minutes, then transfer to steamer basket. Press the Cancel button.
3. Add water to the Instant Pot and insert basket. Lock lid.
4. Press the Manual or Pressure Cook button and adjust time to 1 minute. When timer beeps, quick-release pressure until float valve drops. Unlock lid.
5. Transfer beef to bowls and garnish with tomatoes, onion, and hummus. Serve warm.

Melt-in-your-mouth Meatballs

Servings:4 | Cooking Time: 16 Minutes

Ingredients:
- 1 pound 80/20 ground beef
- ¼ cup grated Parmesan cheese
- 1 large egg, lightly beaten
- 1 tablespoon Italian seasoning
- 1 cup panko bread crumbs
- ½ teaspoon garlic salt
- ½ teaspoon ground black pepper
- 2 tablespoons olive oil
- 1 cup marinara sauce
- 2 cups water

Directions:
1. In a medium bowl, combine beef, cheese, egg, Italian seasoning, bread crumbs, garlic salt, and pepper. If stiff, add 1–2 tablespoons water. Form mixture into eight meatballs. Set aside.
2. Press the Sauté button on the Instant Pot and heat oil. Place meatballs around the edge of pot. Sear all sides of meatballs, about 4 minutes total. Press the Cancel button.
3. Transfer seared meatballs to a 7-cup glass baking dish. Top with marinara sauce. Discard extra juice and oil from pot.
4. Add water to the Instant Pot and insert steam rack. Place glass baking dish on top of steam rack. Lock lid.
5. Press the Manual or Pressure Cook button and adjust time to 12 minutes. When timer beeps, let pressure release naturally for 10 minutes. Quick-release any additional pressure until float valve drops. Unlock lid.
6. Transfer meatballs to plates. Serve warm.

Italian Sausage & Lentil Pot

Servings: 4 | Cooking Time: 40 Minutes

Ingredients:
- 1 cup canned tomatoes, diced
- 1 red bell pepper, cut into strips
- 1 lb Italian sausages, sliced
- 2 tbsp olive oil
- 1 cup lentils, rinsed
- 1 onion, chopped
- 1 tsp paprika
- 4 garlic cloves, minced
- 1 tbsp basil, chopped
- Salt and pepper to taste
- 1 tbsp Italian seasoning

Directions:
1. Warm the olive oil in your Instant Pot on Sauté. Place in sausages and cook for 3-4 minutes. Add in onion, bell pepper, garlic, and and cook for another 4 minutes. Stir in paprika, Italian seasoning, salt, pepper, lentils, tomatoes, and 3 cups of water. Seal the lid, select Manual, and cook for 15 minutes on High. Once over, allow a natural release for 10 minutes. Top with basil and serve.

Spiced Mexican Pork

Servings: 4 | Cooking Time: 55 Minutes + Marinating Time

Ingredients:
- 2 lb pork shoulder, cut into chunks
- 1 chipotle pepper in adobo sauce, chopped
- 3 garlic cloves, minced
- 1 red onion, chopped
- ½ tsp ground coriander
- 1 tsp ground cumin
- 1 tbsp lime juice
- ¼ cup chile enchilada sauce
- 1 tsp Mexican oregano
- Salt and pepper to taste

Directions:
1. Place garlic, onion, ground coriander, cumin, lime juice, Mexican oregano, chipotle pepper, enchilada sauce, salt, pepper, and ½ cup of water in a blender and pulse until smooth. Place the mixture in a large bowl and add in pork chunks; toss to coat. Cover with cling foil and let marinate in the fridge for 30 minutes.
2. Next, remove from the fridge and transfer to your Instant Pot. Pour in ½ cup of water and seal the lid. Select Manual and cook for 25 minutes on High pressure. When ready, allow a natural release for 15 minutes and unlock the lid. Cook for 5 minutes on Sauté until the sauce thickens. Serve warm.

Classic Beef Stroganoff

Servings: 6 | Cooking Time: 45 Minutes

Ingredients:
- 2 lb chuck roast, thin slices
- 2 tbsp butter
- 1 tbsp olive oil
- 1 onion, sliced
- Salt and pepper to taste
- 1 cup mushrooms, sliced
- 2 garlic cloves, minced
- 1 ¼ cups beef broth
- ½ cup crème fraiche
- 2 cup cooked rice

Directions:
1. Warm the olive oil and butter in your Instant Pot on Sauté. Place in onion and cook for 3 minutes. Sprinkle chuck roast with salt and pepper and place it in the pot and brown for 2 minutes on all sides. Add in mushrooms and garlic and cook for another 3 minutes. Stir in beef broth and seal the lid.
2. Select Manual and cook for 20 minutes on High pressure. Once ready, perform a quick pressure release and unlock the lid. Mix in crème fraiche and lock the lid. Let sit for 5 minutes. Serve with rice.

Hearty Beef Stew With Vegetables

Servings: 4 | Cooking Time: 40 Minutes

Ingredients:
- 1 lb beef stew meat, cubed
- 2 onions, peeled, chopped
- 3 potatoes, peeled, chopped
- 1 cup green peas
- 1 tsp salt
- 1 tsp cayenne pepper
- 1 tbsp apple cider vinegar
- 3 tbsp olive oil
- 3 cups beef broth

Directions:
1. Heat oil on Sauté. Stir-fry the onions until translucent. Add the meat and potatoes, and brown for about 10 minutes. Add peas, and season with salt and cayenne pepper. Pour in broth and apple cider. Seal the lid and Set to Meat/Stew for 25 minutes on High. Do a quick release. Carefully unlock the lid. Serve.

Savory Pot Beef Roast With Pancetta

Servings: 4 | Cooking Time: 80 Minutes

Ingredients:
- 1 ½ lb beef brisket, trimmed
- Salt and pepper to taste
- 2 tbsp olive oil
- 1 onion, chopped
- 1 cup beef broth
- ¾ cup dry red wine
- 2 fresh thyme sprigs
- 2 fresh rosemary sprigs
- 4 oz pancetta, chopped
- 1 carrot, chopped
- 1 bay leaf
- 2 tbsp parsley, chopped

Directions:
1. Warm oil on Sauté. Fry the pancetta for 4-5 minutes until crispy. Set aside. Season the beef with pepper and salt and brown for 5-7 minutes; reserve. In the same oil, fry onion for 3 minutes until softened. Pour in red wine and beef broth to deglaze the bottom, scrape the bottom of the pot to get rid of any browned bits of food. Return the beef and pancetta to the pot.
2. Add in rosemary sprigs and thyme. Seal the lid and cook for 50 minutes on High Pressure. Release the pressure quickly. Add carrots and bay leaf to the pot. Seal the lid and cook for an additional 4 minutes on High Pressure. Release the pressure quickly.

Get rid of the thyme, bay leaf, and rosemary sprigs. Place beef on a serving plate and sprinkle with parsley to serve.

Sweet & Spicy Pulled Pork

Servings: 4 | Cooking Time: 60 Minutes

Ingredients:
- 1 lb pork shoulder
- 1 onion, finely chopped
- 2 tbsp butter, unsalted
- 1 tbsp cayenne pepper
- 1 tsp salt
- 1 cup beef broth
- 1 tsp maple syrup
- 2 tbsp soy sauce
- ¼ cup Worcestershire sauce

Directions:
1. Warm butter on Sauté and stir-fry onions, cayenne pepper, and salt for 4 minutes. Add in maple syrup, soy sauce, and Worcestershire sauce and stir. Cook for 5 minutes. Add pork and pour in the broth. Seal the lid and cook on High Pressure for 40 minutes. When done, do a quick release. Divide between plates and serve hot.

Thyme Pork Loin With Apples & Daikon

Servings: 4 | Cooking Time: 40 Minutes

Ingredients:
- 1 lb pork loin, cubed
- 1 onion, diced
- 1 daikon, chopped
- 1 cup vegetable broth
- ½ cup white wine
- 2 apples, peeled and diced
- ½ cup sliced leeks
- 1 tbsp vegetable oil
- 1 celery stalk, diced
- 2 tbsp dried parsley
- ¼ tsp thyme
- ½ tsp cumin
- ¼ tsp lemon zest
- Salt and pepper to taste

Directions:
1. Heat oil on Sauté. Add pork and cook for 6 minutes until browned. Add the onion and cook for 2 more minutes. Stir in daikon, broth, wine, leeks, celery, parsley, thyme, cumin, lemon zest, salt, and pepper. Seal the lid and cook for 15 minutes on Pressure Cook. Release the pressure quickly. Stir in apples, seal the lid again, and cook on High for another 5 minutes. Do a quick release. Carefully unlock the lid. Serve warm.

Mushroom Beef Stroganoff

Servings: 6 | Cooking Time: 1 Hour

Ingredients:
- ¼ cup flour
- Salt and pepper to taste
- 2 lb beef stew meat
- 2 tbsp olive oil
- 1 onion, chopped
- 2 garlic cloves, minced
- 1 cup beef broth
- 3 cups mushrooms, chopped
- 8 oz sour cream
- 1 tbsp chopped parsley
- 1 cup rice, cooked

Directions:
1. In a large bowl, combine salt, pepper, and flour. Add beef and massage to coat beef in flour mixture. Warm oil on Sauté. Brown the beef for 4 to 5 minutes. Add garlic and onion and cook for 3 minutes until fragrant. Add beef broth to the pot.
2. Seal the lid and cook on High Pressure for 35 minutes. Release the pressure quickly. Open the lid and stir mushrooms and sour cream into the beef mixture. Seal the lid and cook on High Pressure for 2 minutes. Release the pressure quickly. Scoop over cooked rice. Season the stroganoff with pepper, parsley, and salt. Serve warm.

Chili-braised Pork Chops With Tomatoes

Servings: 4 | Cooking Time: 30 Minutes

Ingredients:
- 14 oz canned tomatoes with green chilies
- 4 pork chops
- 1 onion, chopped
- 2 tbsp chili powder
- 1 garlic clove, minced
- ½ cup beer
- ½ cup vegetable stock
- 1 tsp olive oil
- Salt and pepper to taste

Directions:
1. Heat oil on Sauté. Add onion, garlic, and chili powder and cook for 2 minutes. Add the pork chops and cook until browned on all sides. Stir in the tomatoes, stock, and beer. Season with salt and pepper. Seal the lid and cook for 20 minutes on Meat/Stew on High. When ready, quick Release the pressure and serve hot.

Beef Short Ribs With Asparagus Sauce

Servings: 6 | Cooking Time: 1 Hour 15 Minutes

Ingredients:
- 3 lb boneless beef short ribs, cut into pieces
- Salt and pepper to taste
- 3 tbsp olive oil
- 1 onion, diced
- 1 cup dry red wine
- 1 tbsp tomato puree
- 2 carrots, chopped
- 2 garlic cloves, minced
- 5 sprigs parsley, chopped
- 2 sprigs rosemary, chopped
- 3 sprigs oregano, chopped
- 4 cups beef stock
- 10 oz mushrooms, quartered
- 1 bunch asparagus, chopped
- 1 tbsp cornstarch

Directions:
1. Season the ribs with black pepper and salt. Warm oil on Sauté. In batches, add the short ribs to the oil and cook for 3 to 5 minutes on each side until browned. Set aside. Add onion and Sauté for 4 minutes until soft. Add tomato puree and red wine into the pot

to deglaze, scrape the bottom to get rid of any browned beef bits. Cook for 2 minutes until wine reduces slightly. Return the ribs to the pot and top with carrots, oregano, rosemary, and garlic. Add in stock and press Cancel.

2. Seal the lid, press Meat/Stew, and cook on High for 35 minutes. Release pressure naturally for 10 minutes. Transfer ribs to a plate. Strain and get rid of herbs and vegetables, and return cooking stock to the inner pot. Add mushrooms and asparagus to the broth. Press Sauté and cook for 2 to 4 minutes until soft.

3. In a bowl, mix ¼ cup cold water and cornstarch until cornstarch dissolves completely. Add the cornstarch mixture into the broth as you stir for 1-3 minutes until the broth thickens slightly. Season the sauce with black pepper and salt. Pour the sauce over ribs, add chopped parsley for garnish before serving.

Pino Noir Beef Pot Roast

Servings: 6 | Cooking Time: 61 Minutes

Ingredients:
- 3 lb beef chuck roast
- 2 tbsp olive oil
- 1 cup beef broth
- 4 carrots, julienned
- 1 lb potatoes, chopped
- 2 celery stalks, chopped
- 3 garlic cloves, peeled
- 1 cup Pino Noir red wine
- 1 onion, sliced
- 2 sprigs rosemary
- 2 tbsp tomato puree
- Salt and pepper to taste

Directions:
1. Warm the olive oil in your Instant Pot on Sauté. Add in the beef roast and brown for 5-6 minutes on all sides. Remove to a plate. Pour in the red wine and scrape any brown bits from the bottom. Stir in onion, garlic, carrots, potatoes, celery, tomato puree, rosemary sprigs, salt, and pepper. Put the beef back on the vegetables and add in the beef broth.

2. Seal the lid. Select Manual and cook for 35 minutes on High. When over, allow a natural release for 10 minutes and unlock the lid. Discard rosemary sprigs and remove beef to a plate. Serve with gravy and vegetables.

Cajun Pork Carnitas

Servings: 4 | Cooking Time: 65 Minutes

Ingredients:
- 1 lb pork shoulder, trimmed of excess fat
- 3 tbsp olive oil
- 1 onion, chopped
- 1 cup chicken stock
- ½ cup sour cream
- 2 tbsp tomato paste
- 1 tbsp lemon juice
- Salt and pepper to taste
- 1 tsp cayenne pepper
- 1 tsp garlic powder
- 1 tbsp Cajun seasoning
- 4 tortillas, warm

Directions:
1. Warm the olive oil in your Instant Pot on Sauté. Place in the

pork and cook for 7-8 minutes on all sides. Stir in onion and cook for 1-2 more minutes. Pour in chicken stock, sour cream, tomato paste, lemon juice, salt, pepper, cayenne pepper, Cajun seasoning, and garlic powder. Seal the lid, select Manual, and cook for 25 minutes on High.

2. When ready, allow a natural release for 10 minutes and unlock the lid. Remove pork and shred it. Put shredded pork back to the pot and cook for 6-8 minutes on Sauté. Serve with warm tortillas.

Sambal Beef Noodles

Servings: 4 | Cooking Time: 65 Minutes

Ingredients:
- 1 lb beef chuck roast, cubed
- 2 tbsp sesame oil
- Salt and pepper to taste
- 1 chopped onion
- 2 minced garlic cloves
- 3 tbsp sambal oelek chili paste
- 2 cups water
- 8 oz egg noodles

Directions:
1. Warm the sesame oil in your Instant Pot on Sauté. Place in the beef roast and cook for 6-7 minutes, stirring often. Add in salt, pepper, onion, sambal oelek chili paste, garlic, and 1 cup of water. Seal the lid, select Manual, and cook for 30 minutes on High pressure.

2. Once done, allow a natural release for 10 minutes, then perform a quick pressure release. Transfer beef roast to a plate. Pour in 1 cup of water in the pot and bring to a boil on Sauté. Add in noodles and cook for 4-5 minutes. Put the beef back to the pot and stir. Serve warm.

Italian Sausage And Peppers Hoagies

Servings:6 | Cooking Time: 20 Minutes

Ingredients:
- 2 tablespoons olive oil, divided
- 1 pound sweet Italian sausage links, uncooked, divided
- 1 large onion, peeled and sliced
- 1 small red bell pepper, seeded and sliced
- 1 small green bell pepper, seeded and sliced
- 1 small yellow bell pepper, seeded and sliced
- 4 cloves garlic, minced
- ½ cup chicken broth
- 1 can diced stewed tomatoes, including juice
- ¼ cup chopped fresh basil
- 2 tablespoons fresh oregano leaves
- 1 teaspoon cayenne pepper
- 1 teaspoon sea salt
- ½ teaspoon ground black pepper
- 6 hoagie rolls

Directions:
1. Press the Sauté button on the Instant Pot. Heat 1 tablespoon olive oil. Add half of the sausage links and brown all sides for about 4–5 minutes. Remove and set aside. Add the remaining 1 tablespoon olive oil and remaining sausages. Brown all sides for another 4–5 minutes. Remove from Instant Pot and set aside.

2. Add onions and bell peppers to Instant Pot and stir-fry for 3–5 minutes until onions are translucent. Add garlic. Cook for an additional minute. Add broth and deglaze Instant Pot by scraping the

sides and bottom of the Instant Pot. Add tomatoes, basil, oregano, cayenne pepper, salt, and pepper. Lock lid.

3. Press the Manual button and adjust time to 5 minutes. When timer beeps, quick-release the pressure until float valve drops and then unlock the lid.

4. Using a slotted spoon, transfer pot ingredients to a serving platter. Slice sausages. Serve on hoagie rolls.

Greek-style Stuffed Peppers

Servings: 4 | Cooking Time: 39 Minutes

Ingredients:
- ¼ cup Halloumi cheese, grated
- 2 tbsp olive oil
- 1 lb ground beef
- 2 onions, chopped
- Salt and pepper to taste
- 4 bell peppers, tops removed
- 1 tsp oregano
- 1 tsp paprika
- ½ tsp ground cinnamon
- 1 cup canned tomato sauce
- 1 tbsp flour

Directions:
1. Mix the cheese, ground beef, onions, paprika, cinnamon, salt, and pepper in a bowl. Stuff each bell pepper with the mixture. Pour the tomato sauce and ½ of water in your Instant Pot and fit in a trivet. Place the peppers on the trivet and seal the lid. Select Manual and cook for 15 minutes on High pressure.
2. When over, allow a natural release for 10 minutes and unlock the lid. Remove peppers to a plate. Whisk the flour and oregano with some cooking sauce in a bowl. Pour it in the pot and select Sauté; cook until the sauce thickens, about 3-4 minutes. Adjust the seasoning before pouring it over the peppers.

Chorizo & Tomato Pork Chops

Servings: 4 | Cooking Time: 40 Minutes

Ingredients:
- 4 pork chops, boneless
- 2 oz chorizo sausage, sliced
- 1 tsp paprika
- 2 garlic cloves, minced
- 2 tbsp olive oil
- 1 yellow onion, sliced
- 2 cups chopped tomatoes

Directions:
1. Place the pork chops in your Instant Pot and sear for 5 minutes on Sauté. Add in onion and garlic and cook for 3 more minutes. Stir in chorizo, paprika, tomatoes, and ½ cup of water. Seal the lid, select Manual, and cook for 15 minutes on High pressure. When done, allow a natural release for 10 minutes, then perform a quick pressure release, and unlock the lid. Serve right away.

Pot Roast, Potatoes, And Gravy

Servings:8 | Cooking Time: 50 Minutes

Ingredients:
- 1 chuck roast, fat trimmed
- 1 teaspoon garlic salt
- 1 teaspoon ground black pepper
- 1 tablespoon olive oil
- 3 cups beef broth
- 1 tablespoon tomato paste
- 2 teaspoons Worcestershire sauce
- 1 tablespoon Italian seasoning
- 2 pounds baby gold potatoes
- 2 tablespoons cornstarch

Directions:
1. Season roast with garlic salt and pepper.
2. Press the Sauté button on the Instant Pot and heat oil. Sear meat on all sides approximately 4–5 minutes. Add broth, scraping brown bits from bottom and sides of pot. Add tomato paste, Worcestershire sauce, Italian seasoning, and potatoes. Press the Cancel button. Lock lid.
3. Press the Manual or Pressure Cook button and adjust time to 45 minutes. When timer beeps, let pressure release naturally for 5 minutes. Quick-release any additional pressure until float valve drops. Unlock lid.
4. Using a slotted spoon transfer meat and potatoes to a platter.
5. Spoon ½ cup liquid from pot into a small bowl and whisk in cornstarch to create a slurry. Whisk slurry back into pot with remaining liquid. Allow to rest and thicken while your roast rests 7 minutes.
6. Slice roast and serve with potatoes and gravy. Serve warm.

Best Pork Chops With Bbq Sauce & Veggies

Servings: 4 | Cooking Time: 25 Minutes

Ingredients:
- 4 pork rib chops
- 1 cup carrots, thinly sliced
- 1 cup turnips, thinly sliced
- 1 cup onions, slice into rings
- 1 ½ cups BBQ sauce
- 2 cups water

Directions:
1. Add the pork chops to your cooker. Pour in ½ cup of BBQ sauce and 2 cups of water. Select Meat/Stew. Stir in the onions, turnips, and carrots. Lock the lid and cook for 20 minutes on High. Once ready, Release the pressure quickly. Open the lid, drizzle with the remaining BBQ sauce and serve warm.

Beef Lasagna With Eggplant & Almonds

Servings: 4 | Cooking Time: 25 Minutes

Ingredients:
- 2 lb stewed beef, boneless, sliced
- 3 oz toasted almonds, chopped
- 3 eggplants, halved
- 2 tomatoes, chopped
- 2 red bell peppers, sliced
- ¼ tbsp tomato paste

- 2 tbsp parsley, chopped
- 2 tbsp capers
- ¼ cup olive oil

Directions:
1. Grease the Instant Pot with 2 tbsp of olive oil. Make the first layer with halved eggplants tucking the ends gently to fit in. Make the second layer with beef slices, tomatoes, and red bell peppers. Spread the tomato paste evenly over, sprinkle with almonds and capers. Add in the remaining olive oil. Pour 1 ½ cups of water and seal the lid. Cook on High Pressure for 13 minutes. Do a quick release. Serve with fresh parsley.

Balsamic Lamb

Servings: 4 | Cooking Time: 45 Minutes

Ingredients:
- 2 lb lamb shanks
- 2 tbsp sesame oil
- 2 garlic cloves, peeled
- 1 onion, chopped
- 1 cup vegetable broth
- 1 tbsp tomato paste
- ½ tsp thyme
- ¼ tsp dried dill weed
- 1 tbsp balsamic vinegar
- 1 tbsp butter

Directions:
1. Warm sesame oil in your Instant Pot on Sauté. Place in onion and garlic and sauté for 3 minutes. Stir in broth, tomato paste, dill, and thyme. Add in the lamb and seal the lid. Select Manual and cook for 25 minutes on High.
2. When ready, allow a natural release for 5 minutes and unlock the lid. Remove the lamb to a bowl. Stir the balsamic vinegar and butter in the pot for 1-2 minutes until the butter melts. Serve the lamb with sauce.

Apple Pork Chops

Servings: 4 | Cooking Time: 42 Minutes

Ingredients:
- 2 leeks, white part only, cut into rings
- 1 lb pork fillets
- ½ lb apples, cut into wedges
- 2 tbsp olive oil
- ¼ cup apple cider vinegar
- 1 tsp chili pepper
- Salt and pepper to taste
- 1 tsp dry rosemary
- 1 tsp dry thyme

Directions:
1. Heat 1 tbsp of olive oil on Sauté. Season the pork with salt, black and chili pepper. Brown the fillets for about 4 minutes per side. Set aside. Heat the remaining oil in the pressure cooker. Add in leeks and Sauté until soft, about 4 minutes. Add in apples, rosemary, and thyme and pour in the vinegar and 1 cup of water. Place the pork loin along with the apples and leeks. Seal the lid.
2. Cook for 20 minutes on Meat/Stew on High. Once cooking is complete, perform a quick pressure release and remove the lid. To serve, arrange the pork on a plate and pour the apple leeks mixture over the pork.

Smoky Shredded Pork With White Beans

Servings: 4 | Cooking Time: 65 Minutes

Ingredients:
- 2 lb pork shoulder, halved
- 2 tbsp vegetable oil
- 1 onion, chopped
- 1 cup vegetable broth
- 2 tbsp liquid smoke
- Salt and pepper to taste
- 1 cup cooked white beans
- 2 tbsp parsley, chopped

Directions:
1. Warm the vegetable oil in your Instant Pot on Sauté. Place in onion and cook for 3 minutes. Sprinkle pork shoulder with salt and pepper, add it to the pot and brown for 5 minutes on all sides. Pour in vegetable broth and liquid smoke and scrape any brown bits from the bottom. Seal the lid, select Manual, and cook for 35 minutes on High.
2. When ready, allow a natural release for 10 minutes, then perform a quick pressure release, and unlock the lid. Remove pork and shred it. Stir white beans in the pot and put shredded pork back. Top with parsley and serve.

Quick French-style Lamb With Sesame

Servings: 4 | Cooking Time: 45 Minutes

Ingredients:
- 12 oz lamb, tender cuts, ½-inch thick
- 1 cup rice
- 1 cup green peas
- 3 tbsp sesame seeds
- 4 cups beef broth
- 1 tsp salt
- ½ tsp dried thyme
- 3 tbsp butter

Directions:
1. Mix the meat in the pot with broth. Seal the lid and cook on High Pressure for 15 minutes. Do a quick release. Remove the meat but keep the liquid. Add rice and green peas. Season with salt and thyme. Stir well and top with the meat. Seal the lid and cook on Manual for 18 minutes on High. Do a quick release. Carefully unlock the lid. Stir in butter and sesame seeds. Serve immediately.

Hawaiian Pulled Pork

Servings:10 | Cooking Time: 95 Minutes

Ingredients:
- 1 bone-in pork butt or shoulder
- Dry Rub
- ½ teaspoon ground ginger
- ½ teaspoon celery seed
- ½ teaspoon cayenne pepper
- 1 teaspoon garlic powder
- 1 teaspoon sea salt
- 1 teaspoon onion powder
- 1 teaspoon ground cumin
- Sauce
- 1 can crushed pineapple
- ¼ cup soy sauce

- ¼ cup tomato sauce
- ¼ cup pure maple syrup
- 1 tablespoon rice wine
- 3 cloves garlic, peeled and halved
- 1 tablespoon grated fresh ginger

Directions:
1. Dry pork butt with paper towels and set aside.
2. For Dry Rub: In a small bowl, combine Dry Rub ingredients. Massage rub into all sides of the pork. Refrigerate covered for 1 hour up to overnight.
3. For Sauce: Combine Sauce ingredients in a small saucepan. Bring to a boil. Reduce heat and simmer for 10 minutes until sauce reduces by a quarter and starts to thicken. Let cool for 5 minutes. Add to a food processor and pulse until smooth.
4. Place the pork butt in the Instant Pot and pour the sauce over the meat. Lock lid.
5. Press the Manual button and adjust time to 85 minutes. When timer beeps, let the pressure release naturally until float valve drops and then unlock lid. Check the pork to make sure it can easily pull apart. If not, press the Sauté button and simmer unlidded for an additional 10 minutes.
6. With the meat still in the Instant Pot, use two forks and pull pork apart. Remove bone and discard. Stir pork with sauce in the Instant Pot. Serve using a slotted spoon.

Spicy Garlic Pork

Servings: 4 | Cooking Time: 45 Minutes

Ingredients:
- 1 lb pork shoulder
- 2 tbsp olive oil
- 3 Jalapeño peppers, minced
- 1 tsp ground cumin
- 1 large onion, chopped
- 2 garlic cloves, crushed
- 3 cups beef broth
- Salt and pepper to taste

Directions:
1. Heat oil on Sauté in your Instant Pot and cook the jalapeño peppers for 3 minutes. Add in cumin, salt, pepper, garlic, and onion and stir-fry for another 2 minutes until soft. Add in the pork shoulder, and beef broth. Seal the lid, and cook on Meat/Stew for 30 minutes on High. Release the pressure quickly and serve hot.

T-bone Steaks With Basil & Mustard

Servings: 4 | Cooking Time: 40 Minutes + Marinating Time

Ingredients:
- 1 lb T-bone steak
- Salt and pepper to taste
- 2 tbsp Dijon mustard
- ¼ cup oil
- ½ tsp dried basil, crushed

Directions:
1. Whisk together oil, mustard, salt, pepper, and basil. Brush each steak and Refrigerate for 1 hour. Then, insert a steamer tray in the Instant Pot. Pour in 1 cup of water and arrange the steaks on the tray. Seal the lid and cook on Manual for 25 minutes on High. Do a quick release. Discard the liquid, remove the tray, and hit Sauté. Brown the steaks for 5 minutes, turning once.

Apricot Jam-glazed Ham

Servings: 6 | Cooking Time: 40 Minutes

Ingredients:
- 4 lb smoked ham
- ¾ cup apricot jam
- ½ cup brown sugar
- Juice from 1 lime
- 2 tsp Dijon mustard
- ½ tsp ground cardamom
- ¼ tsp ground nutmeg
- Black pepper to taste

Directions:
1. Pour 1 cup of water in your Instant Pot and add a trivet. Lay the ham on the trivet. In a bowl, mix the remaining ingredients until the sugar is dissolved. Pour the mixture all over the ham. Seal the lid and cook on High Pressure for 10 minutes. Release the pressure quickly.
2. Transfer the ham to a cutting board. Allow to sit for 10 minutes before slicing. Press Sauté. Simmer the liquid and cook for 4 to 6 minutes until thickened into a sauce. Plate the sliced ham and drizzle with sauce before serving.

Cherry-rosemary Pork Tenderloin

Servings:6 | Cooking Time: 30 Minutes

Ingredients:
- 2 tablespoons avocado oil
- 2 pork tenderloins, halved
- ½ cup balsamic vinegar
- ¼ cup olive oil
- ¼ cup cherry preserves
- ½ teaspoon sea salt
- ¼ teaspoon ground black pepper
- ¼ cup finely chopped fresh rosemary
- 4 garlic cloves, minced

Directions:
1. Press the Sauté button on the Instant Pot. Heat oil. Brown pork on all sides, about 2 minutes per side.
2. In a small bowl, whisk remaining ingredients together and pour over the pork. Lock lid.
3. Press the Manual button and adjust time to 20 minutes. When timer beeps, let the pressure release naturally for 5 minutes. Quick-release any additional pressure until float valve drops and then unlock lid.
4. Transfer tenderloin to a cutting board. Let rest for 5 minutes. Slice into medallions and serve.

Traditional French Beef Stew

Servings: 5 | Cooking Time: 55 Minutes

Ingredients:
- 1 lb boneless chuck steak, cut into chunks
- 2 cups portobello mushrooms, quartered
- ¼ cup flour
- Salt and pepper to taste
- 1 cup pancetta, chopped
- ½ cup red burgundy wine
- 1 ¼ cups beef broth
- 1 carrot, diced
- 4 shallots, chopped

- 3 garlic cloves, crushed
- 2 tbsp parsley, chopped

Directions:
1. Toss beef with black pepper, salt, and flour in a large bowl to coat. Set the Instant Pot to Sauté. Cook pancetta for 5 minutes until brown and crispy. Pour in approximately half the beef and cook for 5 minutes on each side until browned all over. Transfer the pancetta and beef to a plate. Sear remaining beef and transfer to the plate.
2. Add beef broth and wine to the cooker to deglaze the pan, scrape the pan's bottom to get rid of any browned bits of food. Return beef and pancetta to cooker and stir in garlic, carrot, shallots, and mushrooms. Seal the lid and cook on High Pressure for 32 minutes. Release the pressure quickly. Garnish with parsley and serve.

Prune & Shallot Pork Tenderloin

Servings: 6 | Cooking Time: 45 Minutes

Ingredients:
- 3 lb pork tenderloins, cut into large chunks
- 2 tbsp olive oil
- 2 shallots, chopped
- Salt and pepper to taste
- ½ cup vegetable broth
- ½ cup balsamic vinegar
- ½ cup dried pitted prunes
- 1 carrot, sliced diagonally
- 2 garlic cloves, minced
- 2 tbsp rosemary, chopped

Directions:
1. Warm the olive oil in your Instant Pot on Sauté. Sprinkle pork tenderloins with salt and pepper, place them in the pot, and brown for 2-3 minutes. Add in shallots, garlic, and carrots and cook for 3 minutes. Stir in vegetable broth, balsamic vinegar, prunes, and rosemary. Seal the lid, select Manual, and cook for 20 minutes on High pressure. When done, allow a natural release for 10 minutes, then perform a quick pressure release, and unlock the lid.

Calf's Liver Venetian-style

Servings: 2 | Cooking Time: 55 Minutes

Ingredients:
- 1 lb calf's liver, rinsed
- 3 tbsp olive oil
- 2 garlic cloves, crushed
- 1 tbsp mint, chopped
- ½ tsp cayenne pepper
- ½ tsp Italian seasoning

Directions:
1. In a bowl, mix oil, garlic, mint, cayenne, and Italian seasoning. Brush the liver and chill for 30 minutes. Remove from the fridge and pat dry with paper. Place the liver into the inner pot. Seal the lid and cook on High Pressure for 5 minutes. When ready, release the steam naturally for about 10 minutes.

Garlic-spicy Ground Pork With Peas

Servings: 6 | Cooking Time: 55 Minutes

Ingredients:
- 2 lb ground pork
- 1 onion, diced
- 1 can diced tomatoes
- 1 can peas
- 5 garlic cloves, minced
- 3 tbsp butter
- 1 serrano pepper, chopped
- 1 cup beef broth
- 1 tsp ground ginger
- 2 tsp ground coriander
- Salt and pepper to taste
- ¾ tsp cumin
- ¼ tsp cayenne pepper
- ½ tsp turmeric

Directions:
1. Melt butter on Sauté. Add onion and cook for 3 minutes until soft. Stir in ginger, coriander, salt, pepper, cumin, cayenne pepper, turmeric and garlic and cook for 2 more minutes. Add pork and cook until browned. Pour broth and add serrano pepper, peas, and tomatoes. Seal the lid and cook for 30 minutes on Meat/Stew on High. When ready, release the pressure naturally for 10 minutes. Carefully unlock the lid. Serve immediately.

Pork Medallions With Porcini Sauce

Servings: 4 | Cooking Time: 60 Minutes

Ingredients:
- 1 oz dried porcini mushrooms
- 4 boneless pork loin chops
- ½ cup dry Marsala wine
- 1 garlic clove, minced
- 1 tbsp paprika
- ½ tsp rosemary
- 1 onion, sliced
- 2 tbsp butter
- Salt and pepper to taste
- 2 tbsp chopped parsley

Directions:
1. Cover the porcini mushrooms with 1 cup of boiling water in a bowl and let soak for 10-15 minutes. Sprinkle pork chops with paprika, salt, and pepper. Melt butter in your Instant Pot on Sauté. Place the pork chops in the pot and sear for 6 minutes on all sides. Set aside.
2. Add onion and garlic to the pot and cook for 3 minutes. Put pork on top along with Marsala wine, rosemary, and porcini mushrooms with the water. Seal the lid, select Manual, and cook for 15 minutes on High pressure. When over, allow a natural release for 10 minutes and unlock the lid. Garnish with parsley and serve.

Swiss Steak And Potatoes

Servings:6 | Cooking Time: 35 Minutes

Ingredients:
- 2½ pounds beef round steak
- 1 teaspoon sea salt
- ½ teaspoon ground black pepper
- 2 tablespoons olive oil, divided
- 1 medium yellow onion, peeled and diced
- 2 stalks celery, diced
- 1 large green bell pepper, seeded and diced
- 1 cup tomato juice
- 1 cup beef broth
- 6 large carrots, peeled and cut into 1" pieces
- 6 medium Yukon gold potatoes, diced large
- 4 teaspoons butter

Directions:
1. Cut the round steak into 6 serving-sized pieces and season both sides with salt and pepper.
2. Press the Sauté button on the Instant Pot. Heat 1 tablespoon oil. Add 3 pieces of meat and sear for 3 minutes on each side. Move to a platter and repeat with the remaining 1 tablespoon oil and the other 3 pieces of meat.
3. Leave the last 3 pieces of browned meat in the Instant Pot; add the onion, celery, and green pepper on top of them. Lay in the other 3 pieces of meat and pour the tomato juice and broth over them. Place the carrots and potatoes on top of the meat. Lock lid.
4. Press the Manual button and adjust time to 20 minutes. When timer beeps, quick-release pressure until float valve drops and then unlock lid.
5. Transfer the potatoes, carrots, and meat to a serving platter. Cover and keep warm.
6. Skim any fat from the juices remaining in the Instant Pot. Press the Sauté button on the Instant Pot, press Adjust button and change temperature to Less, and simmer the juices unlidded for 5 minutes.
7. Whisk in the butter 1 teaspoon at a time. Serve the resulting gravy available at the table to pour over the meat. Serve immediately.

Beef With Potatoes & Mushrooms

Servings: 6 | Cooking Time: 40 Minutes

Ingredients:
- 2 lb round roast
- 2 tbsp olive oil
- 2 cups vegetable broth
- 2 garlic cloves, minced
- 1 celery stalk, chopped
- Salt and pepper to taste
- 1 tsp oregano
- 2 cups sliced mushrooms
- 1 large white onion, diced
- 1 lb potatoes, quartered

Directions:
1. Place the olive oil, vegetable broth, garlic, salt, pepper, and oregano in your Instant Pot and stir. Mix in the round roast, mushrooms, potatoes, celery, and onion. Seal the lid, select Manual, and cook for 25 minutes on High pressure. When done, perform a quick pressure release and unlock the lid. Serve immediately.

Chorizo With Macaroni & Cheddar Cheese

Servings: 6 | Cooking Time: 20 Minutes

Ingredients:
- 1 lb macaroni
- 3 oz chorizo, chopped
- 3 cups water
- 1 tbsp garlic powder
- 2 tbsp minced garlic
- 2 cups milk
- 2 cups cheddar, shredded
- Salt to taste

Directions:
1. On Sauté and stir-fry chorizo until crispy for about 6 minutes. Set aside. Wipe the pot with kitchen paper. Add in water, macaroni, garlic, and salt. Seal lid and cook for 5 minutes on High Pressure. Release the pressure quickly. Stir in cheese, garlic powder, and milk until the cheese melts. Top with chorizo and serve.

Butternut Squash & Beef Stew

Servings: 6 | Cooking Time: 40 Minutes

Ingredients:
- 2 lb stew beef, cut into 1-inch chunks
- ½ butternut pumpkin, chopped
- 2 tbsp canola oil
- 1 cup red wine
- 1 onion, chopped
- 1 tsp garlic powder
- 1 tsp salt
- 3 whole cloves
- 1 bay leaf
- 3 carrots, chopped
- 2 tbsp cornstarch
- 3 tbsp water

Directions:
1. Warm oil on Sauté. Brown the beef for 5 minutes on each side. Deglaze the pot with wine, scrape the bottom to get rid of any browned beef bits. Add in onion, salt, bay leaf, cloves, and garlic powder. Seal the lid, press Meat/Stew, and cook on High for 15 minutes. Release the pressure quickly. Add in pumpkin and carrots without stirring.
2. Seal the lid. Cook on High Pressure for 5 minutes. Release the pressure quickly. In a bowl, mix water and cornstarch until cornstarch dissolves completely and mix into the stew. Allow to simmer on Sauté for 5 minutes until you attain the desired thickness.

Pork Belly With Tamari Sauce

Servings: 6 | Cooking Time: 35 Minutes

Ingredients:
- 4 garlic cloves, sliced
- ½ tsp ground cloves
- 1 tsp grated fresh ginger
- 1 ½ lb pork belly, sliced
- 2 ¼ cups water
- ¼ cup white wine
- ½ cup onions, chopped
- ¼ cup tamari sauce

- 1 tsp sugar maple syrup
- 4 cups white rice, cooked
- Salt and pepper to taste

Directions:

1. Brown pork belly for about 6 minutes per side on Sauté. Add garlic, cloves, ginger, water, wine, onions, tamari sauce, maple syrup, rice, salt, and pepper. Seal the lid and cook for 25 minutes on Pressure Cook. When ready, do a quick pressure release. Serve immediately.

Merlot Pork Chops

Servings: 4 | Cooking Time: 50 Minutes

Ingredients:
- 4 pork chops
- 3 carrots, chopped
- 1 tomato, chopped
- 1 onion, chopped
- 2 garlic cloves, minced
- ¼ cup merlot red wine
- ½ cup beef broth
- 1 tsp dried oregano
- 2 tbsp olive oil
- 2 tbsp flour
- 2 tbsp water
- 2 tbsp tomato paste
- 1 beef bouillon cube
- Salt and pepper to taste

Directions:

1. Heat the oil on Sauté. In a bowl, mix in flour, pepper, and salt. Coat the pork chops. Place them in the pressure cooker and cook for a few minutes until browned on all sides. Add the carrots, onion, garlic, and oregano.

2. Cook for 2 more minutes. Stir in tomato, wine, broth, water, tomato paste, and bouillon cube and seal the lid. Cook on Soup/Broth and cook for 25 minutes on High. When ready, do a natural pressure release for 10 minutes, and serve immediately.

Bacon & Potato Brussels Sprouts

Servings: 4 | Cooking Time: 20 Minutes

Ingredients:
- 4 bacon slices, chopped
- 1 lb Brussels sprouts, halved
- 1 cup potatoes, cubed
- ½ cup chicken stock
- Salt and pepper to taste

Directions:

1. Set to Sauté your Instant Pot and add the bacon. Cook for 5-6 minutes until crispy; remove to a paper-lined plate. Add potatoes, Brussels sprouts, chicken stock, salt, and pepper to the pot. Seal the lid, select Manual, and cook for 5 minutes on High. When done, perform a quick pressure release.Top with bacon. Serve warm.

Short Ribs With Wine Mushroom Sauce

Servings: 4 | Cooking Time: 75 Minutes

Ingredients:
- 2 lb boneless pork short ribs, cut into 3-inch pieces
- Salt and pepper to taste
- ½ onion, chopped
- ½ cup red wine
- 3 tbsp olive oil
- ½ tbsp tomato paste
- 2 carrots, sliced
- 2 cups mushrooms, sliced
- 1 tbsp cornstarch
- Minced parsley to garnish

Directions:

1. Rub the ribs on all sides with salt and pepper. Heat the oil on Sauté in your Instant Pot and brown short ribs on all sides, about 6-7 minutes. Remove to a plate. Add onion to the pot and cook for 3-5 minutes. Pour in wine and tomato paste to deglaze by scraping any browned bits from the bottom of the cooker. Cook for 2 minutes until the wine has reduced slightly. Return ribs to the pot and cover with carrots. Pour 1 cup of water over.

2. Seal the lid, and select Manual on High Pressure for 35 minutes. When ready, let the pressure release naturally for 10 minutes. Carefully unlock the lid. Transfer ribs and carrots to a plate. To the pot, add mushrooms. Press Sauté and cook them for 2-4 minutes. In a bowl, add 2 tbsp of water and cornstarch and mix until smooth. Pour this slurry into the pot, stirring constantly until it thickens slightly, 2 minutes. Season the gravy with salt and pepper. Pour over the ribs and garnish with parsley.

Savory Herb Meatloaf

Servings: 4 | Cooking Time: 45 Minutes

Ingredients:
- 1 lb ground beef
- 1 egg, beaten
- 1 tsp garlic powder
- 1 tsp onion powder
- 1 shredded potato
- ½ tsp rosemary
- ½ tsp thyme
- 1 ½ tsp parsley
- Salt and pepper to taste
- Dill pickles, to serve

Directions:

1. Add the ground beef, egg, onion powder, garlic powder, shredded potato, rosemary, thyme, parsley, salt, and pepper to a bowl and combine them until everything is well mixed. Press the meatloaf mixture to a greased cooking pan. Pour 1 cup of water into your Instant Pot and fit in a trivet. Place the pan on the trivet and seal the lid. Select Manual and cook for 25 minutes on High.

2. When ready, allow a natural release for 10 minutes, then perform a quick pressure release, and unlock the lid. Remove the meatloaf to a plate and let cool before slicing. Serve with dill pickles.

Pork Loin With Pineapple Sauce

Servings: 6 | Cooking Time: 35 Minutes

Ingredients:
- 2 lb pork loin, cut into 6 equal pieces
- 16 oz canned pineapples
- 1 cup vegetable broth
- 1 tbsp brown sugar
- 3 tbsp olive oil
- ½ cup tomato paste
- 1 cup sliced onions
- ½ tsp ginger, grated
- Salt and pepper to taste
- ¼ cup tamari
- ¼ cup rice wine vinegar
- ½ tbsp cornstarch

Directions:
1. Heat the 2 tbsp oil on Sauté. Cook the onions for 3 minutes until translucent. Add the pork and stir in pineapples, sugar, broth, tomato paste, ginger, salt, pepper, tamari, and rice vinegar. Seal the lid and cook for 20 minutes on Soup/Broth on High. Release the pressure quickly. Mix cornstarch and 1 tbsp water and stir it in the pot. Cook for 2 minutes or until thickened on Sauté. Serve hot.

Savory Irish Lamb Stew

Servings: 4 | Cooking Time: 36 Minutes

Ingredients:
- 1 lb lamb, cut into pieces
- 1 ½ tbsp canola oil
- 1 onion, sliced
- 2 tbsp cornstarch
- 2 potatoes, cubed
- 2 carrots, chopped
- 2 ½ cups beef broth
- ½ tsp dried oregano
- Salt and pepper to taste

Directions:
1. Season the lamb with salt and pepper. Heat the canola oil in your Instant Pot on Sauté. Sear the lamb until browned on all sides, about 4-5 minutes. Add onion, potatoes, carrots, broth, and oregano, and stir. Seal the lid and cook on High Pressure for 18 minutes. When ready, do a quick pressure release. Whisk the cornstarch with a little bit of water and stir it into the stew. Cook on Sauté for 3 more minutes. Serve hot.

Homemade Braised Pork Belly

Servings: 4 | Cooking Time: 30 Minutes

Ingredients:
- 1 lb pork belly, sliced
- 2 tbsp oil
- ½ tsp cinnamon, ground
- ¼ tsp nutmeg, ground
- ¼ cup honey
- ¼ cup red wine
- 2 cups orange juice
- 1 cup water

Directions:
1. Heat oil on Sauté, and brown the pork for 3 minutes. Add cinnamon, nutmeg, honey, wine, orange juice and water, seal the lid, and cook on High Pressure for 20 minutes. Do a quick release. Press Sauté and bring it to a boil. Let simmer until the excess liquid evaporates. Serve.

Easy Lamb & Spinach Soup

Servings: 5 | Cooking Time: 45 Minutes

Ingredients:
- 1 lb lamb shoulder, cubed
- 10 oz spinach, chopped
- 3 eggs, beaten
- 5 cups vegetable broth
- 3 tbsp olive oil
- 1 tsp salt

Directions:
1. Place in your Instant Pot the lamb, spinach, eggs, broth, olive oil, and salt. Seal the lid, press Soup/Broth, and cook for 30 minutes on High Pressure. Do a natural pressure release for about 10 minutes. Serve warm.

Pulled Bbq Beef

Servings: 6 | Cooking Time: 65 Minutes

Ingredients:
- 3 lb beef chuck roast
- 2 tbsp olive oil
- 1 cup BBQ sauce
- 1 tbsp Dijon mustard
- 1 tsp smoked paprika
- Salt and pepper to taste
- 2 cups beef broth
- 3 tbsp cilantro, chopped

Directions:
1. Warm the olive oil in your Instant Pot on Sauté. Sprinkle beef with salt and pepper and place it in the pot and cook for 8-10 minutes on all sides. Add in BBQ sauce, Dijon mustard, smoked paprika, salt, pepper, and beef broth and seal the lid. Select Manual and cook for 35 minutes on High pressure.
2. Once ready, allow a natural release for 10 minutes, then perform a quick pressure release, and unlock the lid. Remove beef and shred it using 2 forks. Put it back to the pot and mix with the remaining liquid. Top with cilantro and serve.

Tandoori Pork Butt

Servings: 4 | Cooking Time: 61 Minutes

Ingredients:
- 2 lb pork butt, boneless, trimmed of excess fat
- 1 tsp ground cumin
- 1 tsp ground coriander
- 1 tsp paprika
- 1 green chili, minced
- 1 tsp garam masala
- 2 tbsp ghee
- 1 onion, chopped
- 2 garlic cloves, minced
- 1-inch piece ginger, grated
- 1 can coconut milk
- Salt and pepper to taste
- Lime wedges for garnish

Directions:
1. Mix the salt, pepper, ground coriander, paprika, cumin, and garam masala in a bowl. Sprinkle pork butt with this mixture. Melt ghee in your Instant Pot on Sauté. Place in green chili, ginger, onion, and garlic and cook for 2 minutes. Add in pork butt and cook for 3-4 minutes.
2. Pour in coconut milk and ½ cup of water and seal the lid. Select Manual and cook for 35 minutes on High pressure. Once ready, allow a natural release for 10 minutes, then perform a quick pressure release, and unlock the lid. Cut the butt into slices and serve with lemon wedges.

Hot Pork Chops With Cheddar Cheese

Servings: 4 | Cooking Time: 30 Minutes

Ingredients:
- 4 boneless pork chops
- 2 tbsp olive oil
- 1 cup water
- 4 tbsp habanero pepper sauce
- 2 tbsp butter
- 1 cup cheddar, grated
- Salt and pepper to taste
- 2 tbsp parsley, chopped

Directions:
1. Warm the olive oil in your Instant Pot on Sauté. Sprinkle pork chops with salt and pepper. Place the chops in the pot and brown for 3 minutes on all sides. Add in 1 cup of water and habanero pepper sauce. Top each pork chop with butter and seal the lid. Select Manual and cook for 15 minutes on High pressure.
2. When done, perform a quick pressure release and unlock the lid. Scatter pork chops with cheddar cheese and broil in the oven for a few minutes. Top with parsley and serve.

Beef Gyros With Yogurt & Dill

Servings: 4 | Cooking Time: 55 Minutes

Ingredients:
- 1 lb beef sirloin, cut into thin strips
- 1 onion, chopped
- 1/3 cup beef broth
- 2 tbsp fresh lemon juice
- 2 tbsp olive oil
- 2 tsp dry oregano
- 1 clove garlic, minced
- Salt and pepper to taste
- 4 slices pita bread
- 1 cup Greek yogurt
- 2 tbsp fresh dill, chopped

Directions:
1. In your Instant Pot, mix beef, beef broth, oregano, garlic, lemon juice, pepper, onion, olive oil, and salt. Seal the lid and cook on High Pressure for 30 minutes. Release pressure naturally for 15 minutes. Carefully unlock the lid. Divide the beef mixture between the pita bread. Top with yogurt and dill and roll up to serve.

Tasty Spicy Beef

Servings: 6 | Cooking Time: 33 Minutes

Ingredients:
- 2 lb lean beef, cut into bite-sized pieces
- 5 onions, chopped
- 5 garlic cloves, minced
- 1 jalapeño pepper, chopped
- Salt and pepper to taste
- 1 tsp cayenne pepper
- 2 tbsp tomato sauce
- 2 tbsp vegetable oil

Directions:
1. Heat oil on Sauté. Stir-fry onions and garlic for 3 minutes. Add in the meat, salt, pepper, cayenne pepper, jalapeño pepper, and tomato sauce. Mix and cover with water. Seal the lid. Cook for 20 minutes on High Pressure. Do a quick pressure release. Carefully unlock the lid. Serve.

Paprika Pork Fajitas With Cotija Cheese

Servings: 4 | Cooking Time: 1 Hour 30 Minutes

Ingredients:
- ½ cup queso Cotija, crumbled
- 1 tbsp ground cumin
- 2 tsp dried oregano
- 1 tsp paprika
- 1 tsp onion powder
- Salt and pepper to taste
- ½ tsp ground cinnamon
- 2 lb boneless pork shoulder
- ¾ cup vegetable broth
- ¼ cup pineapple juice
- 1 lime, juiced
- 4 cloves garlic, crushed
- 2 bay leaves
- 4 corn tortillas, warmed

Directions:
1. In a bowl, combine cumin, paprika, pepper, onion powder, oregano, salt, and cinnamon; toss in pork to coat. Place the pork, broth, garlic, lime juice, bay leaves, and pineapple juice in the Instant Pot. Seal the lid. Cook on High Pressure for 50 minutes. Release pressure quickly. Transfer the pork to a baking sheet and shred it with 2 forks. Reserve juices in the pot.
2. Preheat oven to 450 F. Bake in the oven for 10 minutes until crispy. Skim and get rid of fat from the liquid remaining in the pot. Dispose of the bay leaves. Over the pork, pour the liquid and serve alongside warm corn tortillas and queso Cotija.

Caribean-style Pork With Mango Sauce

Servings: 6 | Cooking Time: 70 Minutes

Ingredients:
- 1 ½ tsp onion powder
- 1 tsp dried thyme
- Salt and pepper to taste
- 1 tsp cayenne pepper
- 1 tsp ground allspice
- ½ tsp ground nutmeg
- ½ tsp ground cinnamon
- 2 lb pork shoulder

- 1 mango, cut into chunks
- 1 tbsp olive oil
- ½ cup water
- 2 tbsp cilantro, minced

Directions:
1. In a bowl, combine onion, thyme, allspice, cinnamon, pepper, sea salt, cayenne, and nutmeg. Coat the pork with olive oil. Season with seasoning mixture. Warm oil on Sauté in your Instant Pot. Add in the pork and cook for 5 minutes until browned completely. To the pot, add water and mango chunks. Seal the lid, press Meat/Stew, and cook on High Pressure for 45 minutes.
2. Release the pressure naturally for 10 minutes. Transfer the pork to a cutting board to cool. To make the sauce, pour the cooking liquid into a food processor and pulse until smooth. Shred the pork and arrange it on a serving platter. Serve topped with mango salsa and cilantro.

Beef Neapolitan Ragù

Servings: 4 | Cooking Time: 53 Minutes

Ingredients:
- 1 ½ lb beef steak, cut into strips
- 2 tbsp lard
- 1 onion, chopped
- 2 cups crushed tomatoes
- 1 carrot, chopped
- 1 celery stalk, chopped
- 1 cup beef broth
- ½ cup red wine
- 1 tbsp passata
- Salt and pepper to taste

Directions:
1. Melt lard in your Instant Pot on Sauté. Place in onion, carrot, and celery and sauté until fragrant. Add in beef steak and cook for 3 minutes, stirring often. Pour in tomatoes, beef broth, red wine, passata, salt, and pepper and seal the lid. Select Meat/Stew.
2. Cook for 30 minutes on High pressure. When over, allow a natural release for 10 minutes, then perform a quick pressure release, and unlock the lid. Serve immediately.

Braised Beef Ribs With Mushrooms

Servings: 4 | Cooking Time: 1 Hour

Ingredients:
- 1 cup crimini mushrooms, chopped
- 2 lb beef short ribs
- 1 tsp smoked paprika
- ½ tsp cayenne pepper
- Salt and pepper to taste
- 1 tbsp olive oil
- 1 small onion, chopped
- 4 garlic cloves, smashed
- 1 cup beer
- 1/3 cup beef broth
- 1 tbsp soy sauce
- 1 bell pepper, diced

Directions:
1. In a bowl, combine pepper, paprika, cayenne, and salt. Rub the seasoning mixture on all sides of the short ribs. Warm oil the Instant Pot on Sauté. Add mushrooms and cook until browned, about 6-8 minutes. Set aside. Add short ribs in the pot and cook

for 3 minutes for each side until browned; reserve. Throw garlic and onion in the oil and stir-fry for 2 minutes.
2. Add in beer to deglaze, scraping the pot's bottom to get rid of any browned bits of food. Bring to a simmer and cook for 2 minutes until reduced slightly. Stir in soy sauce, bell pepper, and broth. Dip short ribs into the liquid. Seal the lid, press Meat/Stew, and cook on High for 40 minutes. Release pressure quickly. Top the ribs and sauce fried mushrooms and serve.

Beef Steaks With Onion Gravy

Servings: 4 | Cooking Time: 35 Minutes

Ingredients:
- 4 round beef steaks
- 2 onions, sliced
- 1 ½ cups beef broth
- 1 tsp garlic, minced
- 1 tbsp dried parsley
- ½ tsp rosemary
- 1 tbsp oil
- ½ tsp red pepper flakes
- ¼ cup half and half
- 2 tbsp flour
- Salt and pepper to taste

Directions:
1. Heat the oil on Sauté. Add the beef and brown the steaks on all sides; set aside. Sauté the onions and garlic for 2 minutes until translucent and fragrant. Return the steaks to the pressure cooker. Stir in salt, pepper, pepper flakes, and rosemary. Pour in broth. Seal the lid.
2. Cook for 20 minutes on Meat/Stew on High. When ready, do a quick pressure release, and stir in the flour and half and half. Cook for 3 more minutes until thickened on Sauté. Serve topped with parsley.

Chapter 7 : Fish & Seafood Recipes

Chapter 7 : Fish & Seafood Recipes

Chili Steamed Catfish

Servings: 4 | Cooking Time: 70 Minutes

Ingredients:
- 1 lb flathead catfish
- 1 cup orange juice
- ¼ cup lemon juice
- ½ cup olive oil
- 1 tbsp dried thyme
- 1 tbsp dried rosemary
- 1 tsp chili flakes
- 1 tsp sea salt

Directions:
1. In a bowl, mix orange juice, lemon juice, olive oil, thyme, rosemary, chili flakes, and salt. Brush the fish with the mixture and refrigerate for 30 minutes. Remove from the fridge, drain, and reserve the marinade. Insert a trivet in the pot. Pour in 1 cup of water and marinade. Place the fish onto the top. Seal the lid and cook on High Pressure for 10 minutes. Do a quick release. Serve immediately.

Mussels With Chorizo And Tomato Broth

Servings:4 | Cooking Time: 11 Minutes

Ingredients:
- 2 tablespoons olive oil
- 1 medium yellow onion, peeled and diced
- ½ pound chorizo, loose or removed from casings
- 1 ½ cups chicken broth
- 1 can diced tomatoes, including juice
- 2 pounds fresh mussels, cleaned and debearded
- 4 tablespoons chopped fresh parsley

Directions:
1. Press the Sauté button on the Instant Pot and heat oil. Add onion and sauté 3–5 minutes until translucent. Add chorizo. Stir-fry 3–4 minutes until chorizo is browned. Stir in broth and let cook 2 minutes, then add tomatoes. Press the Cancel button.
2. Insert steamer basket and place mussels in basket. Lock lid.
3. Press the Manual or Pressure Cook button and adjust time to 0 minutes. When timer beeps, quick-release pressure until float valve drops. Unlock lid.
4. Remove mussels and discard any that haven't opened. Transfer mussels to four bowls and pour liquid from the Instant Pot equally among bowls. Garnish each bowl with 1 tablespoon parsley. Serve immediately.

Clam & Corn Chowder

Servings: 4 | Cooking Time: 30 Minutes

Ingredients:
- 2 tbsp olive oil
- 1 onion, chopped
- 3 potatoes, cubed
- 4 cups corn kernels
- 12 oz canned clams, chopped
- 1 green bell pepper, diced
- 1 red bell pepper, diced
- Salt and pepper to taste
- 4 cups chicken broth
- 1 cup milk
- 1 tbsp flour
- 3 tbsp butter

Directions:
1. Warm the olive oil in your Instant Pot on Sauté. Add in onion and bell peppers and cook for 3-4 minutes until tender. Stir in potatoes, corn kernels, clams with their juice, and chicken broth.
2. Seal the lid, select Manual, and cook for 12 minutes on High. Once ready, perform a quick pressure release. Combine milk with flour and pour it into the pot. Press Sauté and stir in butter. Let simmer for 3-4 minutes.

Herby Trout With Farro & Green Beans

Servings: 4 | Cooking Time: 20 Minutes

Ingredients:
- 1 cup farro
- 2 cups water
- 4 skinless trout fillets
- 8 oz green beans
- 1 tbsp olive oil
- Salt and pepper to taste
- 4 tbsp melted butter
- ½ tbsp sugar
- ½ tbsp lemon juice
- ½ tsp dried rosemary
- 2 garlic cloves, minced
- ½ tsp dried thyme

Directions:
1. Pour the farro and water into the pot and mix with green beans and olive oil. Season with salt and black pepper. In another bowl, mix the remaining black pepper and salt, butter, sugar, lemon juice, rosemary, garlic, and thyme.
2. Coat the trout with the buttery herb sauce. Insert a trivet in the pot and lay the trout fillets on the trivet. Seal the lid and cook on High Pressure for 12 minutes. Do a quick release and serve immediately.

Paprika Salmon With Dill Sauce

Servings: 2 | Cooking Time: 15 Minutes

Ingredients:
- 2 salmon fillets
- ¼ tsp paprika
- Salt and pepper to taste
- ¼ cup fresh dill
- Juice from ½ lemon
- Sea salt to taste
- ¼ cup olive oil

Directions:
1. In a food processor, blend the olive oil, lemon juice, dill, and seas salt until creamy; reserve. To the cooker, add 1 cup water and place a steamer basket. Arrange salmon fillets skin-side down on the steamer basket. Sprinkle the salmon with paprika, salt, and pepper. Seal the lid and cook for 3 minutes on High Pressure. Release the pressure quickly. Top the fillets with dill sauce to serve.

Galician-style Octopus

Servings: 6 | Cooking Time: 30 Minutes

Ingredients:
- 1 lb potatoes, sliced into rounds
- 2 lb whole octopus, cleaned and sliced
- 1 tbsp Spanish paprika
- 3 tbsp olive oil
- Salt and pepper to taste

Directions:
1. Place the potatoes in your Instant Pot and cover them with water. Place a trivet over the potatoes. Season the octopus with salt and pepper and place it onto the trivet. Seal the lid, select Manual, and cook for 15 minutes.
2. Once done, perform a quick pressure release and unlock the lid. Remove the octopus and let cool, then slice it into slices about half-inch thick. Transfer the sliced potatoes to a baking sheet and arrange octopus slices over the potatoes. Drizzle with olive oil and place under the broiler for 5 minutes. Sprinkle with paprika and serve.

Halibut With Lemon-caper Sauce

Servings:4 | Cooking Time: 12 Minutes

Ingredients:
- Halibut
- 4 halibut fillets
- ½ teaspoon salt
- ½ teaspoon ground black pepper
- 1 cup water
- Sauce
- 2 tablespoons unsalted butter
- 1 medium shallot, peeled and diced
- ¼ cup chicken broth
- ⅛ teaspoon salt
- 2 tablespoons drained capers
- Zest and juice of ½ medium lemon

Directions:
1. Pat halibut fillets dry with a paper towel. Season with salt and pepper.
2. Add water to the Instant Pot. Place fillets in steamer basket and insert into pot. Lock lid.

3. Press the Manual or Pressure Cook button and adjust time to 5 minutes. When timer beeps, quick-release pressure until float valve drops. Press the Cancel button. Unlock lid.
4. Line a baking sheet with parchment paper. Transfer fillets to prepared sheet. Broil fillets 2 minutes until tops are browned.
5. Empty water from the Instant Pot, then press the Sauté button on pot. Add butter and heat until melted. Add shallot and stir-fry 2–3 minutes until tender. Add broth to deglaze pot. Add salt, capers, and zest and juice of lemon. Let cook an additional 2 minutes.
6. Transfer halibut to plates and top with sauce. Serve warm.

Savory Cod Fillets In Maple-lemon Sauce

Servings: 4 | Cooking Time: 15 Minutes

Ingredients:
- 1 lb cod fillets, skinless and boneless
- 1 cup maple syrup
- ½ cup soy sauce
- 3 garlic cloves, chopped
- 1 lemon, juiced
- 1 tbsp butter

Directions:
1. In a bowl, mix maple syrup, soy sauce, garlic, and lemon juice. Stir until combined and set aside. Grease the pot with butter. Place the fillets at the bottom and pour over the maple mixture. Seal the lid and cook on Steam for 8 minutes on High. Release the pressure naturally. Serve.

Cheesy Shrimp Scampi

Servings: 4 | Cooking Time: 10 Minutes

Ingredients:
- 1 lb shrimp, deveined
- 2 tbsp olive oil
- 1 clove garlic, minced
- 1 tbsp tomato paste
- 10 oz canned tomatoes, diced
- ½ cup dry white wine
- 1 tsp red chili pepper
- 1 tbsp parsley, chopped
- Salt and pepper to taste
- 1 cup Grana Padano, grated

Directions:
1. Warm the olive oil in your Instant Pot on Sauté. Add in garlic and cook for 1 minute. Stir in shrimp, tomato paste, tomatoes, white wine, chili pepper, parsley, salt, pepper, and ¼ cup of water and seal the lid. Select Manual and cook for 3 minutes on High pressure. Once done, perform a quick pressure release and unlock the lid. Serve garnished with Grana Padano cheese.

Pizza With Tuna & Goat Cheese

Servings: 4 | Cooking Time: 25 Minutes

Ingredients:
- 1 cup canned tuna, oil-free
- ½ cup mozzarella, shredded
- ¼ cup goat's cheese
- 3 tbsp olive oil
- 1 tbsp tomato paste
- ½ tsp dried rosemary

- 14 oz pizza crust
- 1 cup olives

Directions:

1. Grease the bottom of a baking dish with some olive oil. Line with parchment paper. Flour the working surface and roll out the pizza dough to the approximate size of your Instant Pot. Gently fit the dough in the previously prepared baking dish.

2. In a bowl, combine olive oil, tomato paste, and rosemary. Whisk together and Spread the mixture over the crust. Sprinkle with goat cheese, mozzarella, olives, and tuna.

3. Place a trivet inside the pot and pour in 1 cup of water. Seal the lid, and cook for 15 minutes on High Pressure. Do a quick release. Cut and serve.

Basil Salmon With Artichokes & Potatoes

Servings: 4 | Cooking Time: 25 Minutes

Ingredients:

- 1 cup artichoke hearts, halved
- 4 salmon fillets
- 1 lb new potatoes
- 2 tbsp butter
- Salt and pepper to taste
- 2 tbsp basil, chopped

Directions:

1. Season the potatoes with salt and pepper. Pour 1 cup of water into your Instant Pot and fit in a trivet. Place the potatoes on the trivet and seal the lid. Select Manual and cook for 2 minutes on High pressure. Once over, perform a quick pressure release and unlock the lid. Sprinkle the salmon and artichokes with salt and pepper. Put them on the trivet with the potatoes, sprinkle with basil, and seal the lid. Select Manual and cook for another 5 minutes on High pressure. Once done, allow a natural release for 10 minutes. Remove potatoes to a bowl and stir in butter. Serve the salmon with artichokes and potatoes.

Saucy Clams With Herbs

Servings: 4 | Cooking Time: 15 Minutes

Ingredients:

- 1 lb clams, scrubbed
- 2 tsp olive oil
- 2 garlic cloves, minced
- 1 onion, chopped
- 2 celery stalks, diced
- 1 bell pepper, diced
- 1 tbsp tomato paste
- 28 oz can crushed tomatoes
- ½ tsp basil
- 1 tsp rosemary
- ½ tsp oregano
- Salt and pepper to taste
- ¼ tsp chili pepper

Directions:

1. Warm the olive oil in your Instant Pot on Sauté. Place in garlic, onion, celery, and bell pepper and cook for 3-4 minutes. Add in tomato paste and cook for another 1 minute. Stir in clams, tomatoes, basil, rosemary, oregano, salt, pepper, and chili pepper and seal the lid. Select Manual and cook for 2 minutes on High pressure. Once done, perform a quick pressure release and unlock the lid. Discard unopened clams. Serve with cooked rice.

Rich Shrimp Risotto

Servings: 4 | Cooking Time: 30 Minutes

Ingredients:

- ¾ cup Pecorino Romano cheese, grated
- 1 lb shrimp, deveined
- 4 tbsp butter
- 2 garlic cloves, minced
- 1 yellow onion, chopped
- 1 ½ cups Arborio rice
- 2 tbsp dry white wine
- 4 cups fish broth
- ½ tsp Italian seasoning
- 2 tbsp heavy cream
- Salt and pepper to taste

Directions:

1. Melt half of the butter in your Instant Pot. Add in garlic and onion and cook for 4 minutes. Stir in rice and cook for another minute. Mix in white wine and cook for 3 minutes until the wine evaporates. Pour in 3 cups of fish broth and Italian seasoning and seal the lid. Select Manual and cook for 10 minutes on High pressure.

2. When ready, perform a quick pressure release and unlock the lid. Add in shrimp and the remaining broth and cook for 4-5 minutes on Sauté. Stir in Pecorino Romano cheese, heavy cream, and the remaining butter.

Creole Shrimp With Okra

Servings: 2 | Cooking Time: 10 Minutes

Ingredients:

- 1 lb shrimp, deveined
- 6 oz okra, trimmed
- 2 tbsp olive oil
- 1 tsp garlic powder
- ½ tsp cayenne pepper
- ½ tbsp Creole seasoning
- Salt and pepper to taste

Directions:

1. Pour 1 cup water into your Instant Pot and fit in a trivet. In a baking dish, combine shrimp, okra, olive oil, garlic powder, cayenne pepper, Creole seasoning, salt, and pepper and mix to combine. Place the dish on the trivet. Seal the lid and cook for 2 minutes on Steam on High. When ready, perform a quick pressure release. Serve.

Crab Risotto

Servings:4 | Cooking Time: 15 Minutes

Ingredients:

- 4 tablespoons unsalted butter
- 1 small yellow onion, peeled and finely diced
- 1 ½ cups Arborio rice
- 4 cups vegetable broth
- 3 tablespoons grated Parmesan cheese, divided
- ½ teaspoon garlic salt
- ¼ teaspoon ground black pepper
- 1 cup lump crabmeat, picked over for shells

Directions:

1. Press the Sauté button on the Instant Pot. Add butter and heat until melted. Add onion and stir-fry 3–5 minutes until translucent.

2. Add rice, broth, 2 tablespoons cheese, garlic salt, and pepper. Press the Cancel button. Lock lid.
3. Press the Manual or Pressure Cook button and adjust time to 10 minutes. When timer beeps, let pressure release naturally for 10 minutes. Quick-release any additional pressure until float valve drops. Unlock lid.
4. Stir in crab and remaining cheese. Serve warm.

Seafood Traditional Spanish Paella

Servings: 4 | Cooking Time: 30 Minutes

Ingredients:
- 2 tbsp olive oil
- 1 onion, chopped
- 4 garlic cloves, minced
- ½ cup dry white wine
- 1 cup rice
- 1 ½ cups chicken stock
- 1 ½ tsp sweet paprika
- 1 tsp turmeric powder
- 1 lb small clams, scrubbed
- 1 lb prawns, deveined
- 1 red bell pepper, diced
- 1 lemon, cut into wedges

Directions:
1. Cook onion and garlic in 1 tbsp of oil on Sauté for 3 minutes. Pour in wine to deglaze, scraping the bottom of the pot of any brown. Cook for 2 minutes until the wine is reduced by half. Add in rice and broth. Stir in paprika, turmeric, and bell pepper. Seal the lid and cook on High Pressure for 10 minutes. Do a quick release. Remove to a plate and wipe the pot clean. Heat the remaining oil on Sauté. Cook clams and prawns for 6 minutes until the shrimp are pink. Discard unopened clams. Arrange seafood and lemon wedges over paella to serve.

Seafood Medley With Rosemary Rice

Servings: 4 | Cooking Time: 45 Minutes

Ingredients:
- 1 lb frozen seafood mix
- 1 cup brown rice
- 1 tbsp calamari ink
- 2 tbsp extra virgin olive oil
- 2 garlic cloves, crushed
- 1 tbsp chopped rosemary
- ½ tsp salt
- 3 cups fish stock
- ½ lemon

Directions:
1. Add in seafood mix, rice, calamari ink, olive oil, garlic, rosemary, salt, stock, and lemon, seal the lid and cook on Manual for 25 minutes on High. Release the pressure naturally for 10 minutes. Squeeze lemon juice and serve.

Chilled Lobster Salad

Servings: 4 | Cooking Time: 4 Minutes

Ingredients:
- 1 cup water
- 4 lobster tails, thawed
- ¼ cup mayonnaise
- 1 medium stalk celery, diced
- Juice and zest from ½ medium lemon
- ¼ teaspoon hot sauce
- ½ teaspoon salt
- ¼ teaspoon ground black pepper
- 2 medium avocados, peeled, pitted, and diced

Directions:
1. Add water to the Instant Pot and insert steamer basket. Add lobster tails to basket. Lock lid.
2. Press the Steam button and adjust time to 4 minutes. When timer beeps, quick-release pressure until float valve drops. Unlock lid. Transfer tails to an ice bath, to stop lobster from overcooking.
3. Remove lobster meat from shells. Roughly chop meat and transfer to a medium bowl. Combine lobster with mayonnaise, celery, lemon juice and zest, hot sauce, salt, and pepper.
4. Refrigerate until ready to serve. Spoon salad into bowls and garnish with avocado. Serve.

Orange Roughy With Zucchini

Servings: 2 | Cooking Time: 3 Minutes

Ingredients:
- 1 cup water
- 1 large zucchini, thinly sliced
- 2 orange roughy fillets, cubed
- Juice of 1 medium lemon
- 1 teaspoon salt
- ½ teaspoon ground black pepper
- 4 tablespoons unsalted butter, cut into 8 pats
- 2 tablespoons chopped fresh parsley

Directions:
1. Add water to the Instant Pot and insert steamer basket.
2. Add zucchini to basket in an even layer. Add orange roughy fillets on top. Squeeze lemon juice over fish. Season with salt and pepper. Distribute butter pats on fish and zucchini. Lock lid.
3. Press the Manual or Pressure Cook button and adjust time to 3 minutes. When timer beeps, quick-release pressure until float valve drops. Unlock lid.
4. Transfer fish and zucchini to two plates. Garnish with parsley. Serve warm.

Jalapeño Shrimp With Herbs & Lemon

Servings: 4 | Cooking Time: 25 Minutes

Ingredients:
- 1 lb shrimp, deveined
- ½ cup olive oil
- 1 tsp garlic powder
- 1 tsp rosemary, chopped
- 1 tsp thyme, chopped
- ½ tsp basil, chopped
- ½ tsp sage, chopped
- ½ tsp salt
- 1 tsp jalapeño pepper

Directions:

1. Pour 1 cup of water into the inner pot. In a bowl, mix oil, garlic, rosemary, thyme, basil, sage, salt, and jalapeño pepper. Brush the marinade over the shrimp. Insert a steamer rack in the pot and arrange the shrimp on top.

2. Seal the lid and cook on Steam for 3 minutes on High. Release the steam naturally for 10 minutes. Press Sauté and stir-fry for 2 more minutes or until golden brown.

Seafood Chowder With Oyster Crackers

Servings: 4 | Cooking Time: 40 Minutes

Ingredients:

- 20 oz canned mussels, drained, liquid reserved
- ¼ cup grated Pecorino Romano cheese
- 1 lb potatoes, peeled and cut chunks
- 2 cups oyster crackers
- 2 tbsp olive oil
- ½ tsp garlic powder
- Salt and pepper to taste
- 2 pancetta slices, chopped
- 2 celery stalks, chopped
- 1 medium onion, chopped
- 1 tbsp flour
- ¼ cup white wine
- 1 tsp dried rosemary
- 1 bay leaf
- 1 ½ cups heavy cream
- 2 tbsp chopped fresh chervil

Directions:

1. Fry pancetta on Sauté for 5 minutes until crispy. Remove to a paper towel-lined plate and set aside. Sauté the celery and onion in the same fat for 1 minute, stirring until the vegetables soften. Mix in the flour to coat the vegetables. Pour in the wine simmer. Cook for about 1 minute or until reduced by about one-third.

2. Pour in 1 cup water, the reserved mussel liquid, potatoes, salt, rosemary, and bay leaf. Seal the lid and cook on High Pressure for 4 minutes. Do a natural pressure release for 10 minutes. Stir in mussels and heavy cream.

3. Press Sauté and bring the soup to a simmer to heat the mussels through. Discard the bay leaf. Top with pancetta, chervil, cheese, and crackers and serve.

Seafood Pilaf

Servings: 6 | Cooking Time: 35 Minutes

Ingredients:

- 1 lb chopped catfish fillets
- 2 cups mussels and shrimp
- 4 tbsp olive oil
- 1 onion, diced
- 2 garlic cloves, minced
- ½ tsp cayenne pepper
- ½ tsp basil
- ½ tsp oregano
- 1 red bell pepper, diced
- 1 green bell pepper, diced
- 2 cups Jasmine rice
- A few saffron threads
- 3 cups fish stock
- Salt and pepper to taste

Directions:

1. Warm the olive oil in your Instant Pot on Sauté. Add in onion, garlic, and bell peppers and cook for 4 minutes. Add in catfish, rice, and saffron and cook for another 2 minutes. Add mussels, shrimps, cayenne pepper, basil, oregano, stock, salt, and pepper, stir, and seal the lid. Select Manual and cook for 6 minutes. When done, allow a natural release for 10 minutes. Serve.

Tuna & Veggie Egg Mix

Servings: 4 | Cooking Time: 25 Minutes

Ingredients:

- 2 cans tuna, drained
- 1 carrot, chopped
- 10 oz broccoli, chopped
- 1 diced onion
- 2 eggs, beaten
- 1 can cream of celery soup
- ½ cup vegetable broth
- ¾ cup milk
- 2 tbsp butter
- ½ tsp oregano
- ½ rosemary
- Salt and pepper to taste

Directions:

1. Stir the tuna, carrot, broccoli, onion, eggs, celery soup, vegetable broth, milk, butter, oregano, rosemary, salt, and pepper in your Instant Pot and seal the lid. Select Manual and cook for 15 minutes on High. Perform a quick pressure release.

Red Onion Trout Fillets With Olives

Servings: 6 | Cooking Time: 15 Minutes+ Marinating Time

Ingredients:

- 2 lb trout fillets, skin on
- ½ cup olive oil
- ¼ cup apple cider vinegar
- 1 red onion, chopped
- 1 lemon, sliced
- 2 garlic cloves, crushed
- 1 tbsp rosemary, chopped
- Salt and pepper to taste
- 3 cups fish stock
- 12 black olives

Directions:

1. In a bowl, mix oil, apple cider, onion, garlic, rosemary, sea salt, and pepper. Submerge the fillets into this mixture and refrigerate for 1 hour. Pour 4 tbsp of the marinade into your Instant Pot and add in the stock. Add the fish, seal the lid, and cook on High pressure for 4 minutes. Do a quick release. Serve with lemon and olives.

Steamed Clams

Servings:4 | Cooking Time: 10 Minutes

Ingredients:

- 2 pounds fresh clams, rinsed and purged
- 1 tablespoon olive oil
- 1 small white onion, peeled and diced
- 1 clove garlic, quartered
- ½ cup chardonnay

- ½ cup water

Directions:
1. Place clams in the steamer basket. Set aside.
2. Press the Sauté button on Instant Pot. Heat olive oil. Add onion and sauté 3–5 minutes until translucent. Add garlic and cook another minute. Pour in white wine and water. Insert steamer basket. Lock lid.
3. Press the Manual button and adjust time to 4 minutes. When the timer beeps, quick-release pressure until lid unlocks.
4. Transfer clams to four serving bowls and top with a generous scoop of cooking liquid.

Beer-steamed Mussels

Servings: 4 | Cooking Time: 15 Minutes

Ingredients:
- 3 lb mussels, debearded
- 4 tbsp butter
- 1 shallot, chopped
- 2 garlic cloves, minced
- 2 tbsp parsley, chopped
- 1 cup beer
- 1 cup chicken stock

Directions:
1. Melt butter in your Instant Pot on Sauté. Add in shallot and garlic and cook for 2 minutes. Stir in beer and cook for 1 minute. Mix in stock and mussels and seal the lid.
2. Select Manual and cook for 3 minutes on High pressure. Once ready, perform a quick pressure release. Discard unopened mussels. Serve sprinkled with parsley.

Mussels With Lemon & White Wine

Servings: 5 | Cooking Time: 10 Minutes

Ingredients:
- 2 lb mussels, cleaned and debearded
- 1 cup white wine
- ½ cup water
- 1 tsp garlic powder
- Juice from 1 lemon

Directions:
1. In the pot, mix garlic powder, water, and wine. Put the mussels into the steamer basket; rounded-side should be placed facing upwards to fit as many as possible.
2. Insert a rack into the cooker and lower the steamer basket onto the rack. Seal the lid and cook on Low Pressure for 1 minute. Release the pressure quickly. Remove unopened mussels. Coat the mussels with the wine mixture and lemon juice and serve.

Littleneck Clams In Garlic Wine Broth

Servings:4 | Cooking Time: 8 Minutes

Ingredients:
- 2 pounds fresh littleneck clams, cleaned and debearded
- 2 tablespoons olive oil
- 1 medium yellow onion, peeled and diced
- 4 cloves garlic, peeled and minced
- ½ cup dry white wine
- ½ cup vegetable broth
- ½ teaspoon salt

- 4 tablespoons chopped fresh parsley

Directions:
1. Let clams soak in water 30 minutes. Rinse several times. This will help purge any sand trapped in the shells.
2. Press the Sauté button on the Instant Pot and heat oil. Add onion and sauté 3–5 minutes until translucent. Add garlic and cook an additional 1 minute. Stir in wine, broth, and salt and let cook 2 minutes. Press the Cancel button.
3. Insert steamer basket. Place clams in basket. Lock lid.
4. Press the Manual or Pressure Cook button and adjust time to 0 minutes. When timer beeps, quick-release pressure until float valve drops. Unlock lid.
5. Remove clams and discard any that haven't opened. Transfer clams to four bowls and pour liquid from the Instant Pot equally among bowls. Garnish each bowl with 1 tablespoon parsley. Serve immediately.

Smoky Salmon With Garlic Mayo Sauce

Servings: 6 | Cooking Time: 25 Minutes

Ingredients:
- 2 lb salmon fillets
- ½ cup mayonnaise
- 1 tbsp lemon juice
- 2 garlic cloves, minced
- 1 tsp dill
- 1 tsp smoked paprika
- 2 tbsp olive oil
- 2 tbsp chives, chopped
- Salt and pepper to taste

Directions:
1. Mix the mayonnaise, smoked paprika, lemon juice, garlic, and dill in a bowl. Set aside. Sprinkle salmon with salt and pepper. Warm the olive oil in your Instant Pot on Sauté. Place in salmon and cook for 3-4 minutes per side. Spread the mayonnaise mixture on the salmon and cook for 5 minutes, turning once. Serve topped with chives.

Teriyaki Salmon

Servings:2 | Cooking Time: 5 Minutes

Ingredients:
- 2 salmon fillets
- ½ teaspoon salt
- 2 tablespoons teriyaki sauce
- 1 cup water
- 1 teaspoon toasted sesame seeds
- 2 tablespoons sliced green onion (greens only)

Directions:
1. Pat fillets dry with a paper towel and place in a steamer basket. Season salmon with salt. Brush teriyaki sauce on tops of salmon.
2. Add water to the Instant Pot and insert steam rack. Place steamer basket on steam rack. Lock lid.
3. Press the Manual or Pressure Cook button and adjust time to 5 minutes. When timer beeps, quick-release pressure until float valve drops. Unlock lid.
4. Transfer fish to plates and garnish with sesame seeds and onion greens. Serve immediately.

Dilly Lemon Salmon

Servings:2 | Cooking Time: 5 Minutes

Ingredients:
- 2 salmon fillets
- ½ teaspoon sea salt
- 4 lemon slices
- 2 teaspoons chopped fresh dill
- 1 cup water

Directions:
1. Pat fillets dry with a paper towel and place on a steamer basket. Season salmon with salt. Place 2 lemon slices on each fillet. Sprinkle with chopped dill.
2. Place water in Instant Pot. Insert trivet. Place steamer basket onto trivet. Lock lid.
3. Press the Manual button and adjust time to 5 minutes. When timer beeps, quick-release the pressure until float valve drops and then unlock lid.
4. Remove fish to plates and serve immediately.

Low-country Boil

Servings:6 | Cooking Time: 5 Minutes

Ingredients:
- 1 large sweet onion, peeled and chopped
- 4 cloves garlic, quartered
- 6 small red potatoes, cut in sixths
- 3 ears corn, cut in thirds
- 1½ pounds fully cooked andouille sausage, cut in 1" sections
- 1 pound frozen tail-on shrimp
- 1 tablespoon Old Bay Seasoning
- 2 cups chicken broth
- 1 lemon, cut into 6 wedges
- ½ cup chopped fresh parsley

Directions:
1. Layer onions in an even layer in the Instant Pot. Scatter the garlic on top of onions. Add red potatoes in an even layer, then do the same for the corn and sausage. Add the shrimp and sprinkle with Old Bay Seasoning. Pour in broth.
2. Squeeze lemon wedges into the Instant Pot and place squeezed lemon wedges into the Instant Pot. Lock lid.
3. Press the Manual button and adjust time to 5 minutes. When timer beeps, quick-release the pressure until float valve drops and then unlock lid. Transfer ingredients to a serving platter and garnish with parsley.

Mediterranean Cod

Servings:2 | Cooking Time: 6 Minutes

Ingredients:
- 2 cod fillets, divided
- 2 teaspoons olive oil, divided
- 1½ teaspoons sea salt, divided
- 10 pitted kalamata olives, divided
- 1 small Roma tomato, diced, divided
- 3 tablespoons chopped fresh basil leaves, divided

Directions:
1. Place a piece of cod on a 10" × 10" square of aluminum foil. Drizzle with 1 teaspoon olive oil. Sprinkle with ½ teaspoon salt. Scatter 5 olives, ½ the tomatoes, and 1 tablespoon basil on top of fish. Bring up the sides of the foil and crimp at the top to create a foil pocket.
2. Repeat with remaining piece of fish. Place both fish packs in the Instant Pot. Lock lid.
3. Press the Manual button and adjust time to 6 minutes. When the timer beeps, quick-release pressure until float valve drops and then unlock lid.
4. Remove foil packets and transfer fish and toppings to two plates. Garnish each plate with ½ tablespoon basil and ¼ teaspoon salt.

Trout Fillets With Tri-color Pasta & Capers

Servings: 5 | Cooking Time: 50 Minutes

Ingredients:
- 16 oz tri-color rotini pasta
- 6 oz trout fillets
- 1 cup olive oil
- ½ cup lemon juice
- 1 tsp rosemary, chopped
- 3 garlic cloves, crushed
- Salt and pepper to taste
- 2 tbsp parsley, chopped
- Olives, capers for serving

Directions:
1. In a bowl, mix oil, lemon juice, rosemary, 2 garlic cloves, black pepper, and salt. Stir well and submerge fillets in this mixture. Refrigerate for 30 minutes. Remove from the fridge. Place the fillets and marinade in the pot. Add in 1 cup of water. Seal the lid and cook on High pressure for 4 minutes. Do a quick release. Add in the pasta and 1 cup of water. Seal the lid and cook for 3 minutes on High. Do a quick release. Serve with capers and parsley.

Lime & Honey Scallops

Servings: 2 | Cooking Time: 15 Minutes

Ingredients:
- 1 lb sea scallops, shells removed
- 1 cup water
- 1 tbsp olive oil
- 3 tbsp honey
- 1 lime, juiced and zested
- ½ cup soy sauce
- ½ tsp ground ginger
- ½ tsp garlic powder
- Salt to taste

Directions:
1. Pour 1 cup of water into your Instant Pot and fit in a trivet. Place scallops, olive oil, honey, soy sauce, ginger, garlic powder, lime zest, and salt in a small pan and put it on the trivet. Seal the lid and cook for 6 minutes on Steam. Once ready, perform a quick pressure release and unlock the lid. Serve drizzled with lime juice

Mackerel With Potatoes & Spinach

Servings: 4 | Cooking Time: 20 Minutes

Ingredients:
- 4 mackerels, skin on
- 1 lb spinach, torn
- 5 potatoes, peeled, chopped
- 3 tbsp olive oil
- 2 garlic cloves, crushed
- 2 tbsp mint leaves, chopped
- 1 lemon, juiced
- Sea salt to taste

Directions:
1. Heat 2 tbsp of the olive oil on Sauté. Stir-fry garlic for 1 minute. Stir in spinach and salt and cook for 4-5 minutes until wilted; set aside. Make a layer of potatoes in the pot. Top with fish and drizzle with lemon juice, remaining olive oil, and salt. Pour in 1 cup of water, seal the lid, and cook on Steam for 7 minutes on High. When ready, do a quick release. Carefully unlock the lid. Plate the fish and potatoes with spinach and serve topped with mint leaves.

Quick Shrimp Gumbo With Sausage

Servings: 4 | Cooking Time: 30 Minutes

Ingredients:
- 1 lb jumbo shrimp
- 2 tbsp olive oil
- 1/3 cup flour
- 1 ½ tsp Cajun seasoning
- 1 onion, chopped
- 1 red bell pepper, chopped
- 2 celery stalks, chopped
- 2 garlic cloves, minced
- 1 serrano pepper, minced
- 2 ½ cups chicken broth
- 6 oz andouille sausage, sliced
- 2 green onions, finely sliced
- Salt and pepper to taste

Directions:
1. Heat olive oil on Sauté. Whisk in the flour with a wooden spoon and cook 3 minutes, stirring constantly. Stir in Cajun seasoning, onion, bell pepper, celery, garlic, and serrano pepper for about 5 minutes. Pour in the chicken broth, ¾ cup water, and andouille sausage. Seal and cook for 6 minutes on High Pressure. Do a natural pressure for 5 minutes. Stir the shrimp into the gumbo to eat it up for 3 minutes. Adjust the seasoning. Ladle the gumbo into bowls and garnish with the green onions.

Thyme For Lemon-butter Sea Bass

Servings: 2 | Cooking Time: 7 Minutes

Ingredients:
- 2 tablespoons unsalted butter, melted
- 1 tablespoon lemon juice
- 2 teaspoons fresh thyme leaves
- ¼ cup Italian bread crumbs
- 2 sea bass fillets
- ½ teaspoon salt
- ¼ teaspoon ground black pepper
- 1 cup water

Directions:
1. In a small bowl, combine butter, lemon juice, thyme, and bread crumbs to form a thick paste.
2. Pat sea bass fillets dry with a paper towel. Season sea bass with salt and pepper. Press paste on top of each fillet and place in steamer basket.
3. Add water to the Instant Pot and insert steam rack. Place basket on steam rack. Lock lid.
4. Press the Manual or Pressure Cook button and adjust time to 5 minutes. When timer beeps, quick-release pressure until float valve drops. Unlock lid.
5. Line a baking sheet with parchment paper. Transfer fillets to prepared baking sheet. Broil approximately 1–2 minutes until tops are browned.
6. Remove from heat. Serve warm.

Stewed Cod And Peppers

Servings:2 | Cooking Time: 3 Minutes

Ingredients:
- 1 can fire-roasted diced tomatoes, including juice
- ½ cup chicken broth
- 2 teaspoons smoked paprika
- 1 medium green bell pepper, seeded and diced small
- ½ cup diced yellow onion
- 1 teaspoon garlic salt
- ¼ teaspoon ground black pepper
- 1 pound cod fillets, cut into bite-sized pieces

Directions:
1. Place all ingredients except cod in the Instant Pot and stir. Once mixed, add fish on top. Lock lid.
2. Press the Manual or Pressure Cook button and adjust time to 3 minutes. When timer beeps, quick-release pressure until float valve drops. Unlock lid.
3. Transfer to bowls. Serve warm.

Tilapia With Basil Pesto & Rice

Servings: 2 | Cooking Time: 15 Minutes

Ingredients:
- 2 tilapia fillets
- 2 tbsp basil pesto
- ½ cup basmati rice
- Salt and pepper to taste

Directions:
1. Place the rice and 1 cup of water in your Instant Pot and season with salt and pepper; fit in a trivet. Place tilapia fillets in the middle of a parchment paper sheet. Top each fillet with pesto and roll all the edges to form a packet. Place it on the trivet and seal the lid.
2. Select Manual and cook for 6 minutes on Low pressure. Once ready, perform a quick pressure release. Carefully unlock the lid. Fluff the rice with a fork and transfer to a plate. Top with tilapia and serve.

Salmon Steaks With Garlic & Lemon

Servings: 3 | Cooking Time: 60 Minutes

Ingredients:
- 1 lb salmon steaks
- 1 tsp garlic powder
- 2 tbsp olive oil
- Salt and pepper to taste
- ¼ cup lemon juice

Directions:
1. In a bowl, mix garlic powder, olive oil, salt, lemon juice, and pepper. Pour the mixture into a Ziploc bag along with the salmon. Seal the bag and shake to coat well. Refrigerate for 30 minutes. Pour in 1 cup of water in the Instant Pot and insert the trivet. Remove the fish from the Ziploc bag and place it on top. Reserve the marinade. Seal the lid and select Steam.
2. Cook for 15 minutes on High. When ready, do a quick release and remove the steaks. Discard the liquid. Wipe clean the pot. Pour in the marinade and hit Sauté. Cook for 3-4 minutes. Serve the salmon drizzled with the sauce.

Mediterranean Cod With Cherry Tomatoes

Servings: 4 | Cooking Time: 20 Minutes

Ingredients:
- 1 lb cherry tomatoes, halved
- 1 bunch fresh thyme sprigs
- 4 fillets cod
- 2 tbsp olive oil
- 1 clove garlic, pressed
- Salt and pepper to taste
- 1 cup white rice
- 1 cup kalamata olives
- 2 tbsp pickled capers

Directions:
1. Line a parchment paper on the basket of the pot. Place about half the tomatoes in a single layer on the paper. Sprinkle with thyme, reserving some for garnish. Arrange cod fillets on top. Sprinkle with some olive oil. Spread the garlic, pepper, salt, and remaining tomatoes over the fish. In the pot, mix rice and 2 cups of water. Lay a trivet over the rice and water.
2. Lower steamer basket onto the trivet. Seal the lid, and cook for 7 minutes on Low Pressure. Release the pressure quickly. Remove the steamer basket and trivet from the pot. Use a fork to fluff the rice. Plate the fish fillets and apply a garnish of olives, reserved thyme, remaining olive oil, and capers. Serve with rice.

Mediterranean Cod With Capers

Servings: 4 | Cooking Time: 15 Minutes

Ingredients:
- 4 cod fillets, boneless
- ½ cup white wine
- 1 tsp oregano
- Salt and pepper to taste
- ¼ cup capers

Directions:
1. Pour the white wine and ½ cup of water in your Instant Pot and fit in a trivet. Place cod fillets on the trivet.

2. Sprinkle with oregano, salt, and pepper. Seal the lid, select Steam, and cook for 3 minutes on Low. Once ready, perform a quick pressure release. Top the cod with capers and drizzle with the sauce to serve.

Shrimp With Okra & Brussels Sprouts

Servings: 4 | Cooking Time: 40 Minutes

Ingredients:
- 1 lb large shrimp, cleaned, rinsed
- 6 oz Brussels sprouts
- 4 oz okra, whole
- 2 carrots, chopped
- 2 cups vegetable broth
- 2 tomatoes, diced
- 2 tbsp tomato paste
- ½ tsp cayenne pepper
- Salt and pepper to taste
- 2 tbsp olive oil
- ¼ cup balsamic vinegar
- 1 tbsp rosemary, chopped
- 2 tbsp sour cream

Directions:
1. Mix olive oil, vinegar, rosemary, salt, and pepper in a large bowl. Stir the shrimp into the mixture. Toss well to coat. Mix tomatoes, tomato paste, and cayenne pepper in the pressure cooker. Cook on Sauté for 5 minutes, stirring constantly. Set aside. Pour broth, Brussels sprouts, carrots, and okra into the pot. Cook on High pressure for 15 minutes. Do a quick release.
2. Remove the vegetables and add the shrimp to the remaining broth in the pot. Press Sauté and cook for 5 minutes. Add in the cooked vegetables. Cook for 2-3 minutes, stirring constantly. Stir in sour cream and serve.

Thai-inspired Poached Salmon

Servings:4 | Cooking Time: 3 Minutes

Ingredients:
- 1 can coconut milk
- Juice and zest of 1 medium lime
- 1 teaspoon lemongrass paste
- 1 tablespoon hot sauce
- ½ teaspoon salt
- 4 salmon fillets
- ½ cup fresh basil chiffonade, divided

Directions:
1. In the Instant Pot, whisk together coconut milk, lime juice and zest, lemongrass paste, hot sauce, and salt. Add salmon and ¼ cup basil. Lock lid.
2. Press the Manual or Pressure Cook button and adjust time to 3 minutes. When timer beeps, quick-release pressure until float valve drops. Unlock lid.
3. Transfer fish and broth to bowls and garnish with remaining basil. Serve warm.

Chili Steamed Salmon

Servings: 2 | Cooking Time: 25 Minutes

Ingredients:
- 2 salmon fillets
- 1 red chili, chopped
- 1 tsp sesame oil
- Salt and pepper to taste

Directions:
1. Pour 1 cup of water into your Instant Pot and fit in a trivet. Sprinkle salmon with salt and pepper and place it on the trivet. Seal the lid and cook for 6 minutes on Steam. Once ready, allow a natural release for 10 minutes and unlock the lid. Drizzle with sesame oil and top with red chili. Serve with lemon wedges.

Umami Calamari

Servings:4 | Cooking Time: 20 Minutes

Ingredients:
- 1 tablespoon olive oil
- 1 small onion, peeled and diced
- 2 cloves garlic, minced
- ¼ cup dry red wine
- 1 can diced tomatoes, including juice
- 1 cup chicken broth
- ¼ cup chopped fresh parsley
- 6 tablespoons chopped fresh basil, divided
- 1 teaspoon sea salt
- ½ teaspoon ground black pepper
- 2 teaspoons anchovy paste
- 1 bay leaf
- 1 pound calamari tubes, cut into ¼" rings
- ¼ cup grated Parmesan cheese

Directions:
1. Press the Sauté button on Instant Pot. Add olive oil and heat. Add onion and sauté for 3–5 minutes until onions are translucent. Add garlic and sauté for an additional minute. Add red wine, press Adjust button to change temperature to Less, and simmer unlidded for 5 minutes.
2. Add remaining ingredients except 2 tablespoons basil and Parmesan cheese. Lock lid.
3. Press the Manual button and adjust time to 10 minutes. When timer beeps, let pressure release naturally for 10 minutes. Quick-release any additional pressure until the float valve drops and then unlock lid.
4. Remove bay leaf. Use a slotted spoon to transfer pot ingredients to four bowls. Garnish each bowl with equal amounts Parmesan cheese and ½ tablespoon basil.

Indian Prawn Curry

Servings: 4 | Cooking Time: 30 Minutes

Ingredients:
- 1 ½ lb prawns, deveined
- 2 tbsp ghee
- 2 garlic cloves, minced
- 1 onion, chopped
- 1 tsp ginger, grated
- ½ tsp ground turmeric
- 1 tsp red chili powder
- 2 tsp ground cumin
- 2 tsp ground coriander
- 2 tbsp curry paste
- 2 cups coconut milk
- 1 cup tomatoes, chopped
- 2 habanero peppers, minced
- Salt and pepper to taste
- 1 tbsp fresh lemon juice

Directions:
1. Melt the ghee in your Instant Pot on Sauté. Add in garlic, onion, and ginger and cook for 4 minutes. Stir in the turmeric, chili powder, cumin, coriander, and curry paste and cook for 1 more minute. Stir in coconut milk, prawns, tomatoes, habanero peppers, salt, and pepper.
2. Seal the lid. Select Manual and cook for 5 minutes on Low. Once ready, allow a natural release for 10 minutes, then perform a quick pressure release, and unlock the lid. Top with lemon juice and serve.

Citrus Smelt With Okra & Cherry Tomatoes

Servings: 4 | Cooking Time: 30 Minutes + Cooling Time

Ingredients:
- 1 lb fresh smelt, cleaned, heads removed
- 1 cup extra virgin olive oil
- ½ cup lemon juice
- ¼ cup orange juice
- 1 tbsp Dijon mustard
- 1 tsp rosemary, chopped
- 4 tbsp vegetable oil
- 2 garlic cloves, crushed
- 1 tsp sea salt
- 5 oz okra
- 1 carrot, chopped
- ¼ cup green peas
- 5 oz cherry tomatoes, halved
- 1 cup fish stock

Directions:
1. In a bowl, mix olive oil, lemon and orange juices, Dijon mustard, garlic, salt, and rosemary. Stir well and submerge fish in this mixture. Refrigerate for 1 hour. Heat the vegetable oil on Sauté and stir-fry carrot, peas, cherry tomatoes, and okra for 10 minutes. Add in the fish stock.
2. Place a trivet over the mixture and lower the fish onto the trivet. Pour in the marinade. Seal the lid and cook on Manual for 8 minutes on High. When done, do a quick release. Serve the smelt drizzled with the cooking sauce.

Black Squid Ink Tagliatelle

Servings: 4 | Cooking Time: 25 Minutes

Ingredients:
- 18 oz squid ink tagliatelle, cooked
- 1 lb fresh seafood mix
- ¼ cup olive oil
- 4 garlic cloves, crushed
- 1 tbsp parsley, chopped
- 1 tsp rosemary, chopped
- ½ tbsp white wine

Directions:

1. Heat 3 tbsp olive oil on Sauté and stir-fry the garlic for 1-2 minutes until fragrant. Add seafood, parsley, and rosemary and stir. Add the remaining oil, wine, and ½ cup of water. Seal the lid and cook on High Pressure for 4 minutes. Do a quick release and set aside. Open the lid, add the pasta, and stir. Serve hot.

Steamed Shrimp And Asparagus

Servings:2 | Cooking Time: 1 Minute

Ingredients:
- 1 cup water
- 1 bunch asparagus
- 1 teaspoon sea salt, divided
- 1 pound shrimp, peeled and deveined
- ½ lemon
- 2 tablespoons butter, cut into 2 pats

Directions:
1. Pour water into Instant Pot. Insert trivet. Place steamer basket onto trivet.
2. Prepare asparagus by finding the natural snap point on the stalks and discarding the woody ends.
3. Spread the asparagus on the bottom of the steamer basket. Sprinkle with ½ teaspoon salt. Add the shrimp. Squeeze lemon into the Instant Pot, then sprinkle shrimp with remaining ½ teaspoon salt. Place pats of butter on shrimp. Lock lid.
4. Press the Manual button and adjust time to 1 minute. When the timer beeps, quick-release the pressure until the float valve drops and then unlock lid.
5. Transfer shrimp and asparagus to a platter and serve.

Lemon Salmon With Blue Cheese

Servings: 4 | Cooking Time: 15 Minutes

Ingredients:
- 1 lb salmon fillets
- 2 tbsp olive oil
- 1 garlic clove, minced
- 1 tbsp lemon juice
- ¼ tsp thyme
- 1 tbsp blue cheese, crumbled
- 1 lemon, sliced
- 2 sprigs fresh rosemary
- Salt and pepper to taste

Directions:
1. Mix the olive oil, garlic, lemon juice, thyme, salt, pepper, and blue cheese in a bowl. Pour 1 cup of water into your Instant Pot and fit in a trivet. Place salmon on the trivet and top with cheese mixture, lemon slices, and rosemary sprigs. Seal the lid, select Manual, and cook for 5 minutes on High pressure. When done, perform a quick pressure release and unlock the lid. Discard the rosemary sprigs and serve.

Calamari Poppers

Servings:4 | Cooking Time: 3 Minutes

Ingredients:
- 10–12 calamari tubes
- 1 cup shredded sharp Cheddar cheese
- ¾ cup cream cheese, softened
- ¼ teaspoon garlic powder
- ¼ teaspoon ground black pepper

- 2 medium jalapeño peppers, seeded and diced
- 1 cup water

Directions:
1. Rinse calamari tubes and set aside.
2. In a medium bowl, combine Cheddar cheese, cream cheese, garlic powder, black pepper, and jalapeños. Transfer mixture to a piping bag or plastic bag. Cut the tip off large enough for the mixture to pass through. Pipe cheese mixture into calamari tubes. Fasten opening of each calamari tube with a toothpick.
3. Add water to the Instant Pot and insert steamer basket. Place stuffed calamari in an even row in basket. Lock lid.
4. Press the Manual or Pressure Cook button and adjust time to 3 minutes. When timer beeps, quick-release pressure until float valve drops. Unlock lid.
5. Transfer calamari to a plate. Remove toothpicks. Serve warm.

Crab Pilaf With Broccoli & Asparagus

Servings: 4 | Cooking Time: 30 Minutes

Ingredients:
- ½ lb asparagus, trimmed and cut into 1-inch pieces
- ½ lb broccoli florets
- Salt to taste
- 2 tbsp olive oil
- 1 small onion, chopped
- 1 cup rice
- 1/3 cup white wine
- 2 cups vegetable stock
- 8 oz lump crabmeat

Directions:
1. Heat oil on Sauté and cook the onion for 3 minutes until soft. Stir in rice and cook for 1 minute. Pour in the wine. Cook for 2 to 3 minutes, stirring until the liquid has almost evaporated. Add vegetable stock and salt; stir.
2. Place a trivet on top. Arrange the broccoli and asparagus on the trivet. Seal the lid and cook on High Pressure for 8 minutes. Do a quick release. Remove the vegetables to a bowl. Fluff the rice with a fork and add in the crabmeat, heat for a minute. Taste and adjust the seasoning. Serve immediately topped with broccoli and asparagus.

Louisiana Grouper

Servings:4 | Cooking Time: 20 Minutes

Ingredients:
- 2 tablespoons olive oil
- 1 small onion, peeled and diced
- 1 stalk celery, diced
- 1 small green bell pepper, seeded and diced
- 1 can diced tomatoes
- ¼ cup water
- 1 tablespoon tomato paste
- 1 teaspoon honey
- Pinch of dried basil
- 2 teaspoons Creole seasoning
- 4 grouper fillets, rinsed and cut into bite-sized pieces
- ½ teaspoon sea salt
- ¼ teaspoon ground black pepper

Directions:
1. Press Sauté button on Instant Pot. Heat oil and add onion, celery, and bell pepper. Sauté for 3–5 minutes until onions are trans-

lucent and peppers are tender.

2. Stir in undrained tomatoes, water, tomato paste, honey, basil, and Creole seasoning.

3. Sprinkle fish with salt and pepper. Gently toss the fish pieces into the sauce in the Instant Pot. Lock lid.

4. Press the Manual button and adjust time to 5 minutes. When timer beeps, quick-release the pressure until float valve drops and then unlock lid.

5. Transfer fish to a serving platter. Press Sauté button on Instant Pot, press Adjust button to change the temperature to Less, and simmer juices unlidded for 10 minutes. Transfer tomatoes and preferred amount of sauce over fish. Serve immediately.

Salmon With Coconut Rice

Servings: 2 | Cooking Time: 20 Minutes

Ingredients:
- 1 oz vegetable soup mix, dried
- 2 salmon fillets
- ½ cup jasmine rice
- 1 cup coconut milk
- 1 tbsp ghee
- ½ oz grated ginger
- 1 spring onion, chopped
- Salt and pepper to taste

Directions:
1. Stir the rice, coconut milk, ghee, ginger, and soup mix in your Instant Pot and fit in a trivet. Season salmon with salt and pepper and place it on the trivet. Seal the lid, select Manual, and cook for 5 minutes on High pressure. Once done, allow a natural release for 10 minutes and unlock the lid. Serve topped with spring onion.

Creamed Crab

Servings:4 | Cooking Time: 8 Minutes

Ingredients:
- 4 tablespoons butter
- ½ stalk celery, finely diced
- 1 small red onion, peeled and finely diced
- 1 pound uncooked lump crabmeat
- ¼ cup chicken broth
- ½ cup heavy cream
- ½ teaspoon sea salt
- ½ teaspoon ground black pepper

Directions:
1. Press the Sauté button on Instant Pot. Add the butter and melt. Add the celery and red onion. Stir-fry for 3–5 minutes until celery begins to soften. Stir in the crabmeat and broth. Lock lid.

2. Press the Manual button and adjust time to 3 minutes. Press the Pressure button to change the pressure to Less. When timer beeps, quick-release pressure until float valve drops and then unlock lid.

3. Carefully stir in the cream, add salt and pepper, and serve warm.

White Wine Oysters

Servings: 4 | Cooking Time: 10 Minutes

Ingredients:
- 2 lb in-shell oysters, cleaned
- 1 cup vegetable broth

- 4 tbsp white wine
- 2 tbsp thyme, chopped
- 1 garlic clove, minced
- Salt and pepper to taste
- 4 tbsp butter, melted

Directions:
1. Place the vegetable broth, oysters, white wine, garlic, salt, and pepper in your Instant Pot and seal the lid. Select Manual and cook for 3 minutes on High pressure. Once done, perform a quick pressure release and unlock the lid. Drain the oysters, drizzle with the melted butter, and top with thyme to serve.

Octopus & Shrimp With Collard Greens

Servings: 4 | Cooking Time: 30 Minutes

Ingredients:
- 6 oz octopus, cut into bite-sized pieces
- 1 lb collard greens, chopped
- 1 lb shrimp, whole
- 1 tomato, chopped
- 3 cups fish stock
- 4 tbsp olive oil
- 3 garlic cloves
- 2 tbsp parsley, chopped
- 1 tsp sea salt

Directions:
1. Place shrimp and octopus in the pot. Add tomato and fish stock. Seal the lid and cook on High Pressure for 15 minutes. Do a quick release. Remove shrimp and octopus. Drain the liquid. Heat olive oil on Sauté and add garlic and parsley and cook for 1 minute. Add in collard greens, season with salt, and simmer for 5 minutes. Serve with shrimp and octopus.

Paprika Cod With Orange Sauce

Servings: 4 | Cooking Time: 20 Minutes

Ingredients:
- 4 cod fillets
- 2 tsp ginger, grated
- 1 orange, juiced and zested
- 1 cup fish stock
- 2 tbsp olive oil
- ¼ cup dry white wine
- ½ tsp paprika
- ½ jalapeno pepper, minced
- 1 tbsp arrowroot powder
- Salt and pepper to taste

Directions:
1. Sprinkle fish fillets with olive oil, paprika, salt, and pepper. Mix the ginger, orange juice, orange zest, jalapeño pepper, fish stock, and white wine in your Instant Pot. Fit in a trivet. Place the fillets on the trivet and seal the lid. Select Manual and cook for 6 minutes on High.

2. When done, perform a quick pressure release and unlock the lid. Remove the cod. In a bowl, mix the arrowroot powder with 1 cup of the cooking liquid and pour into the pot. Press Sauté and cook for 4-5 minutes until thickened. Top the fillets with sauce and serve.

Chapter 8 : Poultry Recipes

Chapter 8 : Poultry Recipes

Turkey Cakes With Ginger Gravy

Servings: 4 | Cooking Time: 25 Minutes

Ingredients:
- 1 lb ground turkey
- ¼ cup breadcrumbs
- ¼ cup grated Parmesan
- ½ tsp garlic powder
- 2 green onions, chopped
- Salt and pepper to taste
- 2 tbsp olive oil
- 2 cups tomatoes, diced
- ¼ cup chicken broth
- Ginger sauce
- 4 tbsp soy sauce
- 2 tbsp canola oil
- 2 tbsp rice vinegar
- 1 garlic clove, minced
- 1 tsp ginger, grated
- ½ tbsp honey
- ¼ tsp black pepper
- ½ tbsp cornstarch

Directions:
1. Combine turkey, breadcrumbs, green onions, garlic powder, salt, pepper, and Parmesan cheese in a bowl. Mix with your hands and shape meatballs out of the mixture. In another bowl, mix soy sauce, canola oil, rice vinegar, garlic clove, ginger, honey, pepper, and cornstarch. Warm the olive oil in your Instant Pot on Sauté.
2. Place in meatballs and cook for 4 minutes on all sides. Pour in ginger gravy, tomatoes, and chicken stock and seal the lid. Select Manual and cook for 10 minutes on High pressure. Once over, perform a quick pressure release and unlock the lid. Serve in individual bowls.

Sunday Turkey Lettuce Wraps

Servings: 4 | Cooking Time: 35 Minutes

Ingredients:
- ¾ cup olive oil
- 4 cloves garlic, minced
- 3 tbsp maple syrup
- 2 tbsp pineapple juice
- 1 cup coconut milk
- 3 tbsp rice wine vinegar
- 3 tbsp soy sauce
- 1 tbsp Thai-style chili paste
- 1 lb turkey breast, boneless, cut into strips
- 1 lettuce, leaves separated
- 1/3 cup chopped peanuts
- ¼ cup chopped cilantro

Directions:
1. In your Instant Pot, mix oil, garlic, rice wine vinegar, soy sauce, pineapple juice, maple syrup, coconut milk, and chili paste until smooth; add turkey strips and ensure they are submerged in the sauce. Seal the lid and cook on High Pressure for 12 minutes. Release the pressure quickly. Place the turkey at the center of each lettuce leaf. Top with cilantro and chopped peanuts.

Tasty Indian Chicken Curry

Servings: 6 | Cooking Time: 30 Minutes

Ingredients:
- 1 can coconut milk, refrigerated overnight
- 2 lb boneless, skinless chicken legs
- 2 tbsp butter
- 1 large onion, minced
- 1 tbsp grated fresh ginger
- 1 tbsp minced fresh garlic
- ½ tsp ground turmeric
- 1 tbsp Kashmiri chili powder
- 3 tomatoes, pureed
- 2 tbsp Indian curry paste
- 2 tbsp dried fenugreek
- 1 tsp garam masala
- Salt to taste

Directions:
1. Melt butter on Sauté in your Instant Pot. Add in onion and cook for 3 minutes until fragrant. Stir in ginger, turmeric, garlic, and red chili powder for 2 minutes. Place the water from the coconut milk can in a bowl and mix with pureed tomatoes and chicken. Pour in the onion mixture.
2. Seal the lid and cook on High Pressure for 8 minutes. Release the pressure quickly. Stir in coconut milk, fenugreek, salt, curry paste, and garam masala. Simmer for 10 minutes until the sauce thickens on Sauté. Serve.

Moroccan-inspired Chicken Thighs

Servings:6 | Cooking Time: 7 Minutes

Ingredients:
- 2 teaspoons smoked paprika
- 1 teaspoon cumin
- ½ teaspoon ground ginger
- 1 teaspoon salt
- ½ teaspoon ground black pepper
- 3 pounds boneless, skinless chicken thighs
- 1 cup water
- ½ cup sliced Manzanilla green olives plus ¼ cup juice from jar

Directions:
1. In a small bowl, combine paprika, cumin, ginger, salt, and pepper.
2. Pat chicken dry with a paper towel. Season with spice mixture.
3. Add water to the Instant Pot and insert steam rack. Add olive juice to a 7-cup glass baking dish. Arrange chicken in dish. Scatter olives evenly over chicken. Lock lid.
4. Press the Manual or Pressure Cook button and adjust time to 7 minutes. When timer beeps, quick-release pressure until float valve drops. Unlock lid. Check chicken using a meat thermometer

to ensure internal temperature is at least 165°F.

5. Remove dish from pot. Serve warm.

Bbq Chicken Legs

Servings:5 | Cooking Time: 15 Minutes

Ingredients:
- 1 cup chicken broth
- 3 pounds chicken legs/drumsticks
- ¾ cup barbecue sauce

Directions:
1. Insert trivet into Instant Pot. Add chicken broth. Arrange chicken standing up, meaty-side down, on the trivet. Lock lid.
2. Press the Poultry button and cook for the default time of 15 minutes. When timer beeps, let pressure release naturally for 10 minutes. Quick-release any additional pressure until float valve drops and then unlock lid. Check the chicken using a meat thermometer to ensure the internal temperature is at least 165°F.
3. Remove chicken from pot. In a large bowl, gently toss chicken legs in the barbecue sauce and serve.

Spicy Ground Turkey Chili With Vegetables

Servings: 6 | Cooking Time: 60 Minutes

Ingredients:
- 1 tbsp olive oil
- 1 small onion, diced
- 2 garlic cloves, minced
- 1 lb ground turkey
- 2 bell peppers, chopped
- 6 potatoes, chopped
- 1 cup carrots, chopped
- 1 cup corn kernels, roasted
- 1 cup tomato puree
- 1 cup diced tomatoes
- 1 cup chicken broth
- 1 tbsp ground cumin
- 1 tbsp chili powder
- Salt and pepper to taste

Directions:
1. Warm oil on Sauté in your Instant Pot and stir-fry onion and garlic until soft for about 3 minutes. Stir in turkey and cook until thoroughly browned, about 5-6 minutes. Add the bell peppers, potatoes, carrots, corn, tomato puree, tomatoes, broth, cumin, chili powder, salt, and pepper, and stir to combine. Seal the lid and cook for 25 minutes on High Pressure. Do a quick release. Set to Sauté and cook uncovered for 15 more minutes. Serve.

Hot Chicken With Coriander & Ginger

Servings: 6 | Cooking Time: 45 Minutes

Ingredients:
- 2 lb chicken thighs
- 1 tbsp ancho chili powder
- 1 tsp fresh basil
- Salt and pepper to taste
- 6 cups chicken broth
- 1 tbsp ginger, freshly grated
- 1 tbsp coriander seeds
- 3 garlic cloves, crushed

Directions:
1. Season the chicken with chili powder, salt, and pepper and place in the Instant Pot. Add the chicken broth broth, ginger, garlic, and coriander seeds; stir. Seal the lid and cook on Meat/Stew for 25 minutes on High. Do a natural release for 10 minutes. Serve topped with basil.

Chicken Thighs With Mushrooms & Garlic

Servings: 2 | Cooking Time: 30 Minutes

Ingredients:
- 2 chicken thighs, boneless and skinless
- 6 oz button mushrooms
- 3 tbsp olive oil
- 1 tsp rosemary, chopped
- 2 garlic cloves, crushed
- ½ tsp salt
- 1 tbsp butter
- 1 tbsp Italian seasoning

Directions:
1. Heat a tablespoon of olive oil on Sauté in your Instant Pot. Add chicken thighs and sear for 5 minutes. Set aside. Pour in the remaining oil, and add mushrooms, rosemary, salt, and Italian seasoning mix. Stir-fry for 5 minutes. Add in butter, chicken, and 2 cups of water.
2. Seal the lid and cook on Pressure Cook for 13 minutes on High. Do a quick release. Remove the chicken and mushrooms from the cooker and serve with garlic.

Pea & Rice Chicken With Paprika & Herbs

Servings: 4 | Cooking Time: 30 Minutes

Ingredients:
- 4 chicken breasts, chopped
- 1 garlic clove, minced
- ½ tsp paprika
- ¼ tsp dried oregano
- ¼ tsp dried thyme
- 1 tsp cayenne pepper
- Salt and pepper to taste
- 1 tbsp oil olive
- 1 onion, chopped
- 1 tbsp tomato puree
- 2 cups chicken broth
- 1 cup rice
- 1 celery stalk, diced
- 1 cup frozen green peas

Directions:
1. Season chicken with garlic, oregano, white pepper, thyme, paprika, cayenne pepper, and salt. Warm the oil on Sauté in your Instant Pot. Add in onion and cook for 4 minutes until fragrant. Mix in tomato puree to coat. Add ¼ cup chicken broth into the cooker to deglaze the pan, scrape the pan's bottom to get rid of browned bits of food. Mix in celery, rice, and seasoned chicken. Add in the remaining broth to the chicken mixture. Seal the lid and cook on High Pressure for 8 minutes. Do a quick release. Mix in green peas, cover with the lid, and let sit for 5 minutes. Serve warm.

Chicken With Honey-lime Sauce

Servings: 4 | Cooking Time: 30 Minutes

Ingredients:
- 4 chicken breasts, cut into chunks
- 1 onion, diced
- 4 garlic cloves, smashed
- 1 tbsp honey
- 3 tbsp soy sauce
- 2 tbsp lime juice
- 2 tsp sesame oil
- 1 tsp rice vinegar
- 1 tbsp cornstarch
- Salt and pepper to taste

Directions:
1. Mix garlic, onion, and chicken in your Instant Pot. In a bowl, combine honey, sesame oil, lime juice, soy sauce, and rice vinegar. Pour over the chicken mixture. Seal the lid and cook on High Pressure for 15 minutes. Release the pressure quickly. Mix 1 tbsp water and cornstarch until well dissolved; Stir into the sauce, add salt and pepper to taste. Press Sauté. Simmer the sauce and cook for 2 to 3 minutes as you stir until thickened.

Bourbon Barbecue Chicken

Servings:5 | Cooking Time: 15 Minutes

Ingredients:
- ¼ cup bourbon whiskey
- ¼ cup pure maple syrup
- 1 tablespoon Dijon mustard
- 1 cup ketchup
- 1 teaspoon garlic powder
- 1 teaspoon onion salt
- 1 teaspoon smoked paprika
- 3 pounds chicken legs
- 1 cup water

Directions:
1. In a small bowl, whisk together bourbon, maple syrup, mustard, ketchup, garlic powder, onion salt, and smoked paprika. Place chicken in large zip-top bag and pour mixture over chicken; seal bag and refrigerate for 1 hour.
2. Insert trivet into Instant Pot. Add water. Arrange chicken standing up, meaty-side down, on the trivet. Lock lid.
3. Press the Poultry button and cook for the default time of 15 minutes. When timer beeps, let pressure release naturally for 10 minutes. Quick-release any additional pressure until the float valve drops and then unlock lid. Check the chicken using a meat thermometer to ensure the internal temperature is at least 165°F.
4. Transfer chicken to a serving tray. Brush with remaining 2 tablespoons sauce and serve.

Potato Skins With Shredded Turkey

Servings: 4 | Cooking Time: 30 Minutes

Ingredients:
- 2 cups vegetable broth
- 1 tsp chili powder
- 1 tsp ground cumin
- ½ tsp onion powder
- ½ tsp garlic powder
- 1 lb turkey breast
- 4 potatoes
- 1 Fresno chili, minced
- Salt and pepper to taste

Directions:
1. In the pot, combine broth, cumin, garlic powder, onion powder, and chili powder. Toss in turkey to coat. Place a steamer rack over the turkey. On top of the rack, set the steamer basket. Use a fork to pierce the potatoes and transfer to the steamer basket. Seal the lid and cook for 20 minutes on High. Release the pressure quickly.
2. Remove rack and steamer basket from the cooker. Shred the turkey in a bowl. Place the potatoes on a plate. Cut in half each potato lengthwise and scoop out the insides. Season with salt and pepper. Stuff with shredded turkey. Top with chili pepper.

Cuban Mojo Chicken Tortillas

Servings: 4 | Cooking Time: 80 Minutes + Marinating Time

Ingredients:
- 4 chicken breasts
- 2 tbsp olive oil
- 1 lime, juiced
- 1 grapefruit, juiced
- 4 garlic cloves, minced
- 1 tsp ground cumin
- Salt and pepper to taste
- 2 tbsp chopped cilantro
- 4 tortillas
- 1 avocado, sliced
- 2 tbsp hot sauce

Directions:
1. Combine olive oil, lime juice, grapefruit juice, garlic, cumin, cilantro, salt, and pepper in a bowl. Add in chicken breasts and let marinate covered for 30 minutes. Transfer chicken and marinade to your Instant Pot and pour in 1 cup of water. Seal the lid and cook for 20 minutes on Manual. Once done, allow a natural release for 10 minutes and unlock the lid. Remove the chicken and shred it, then add it back to the pot; stir. Divide the chicken between the tortillas and top with avocado slices and hot sauce. Serve right away.

Tasty Chicken Breasts

Servings: 4 | Cooking Time: 30 Minutes

Ingredients:
- 4 chicken breasts
- Salt and pepper to taste
- 2 tbsp olive oil
- 2 tbsp soy sauce
- 2 tbsp tomato paste
- 2 tbsp honey
- 2 tbsp minced garlic
- 1 tbsp cornstarch
- ½ cup chives, chopped

Directions:
1. Season the chicken with pepper and salt. Warm oil on Sauté in your Instant Pot. Add in chicken and cook for 5 minutes until lightly browned. In a small bowl, mix garlic, soy sauce, honey, and tomato paste. Pour the mixture over the chicken. Stir in ½ cup water.
2. Seal the lid and cook on High Pressure for 12 minutes. Release

the pressure quickly. Remove the chicken. Mix 1 tbsp water and cornstarch to create a slurry. Stir it in the sauce for 2 minutes until thickened. Serve the chicken with sauce and chives.

Island Chicken Legs

Servings:5 | Cooking Time: 21 Minutes

Ingredients:
- 1 can pineapple, including juice
- 2 tablespoons tomato paste
- ¼ cup granulated sugar
- 2 tablespoons soy sauce
- 2 teaspoons grated fresh ginger
- 1 teaspoon garlic salt
- 3 pounds chicken legs/drumsticks
- 1 cup water

Directions:
1. In a blender, combine pineapple, tomato paste, sugar, soy sauce, ginger, and garlic salt. Divide sauce in half. Add chicken legs to half of mixture and refrigerate 30 minutes.
2. Preheat oven to broiler at 500°F.
3. Add water to the Instant Pot and insert steam rack. Arrange chicken standing up, meaty side down, on steam rack. Lock lid.
4. Press the Poultry button and cook for the default time of 15 minutes. When timer beeps, let pressure release naturally for 5 minutes. Quick-release any additional pressure until float valve drops. Unlock lid. Check chicken using a meat thermometer to ensure internal temperature is at least 165°F.
5. Place chicken legs on a parchment paper–lined baking sheet and broil 3 minutes on each side to crisp chicken. Toss chicken in remaining sauce mixture.
6. Transfer chicken to a platte. Serve warm.

Pancetta & Cabbage Chicken Thighs

Servings: 4 | Cooking Time: 30 Minutes

Ingredients:
- 4 chicken thighs, boneless skinless
- 1 tbsp lard
- 4 slices pancetta, diced
- Salt and pepper to taste
- 1 cup chicken broth
- 1 tbsp Dijon mustard
- 1 lb green cabbage, shredded
- 2 tbsp parsley, chopped

Directions:
1. Melt lard on Sauté in your Instant Pot. Fry pancetta for 5 minutes until crisp. Set aside. Season chicken with pepper and salt. Sear in the cooker for 2 minutes on each side until browned. In a bowl, mix mustard and broth.
2. In the cooker, add pancetta, and chicken broth mixture. Seal the lid and cook on High Pressure for 6 minutes. Release the pressure quickly. Open the lid, mix in green cabbage, seal again, and cook again on High Pressure for 2 minutes. Release the pressure quickly. Serve with sprinkled parsley.

Spinach Chicken Thighs

Servings: 4 | Cooking Time: 40 Minutes

Ingredients:
- 1 lb chicken thighs
- 1 lb spinach, chopped
- 2 garlic cloves, minced
- ½ cup soy sauce
- ½ cup white wine vinegar
- 2 bay leaves
- Salt and pepper to taste

Directions:
1. Combine garlic, soy sauce, vinegar, bay leaves, salt, and pepper in a bowl. Add in chicken thighs and toss to coat. Transfer to your Instant Pot. Seal the lid and cook for 15 minutes on Poultry. Once ready, allow a natural release for 10 minutes and unlock the lid. Discard bay leaves and mix in spinach. Cook on Sauté for 4-5 minutes until the spinach wilts. Serve right away.

Chicken With Chili & Lime

Servings: 4 | Cooking Time: 25 Minutes

Ingredients:
- 1 lb chicken breasts
- ¾ cup chicken broth
- Juice and zest of 1 lime
- 1 red chili, chopped
- 1 tsp cumin
- 1 tsp onion powder
- 2 garlic cloves, minced
- 1 tsp mustard powder
- 1 bay leaf
- Salt and pepper to taste

Directions:
1. Place the chicken breasts, chicken broth, lime juice, lime zest, red chili, cumin, onion powder, garlic cloves, mustard powder, bay leaf, salt, and pepper in your Instant Pot. Seal the lid, select Manual, and cook for 10 minutes on High. When ready, allow a natural release. Remove chicken and shred it. Discard the bay leaf. Top the chicken with cooking juices and serve.

Tasty Chicken Breasts With Bbq Sauce

Servings: 6 | Cooking Time: 20 Minutes

Ingredients:
- 2 lb chicken breasts
- 1 tsp salt
- 1 ½ cups barbecue sauce
- 1 small onion, minced
- 1 cup carrots, chopped
- 4 garlic cloves

Directions:
1. Rub salt onto the chicken and place it in the Instant Pot. Add onion, carrots, garlic, and barbeque sauce; toss to coat. Seal the lid, press Manual, and cook on High for 15 minutes. Do a quick release. Shred the chicken and stir into the sauce. Serve.

Sweet & Spicy Bbq Chicken

Servings: 4 | Cooking Time: 35 Minutes

Ingredients:
- 6 chicken drumsticks
- 1 tbsp olive oil
- 1 onion, chopped
- 1 tsp garlic, minced
- 1 jalapeño pepper, minced
- ½ cup sweet BBQ sauce
- 1 tbsp arrowroot

Directions:
1. Warm the olive oil in your Instant Pot on Sauté. Add in the onion and cook for 3 minutes. Add in garlic and jalapeño pepper and cook for another minute. Stir in barbecue sauce and 1/2 cup of water. Put in chicken drumsticks and seal the lid. Select Manual and cook for 18 minutes on High pressure. When over, perform a quick pressure release and unlock the lid. Mix 2 tbsp of water and arrowroot and pour it into the pot. Cook for 5 minutes on Sauté until the liquid thickens. Top with sauce and serve.

Savory Orange Chicken

Servings: 6 | Cooking Time: 25 Minutes

Ingredients:
- 2 tbsp olive oil
- 6 chicken breasts, cubed
- 1/3 cup chicken stock
- ¼ cup soy sauce
- 2 tbsp brown sugar
- 1 tbsp lemon juice
- 1 tbsp garlic powder
- 1 tsp chili sauce
- 1 cup orange juice
- Salt and pepper to taste
- 1 tbsp cornstarch

Directions:
1. Warm oil on Sauté in your Instant Pot. Sear the chicken for 5 minutes until browned, stirring occasionally. Set aside in a bowl. In the pot, mix orange juice, chicken stock, sugar, chili sauce, garlic powder, lemon juice, and soy sauce. Stir in chicken to coat. Seal the lid.
2. Cook on High Pressure for 7 minutes. Release the pressure quickly. Take ¼ cup liquid from the pot to a bowl and stir in cornstarch to dissolve. Pour the sauce in the pot and stir until the color is consistent. Press Sauté and cook the sauce for 2-3 minutes until thickened. Season with pepper and salt. Serve warm.

Chicken Taco Salad Bowls

Servings:4 | Cooking Time: 4 Minutes

Ingredients:
- 2 teaspoons olive oil
- 1 pound ground chicken
- 1 packet taco seasoning mix
- ⅛ teaspoon hot sauce
- ½ cup water
- 4 cups shredded iceberg lettuce
- ¼ cup shredded Mexican-blend cheese
- 1 cup crushed tortilla chips

Directions:

1. Press the Sauté button on the Instant Pot. Heat olive oil. Add chicken and brown 3 minutes.
2. Stir in taco seasoning mix, hot sauce, and water. Press the Cancel button. Lock lid.
3. Press the Manual or Pressure Cook button and adjust time to 1 minute. When timer beeps, quick-release pressure until float valve drops. Unlock lid. Stir mixture.
4. Line four bowls with lettuce. Using a slotted spoon, transfer chicken mixture to bowls. Garnish with cheese and tortilla chips. Serve warm.

Buffalo Turkey Chili

Servings: 4 | Cooking Time: 40 Minutes

Ingredients:
- 1 lb ground turkey
- 2 tbsp olive oil
- 1 onion, diced
- ½ habanero pepper, diced
- ½ cup red bell pepper, diced
- 1 can pinto beans
- ½ cup hot Buffalo sauce
- 2 ½ cups chicken stock
- 1 tsp oregano
- 1 tbsp chili powder
- Salt and pepper to taste
- 2 tbsp cilantro, chopped

Directions:
1. Warm the olive oil in your Instant Pot on Sauté and cook the onion, habanero pepper, and bell pepper until tender, about 3-4 minutes. Stir in ground turkey, beans, chicken stock, buffalo sauce, oregano, chili powder, salt, and pepper. Seal the lid and cook for 15 minutes on Bean/Chili on High pressure. When over, allow a natural release for 10 minutes, then perform a quick pressure release and unlock the lid. Serve topped with cilantro.

Simple Whole Chicken

Servings:4 | Cooking Time: 25 Minutes

Ingredients:
- 1 whole chicken
- 2 teaspoons sea salt
- 1 teaspoon ground black pepper
- 1 medium apple, peeled, quartered, and cored
- 1 medium onion, peeled and roughly chopped
- 3 cloves garlic, halved
- 1 celery stalk, chopped
- 2 large carrots, peeled and chopped
- 3 sprigs thyme
- 2 cups water

Directions:
1. Pat the chicken dry, inside and out, with paper towels. Sprinkle chicken with salt and pepper, then place the apple in the cavity of the bird.
2. In the bottom of the Instant Pot, scatter the onion, garlic, celery, carrots, and thyme. Pour in the water. Place the trivet over the vegetables.
3. Place chicken on the trivet. Lock lid.
4. Press the Manual button and adjust time to 25 minutes. When timer beeps, let pressure release naturally until float valve drops and then unlock lid. Check the chicken using a meat thermometer

to ensure the internal temperature is at least 165°F.

5. Remove chicken and vegetables. Discard apple. Serve warm.

Awesome Chicken In Tikka Masala Sauce

Servings: 4 | Cooking Time: 30 Minutes

Ingredients:
- 2 lb boneless, skinless chicken thighs
- Salt and pepper to taste
- 1 ½ tbsp olive oil
- ½ onion, chopped
- 2 garlic cloves, minced
- 3 tbsp tomato puree
- 1 tsp fresh ginger, minced
- 1 tbsp garam masala
- 2 tsp curry powder
- 1 tsp ground coriander
- ½ tsp ground cumin
- 1 jalapeño pepper, minced
- 29 oz canned tomato sauce
- 3 tomatoes, chopped
- ½ cup natural yogurt
- 1 lemon, juiced
- ¼ cup chopped cilantro
- 4 lemon wedges

Directions:
1. Rub black pepper and salt onto the chicken. Warm oil on Sauté in your Instant Pot. Add garlic and onion and cook for 3 minutes until soft. Stir in tomato puree, garam masala, cumin, curry powder, ginger, coriander, and jalapeño pepper; cook for 30 seconds until fragrant.
2. Stir in tomato sauce and tomatoes. Simmer the mixture as you scrape the bottom to get rid of any browned bits. Stir in chicken to coat. Seal the lid and cook on High Pressure for 10 minutes. Release the pressure quickly.
3. Press Sauté and simmer the sauce and cook for 5 minutes until thickened. Stir lemon juice and yogurt through the sauce. Serve garnished with lemon wedges and cilantro.

Honey-lemon Chicken With Vegetables

Servings: 4 | Cooking Time: 35 Minutes

Ingredients:
- 4 skin-on, bone-in chicken legs
- 2 tbsp olive oil
- Salt and pepper to taste
- 4 cloves garlic, minced
- 1 tsp fresh chopped thyme
- ½ cup dry white wine
- 1 ¼ cups chicken stock
- 1 cup carrots, chopped
- 1 cup parsnips, chopped
- 3 tomatoes, chopped
- 1 tbsp honey
- 4 lemon slices

Directions:
1. Season the chicken with pepper and salt. Warm oil on Sauté in your Instant Pot. Cook the chicken legs for 6-8 minutes on all sides until browned; reserve. Sauté thyme and garlic in the chicken fat for 1 minute until soft and lightly golden. Add in wine to

deglaze, scrape the pot's bottom to get rid of any brown bits of food. Simmer for 2-3 minutes until slightly reduced in volume.
2. Add stock, carrots, parsnip, tomatoes, pepper, and salt into the pot. Lay steam rack over veggies. Put the chicken legs on the rack. Drizzle with honey, then top with lemon slices. Seal the lid and cook on High Pressure for 12 minutes. Release pressure quickly. On a large platter, arrange the chicken legs and drained veggies. Sprinkle with thyme and serve.

Creole Chicken With Rice

Servings: 4 | Cooking Time: 45 Minutes

Ingredients:
- 2 tbsp olive oil
- 1 onion, diced
- 3 garlic cloves, minced
- 1 lb chicken breasts, sliced
- 1 cup chicken broth
- 1 can tomato sauce
- 1 cup white rice, rinsed
- 1 bell pepper, chopped
- 2 tsp creole seasoning
- 1 tbsp hot sauce

Directions:
1. Warm the olive oil in your Instant Pot on Sauté. Place in onion and garlic and cook until fragrant, about 3 minutes. Stir in chicken breasts, bell pepper, hot sauce, and creole seasoning. Cook for 3 more minutes. Mix in chicken broth, tomato sauce, and rice and seal the lid. Select Manual and cook for 20 minutes on High pressure. When ready, allow a natural release for 10 minutes and unlock the lid. Serve warm.

Turkey Sausage With Brussels Sprouts

Servings: 4 | Cooking Time: 40 Minutes

Ingredients:
- 1 lb turkey sausage, sliced
- 2 tbsp olive oil
- 1 yellow onion, chopped
- 2 garlic cloves, minced
- ½ lb Brussels sprouts, sliced
- ¼ cup chicken broth
- 1 tsp yellow mustard
- 1 tsp balsamic vinegar
- Salt and pepper to taste

Directions:
1. Warm the olive oil in your Instant Pot on Sauté. Place in onion and garlic and cook for 2 minutes. Add in turkey sausage and cook for 5 more minutes. Stir in Brussels sprouts, mustard, vinegar, salt, and pepper for 3 minutes. Pour in chicken broth. Seal the lid, select Manual, and cook for 15 minutes on High pressure. When ready, allow a natural release for 5 minutes, then a quick pressure release, and unlock the lid. Serve right away.

Picante Chicken With Lemon

Servings: 2 | Cooking Time: 60 Minutes

Ingredients:
- 1 lb chicken breasts, sliced
- 1 cup olive oil
- 1 cup chicken broth
- ½ cup lemon juice
- 1 tbsp parsley, chopped
- 3 garlic cloves, crushed
- 1 tbsp cayenne pepper
- 1 tsp dried oregano
- ½ tsp salt

Directions:
1. In a bowl, mix olive oil, lemon juice, parsley, garlic, cayenne, oregano, and salt. Add in the chicken slices, toss to coat, and cover. Chill for 30 minutes. Remove from the fridge and place all inside your Instant Pot. Add in the broth. Seal the lid and cook on High Pressure for 7 minutes. Release the pressure naturally for about 10 minutes and serve immediately.

Lemon-butter Chicken And Fingerling Potatoes

Servings:8 | Cooking Time: 10 Minutes

Ingredients:
- 3 pounds boneless and skinless chicken thighs
- 1 teaspoon salt
- ½ teaspoon ground black pepper
- 2 pounds fingerling potatoes, halved
- 1 large sweet onion, peeled and large-chopped
- 1 cup chicken broth
- 1 medium lemon, halved, divided
- 4 tablespoons unsalted butter, cut into 8 pats, divided

Directions:
1. Season chicken with salt and pepper.
2. Layer potatoes and onion in the Instant Pot. Pour in broth. Place chicken on top. Squeeze half of lemon over chicken. Add 4 butter pats. Lock lid.
3. Press the Manual or Pressure Cook button and adjust time to 10 minutes. When timer beeps, let pressure release naturally for 10 minutes. Quick-release any additional pressure until float valve drops. Unlock lid. Check chicken using a meat thermometer to make sure internal temperature is at least 165°F.
4. Using a slotted spoon, remove chicken, potatoes, and onions and transfer to a platter. Squeeze remaining half of lemon over platter. Top with remaining 4 butter pats. Serve warm.

Beer Can Chicken Dijon

Servings:5 | Cooking Time: 20 Minutes

Ingredients:
- ¼ cup Dijon mustard
- 3 pounds chicken legs/drumsticks
- 1 large onion, peeled and chopped
- 1 bottle beer, any brand/variety

Directions:
1. Rub Dijon mustard over the chicken legs.
2. Scatter onion in Instant Pot. Insert trivet. Add beer. Press the Sauté button and simmer unlidded for 5 minutes (press the Adjust button to change the temperature to Less if mixture starts to boil too vigorously). Arrange chicken standing up, meaty-side down, on the trivet. Lock lid.
3. Press the Poultry button and cook for the default time of 15 minutes. When timer beeps, let pressure release naturally for 10 minutes. Quick-release any additional pressure until float valve drops and then unlock lid. Check the chicken using a meat thermometer to ensure the internal temperature is at least 165°F.
4. Remove chicken from pot and serve.

Chicken Marinara And Zucchini

Servings:4 | Cooking Time: 15 Minutes

Ingredients:
- 2 large zucchini, diced large
- 4 chicken breast halves
- 3 cups marinara sauce
- 1 tablespoon Italian seasoning
- ½ teaspoon sea salt
- 1 cup shredded mozzarella

Directions:
1. Scatter zucchini into Instant Pot. Place chicken on zucchini. Pour marinara sauce over chicken. Sprinkle with Italian seasoning and salt. Lock lid.
2. Press the Poultry button and cook for the default time of 15 minutes. When timer beeps, let pressure release naturally for 10 minutes. Quick-release any additional pressure until float valve drops and then unlock lid. Check chicken using a meat thermometer to ensure the internal temperature is at least 165°F.
3. Sprinkle chicken with mozzarella. Press Keep Warm button, lock lid back in place, and warm for 5 minutes to allow the cheese to melt.
4. Transfer chicken and zucchini to a serving platter.

Corn & Sweet Potato Soup With Chicken

Servings: 4 | Cooking Time: 25 Minutes

Ingredients:
- 4 oz canned diced green chiles, drained
- 2 chicken breasts, diced
- 2 garlic cloves, minced
- 1 cup chicken stock
- 1 cup corn kernels
- 1 sweet potato, peeled, cubed
- 2 tsp chili powder
- 1 tsp ground cumin
- 2 cups cheddar, shredded
- 2 cups creme fraiche
- Salt and pepper to taste
- Cilantro leaves, chopped

Directions:
1. Add chicken, corn, chili powder, cumin, chicken stock, sweet potato, green chiles, and garlic to your Instant Pot. Mix well. Seal the lid and cook on High Pressure for 10 minutes. Release the pressure quickly. Set the chicken to a cutting board and shred it. Return to the pot and stir well into the liquid. Stir in cheese and creme fraiche; Season with pepper and salt. Cook for 2-3 minutes until the cheese is melted. Place chowder into plates and top with cilantro. Serve warm.

Buffalo Chicken With Blue Cheese Sauce

Servings: 4 | Cooking Time: 30 Minutes

Ingredients:
- 1 lb chicken breasts, cut into thin strips
- 2 tbsp olive oil
- 1 tsp paprika
- 1 yellow onion, chopped
- ½ cup celery, chopped
- ½ cup buffalo sauce
- ½ cup chicken stock
- ¼ cup blue cheese, crumbled
- 4 tbsp sour cream

Directions:
1. Place the chicken breasts, olive oil, paprika, onion, celery, buffalo sauce, and chicken stock in your Instant Pot. Seal the lid, select Manual, and cook for 12 minutes on High.
2. When ready, allow a natural release for 10 minutes and unlock the lid. In a bowl, combine the crumbled blue cheese and sour cream and add 1 cup of the cooking juice and stir. Pour into the pot. Serve right away.

Rosemary Chicken With Asparagus Sauce

Servings: 4 | Cooking Time: 40 Minutes

Ingredients:
- 1 whole chicken
- 4 garlic cloves, minced
- 2 tbsp olive oil
- 4 fresh thyme, minced
- 3 fresh rosemary, minced
- 2 lemons, zested, quartered
- Salt and pepper to taste
- 2 tbsp olive oil
- 8 oz asparagus, chopped
- 1 onion, chopped
- 1 cup chicken stock
- 1 tbsp soy sauce
- 1 fresh thyme sprig
- 1 tbsp flour
- Chopped parsley to garnish

Directions:
1. Rub all sides of the chicken with garlic, rosemary, black pepper, lemon zest, thyme, and salt. Into the chicken cavity, insert lemon wedges. Warm the olive oil on Sauté in your Instant Pot. Add in onion and asparagus, and sauté for 5 minutes until softened. Mix chicken stock, thyme sprig, black pepper, soy sauce, and salt. Into the inner pot, set trivet over asparagus mixture.
2. On top of the trivet, place the chicken with breast-side up. Seal the lid, select Manual, and cook for 20 minutes on High. Do a quick release. Remove the chicken to a serving platter. In the inner pot, sprinkle flour over asparagus mixture and blend the sauce with an immersion blender until desired consistency. Top the chicken with asparagus sauce and garnish with parsley.

Lemongrass Chicken

Servings:8 | Cooking Time: 10 Minutes

Ingredients:
- 1 tablespoon fish sauce
- 1 tablespoon soy sauce
- ⅛ cup freshly squeezed lime juice
- 1 tablespoon honey
- ½ teaspoon sea salt
- ¼ teaspoon ground turmeric
- ⅛ teaspoon red pepper flakes
- ¼ cup minced lemongrass, tough layers removed
- 3 pounds boneless, skinless chicken thighs
- 1 cup chicken broth
- ¼ cup chopped fresh cilantro

Directions:
1. In a large bowl, whisk together fish sauce, soy sauce, lime juice, honey, salt, turmeric, red pepper flakes, and lemongrass. Toss chicken in sauce and refrigerate covered for 1 hour.
2. Place trivet in Instant Pot. Pour in chicken broth. Arrange chicken on a steamer basket and lower onto the trivet. Lock lid.
3. Press the Manual button and adjust time to 10 minutes. When timer beeps, let pressure release naturally for 10 minutes. Quick-release any additional pressure until the float valve drops and then unlock lid. Check the chicken using a meat thermometer to ensure the internal temperature is at least 165°F.
4. Using a slotted spoon, transfer chicken to a serving tray. Garnish with chopped cilantro.

Mediterranean Duck With Olives

Servings: 4 | Cooking Time: 20 Minutes

Ingredients:
- ½ cup sun-dried tomatoes, chopped
- 1 lb duck breasts, halved
- 2 tbsp olive oil
- ½ tbsp Italian seasoning
- Salt and pepper to taste
- 2 garlic cloves, minced
- ½ cup chicken stock
- ¾ cup heavy cream
- 1 cup kale, chopped
- ½ cup Parmesan, grated
- 10 Kalamata olives, pitted

Directions:
1. Combine olive oil, Italian seasoning, pepper, salt, and garlic in a bowl. Add in the duck breasts and toss to coat. Set your Instant Pot to Sauté. Place in duck breasts and cook for 5-6 minutes on both sides. Pour in chicken stock and seal the lid. Select Manual and cook for 4 minutes.
2. When done, perform a quick pressure release and unlock the lid. Mix in heavy cream, tomatoes, Kalamata olives, and kale and cook for 5 minutes on Sauté. Serve topped with Parmesan cheese.

Macaroni With Chicken & Pesto Sauce

Servings: 4 | Cooking Time: 20 Minutes

Ingredients:
- 3 ½ cups water
- 4 chicken breasts, cubed
- 8 oz macaroni pasta
- 1 tbsp butter
- Salt and pepper to taste
- 1 lb collard greens, trimmed
- 1 cup cherry tomatoes, halved
- ½ cup basil pesto sauce
- ¼ cup cream cheese
- 1 garlic clove, minced
- ¼ cup asiago cheese, grated
- 2 tbsp chopped basil

Directions:
1. Mix water, chicken, salt, butter, and macaroni in the Instant Pot. Seal the lid and cook for 2 minutes on High Pressure. Release the pressure quickly. Carefully open the lid, get rid of ¼ cup water from the pot. Set to Sauté.
2. Into the pot, mix in collard greens, pesto sauce, garlic, salt, cream cheese, cherry tomatoes, and black pepper. Cook for 1-2 minutes as you stir until sauce is creamy. Place the pasta into serving plates. Top with asiago cheese and basil before serving.

Thai Chicken

Servings: 4 | Cooking Time: 25 Minutes

Ingredients:
- 1 lb chicken thighs
- 1 cup lime juice
- 4 tbsp red curry paste
- ½ cup fish sauce
- 2 tbsp brown sugar
- 1 red chili pepper, sliced
- 2 tbsp olive oil
- 1 tsp ginger, grated
- 2 tbsp cilantro, chopped

Directions:
1. Combine lime juice, red curry paste, fish sauce, olive oil, brown sugar, ginger, and cilantro in a bowl. Add in chicken thighs and toss to coat. Transfer to your Instant Pot and pour in 1 cup water.
2. Seal the lid, select Manual, and cook for 15 minutes on High. When done, perform a quick pressure release. Top with red chili slices and serve.

Bbq Shredded Chicken Sandwiches

Servings:6 | Cooking Time: 15 Minutes

Ingredients:
- 1 cup chicken broth
- 2 pounds boneless, skinless chicken breasts
- 2 cups barbecue sauce
- 1 small sweet onion, peeled and grated
- 6 hamburger buns
- 24 dill pickle slices

Directions:
1. Add broth, chicken breasts, barbecue sauce, and onion to the Instant Pot. Lock lid.

2. Press the Manual or Pressure Cook button and adjust time to 15 minutes. When timer beeps, let pressure release naturally for 10 minutes. Quick-release any additional pressure until float valve drops. Unlock lid. Check chicken using a meat thermometer to ensure internal temperature is at least 165°F.
3. Using two forks, pull apart chicken in pot. Using a slotted spoon, transfer chicken to hamburger buns and place 4 pickle slices on each. Serve warm.

Chicken With Port Wine Sauce

Servings: 6 | Cooking Time: 41 Minutes

Ingredients:
- 1 chicken, cut into pieces
- 2 tbsp olive oil
- 1 large onion, finely diced
- 1 cup mushrooms
- ¼ cup Port wine
- Salt and pepper to taste
- 2 tbsp parsley, chopped

Directions:
1. Warm olive oil in your IP on Sauté. Add in the chicken pieces and cook until the chicken is light brown, about 6-7 minutes; set aside. Add onion and mushrooms to the pot and sauté for 3-4 minutes. Deglaze with Port wine and pour in 1 cup of water. Season with salt and pepper and return the chicken. Seal the lid, select Manual, and cook for 20 minutes on High. Once ready, release pressure naturally. Sprinkle with parsley and serve.

Curried Chicken With Mushrooms

Servings: 4 | Cooking Time: 25 Minutes

Ingredients:
- 1 cup shiitake mushrooms, sliced
- 1 cup white mushrooms, sliced
- 1 lb chicken breasts, cubed
- 2 tbsp olive oil
- 1 yellow onion, thinly sliced
- 1 tbsp curry paste
- 1 cup chicken stock
- ½ bunch cilantro, chopped

Directions:
1. Warm the olive oil in your Instant Pot on Sauté. Add in the chicken breasts and cook for 2 minutes until browned. Stir in onion and mushrooms and cook for another 3 minutes. Mix curry paste and chicken stock in a bowl and pour into the pot. Seal the lid, select Manual, and cook for 15 minutes on High pressure. Once ready, perform a quick pressure release and unlock the lid. Serve topped with cilantro.

Garlic Chicken

Servings: 4 | Cooking Time: 35 Minutes

Ingredients:
- 1 lb chicken breasts
- Salt and pepper to taste
- 2 tbsp butter
- 1 cup chicken broth
- 2 garlic cloves, minced
- 2 tbsp tarragon, chopped

Directions:
1. Place chicken breasts in your Instant Pot. Sprinkle with garlic, salt, and pepper. Pour in the chicken broth and butter. Seal the lid, select Manual, and cook for 15 minutes on High pressure.
2. When over, allow a natural release for 10 minutes and unlock the lid. Remove the chicken and shred it. Top with tarragon and serve.

Tarragon Whole Chicken

Servings: 6 | Cooking Time: 45 Minutes

Ingredients:
- 1 whole chicken
- 1 tsp tarragon, chopped
- 3 tbsp butter, softened
- 1 tbsp onion powder
- 1 tbsp garlic powder
- 1 tbsp paprika
- Salt and pepper to taste
- 1 cup chicken broth
- 1 tbsp white wine
- 2 tsp soy sauce
- 1 minced green onion

Directions:
1. Combine butter, tarragon, onion powder, garlic powder, paprika, salt, and pepper in a bowl. Pour the chicken broth, white wine, and soy sauce in your Instant Pot and fit in a trivet. Brush chicken with the butter mixture on all sides and place it on the trivet. Seal the lid, select Manual, and cook for 25 minutes on High pressure. When done, allow a natural release for 10 minutes and unlock the lid. Serve topped with minced green onion.

Za'atar Chicken With Baby Potatoes

Servings: 4 | Cooking Time: 30 Minutes

Ingredients:
- 1 lb chicken thighs
- ½ lb baby potatoes, halved
- 2 tbsp olive oil
- 1 tbsp za'atar seasoning
- 1 garlic clove, minced
- 1 large onion, sliced
- Salt and pepper to taste

Directions:
1. Warm the olive oil in your Instant Pot on Sauté. Place in onion and garlic and cook for 2 minutes. Add in chicken thighs and cook for 4-6 minutes on both sides. Scatter with za´atar seasoning, salt, pepper, potatoes, and pour in 1 cup of water. Seal the lid, select Manual, and cook for 15 minutes on High pressure.
2. Once ready, perform a quick pressure release and unlock the lid. Remove the chicken and shred it. Put chicken back to the pot and toss to coat. Serve right away.

Citrus-spiced Chicken

Servings:8 | Cooking Time: 15 Minutes

Ingredients:
- 2 tablespoons olive oil
- 3 pounds boneless, skinless chicken thighs
- 1 teaspoon smoked paprika
- ½ teaspoon sea salt
- ⅛ teaspoon ground cinnamon
- ⅛ teaspoon ground ginger
- ⅛ teaspoon ground nutmeg
- ½ cup white raisins
- ½ cup slivered almonds
- 1 cup freshly squeezed orange juice
- ⅛ cup freshly squeezed lemon juice
- ⅛ cup freshly squeezed lime juice
- 1 pound carrots, peeled and diced large
- 2 tablespoons water
- 1 tablespoon arrowroot powder

Directions:
1. Press the Sauté button on Instant Pot. Heat olive oil and fry chicken thighs for 2 minutes on each side until browned.
2. Add the paprika, salt, cinnamon, ginger, nutmeg, raisins, almonds, orange juice, lemon juice, lime juice, and carrots. Lock lid.
3. Press the Manual button and adjust time to 10 minutes. When timer beeps, let pressure release naturally for 5 minutes. Quick-release any additional pressure until the float valve drops and then unlock lid. Check the chicken using a meat thermometer to make sure the internal temperature is at least 165°F.
4. Use a slotted spoon to remove chicken, carrots, and raisins and transfer to a serving platter.
5. In a small bowl, whisk together water and arrowroot to create a slurry. Add to liquid in the Instant Pot and stir to combine. Press Sauté button on Instant Pot, press Adjust button to change the temperature to Less, and simmer unlidded for 3 minutes until sauce is thickened. Pour sauce over chicken and serve.

Parsley & Lemon Turkey Risotto

Servings: 4 | Cooking Time: 40 Minutes

Ingredients:
- 2 boneless turkey breasts, cut into strips
- 2 lemons, zested and juiced
- 1 tbsp dried oregano
- 2 garlic cloves, minced
- 1 ½ tbsp olive oil
- 1 onion, diced
- 2 cups chicken broth
- 1 cup arborio rice, rinsed
- Salt and pepper to taste
- ¼ cup chopped parsley
- 8 lemon slices

Directions:
1. In a Ziploc bag, mix turkey, oregano, salt, garlic, juice and zest of two lemons. Marinate for 10 minutes. Warm oil on Sauté in your Instant Pot. Add onion and cook for 3 minutes. Stir in the rice and chicken broth and season with pepper and salt.
2. Empty the Ziploc having the chicken and marinade into the pot. Seal the lid and cook on High Pressure for 12 minutes. Release the pressure quickly. Garnish with lemon slices and parsley to serve.

Nashville Hot Chicken Patties

Servings:4 | Cooking Time: 10 Minutes

Ingredients:
- 1 pound ground chicken
- ½ medium sweet onion, peeled and grated
- 1 tablespoon hot sauce
- 1 teaspoon chili powder
- 1 teaspoon cayenne pepper
- 1 teaspoon packed light brown sugar
- 1 teaspoon salt
- ½ teaspoon ground black pepper
- 1 cup water

Directions:
1. In a small bowl, combine chicken, onion, hot sauce, chili powder, cayenne pepper, brown sugar, salt, and black pepper. Form into four patties. Wrap each one in aluminum foil.
2. Add water to the Instant Pot and insert steam rack. Arrange patties on steam rack. Lock lid.
3. Press the Manual or Pressure Cook button and adjust time to 10 minutes. When timer beeps, quick-release pressure until float valve drops. Unlock lid. Check chicken using a meat thermometer to ensure internal temperature is at least 165°F.
4. Remove patties from pot. Serve warm.

Chicken And Gnocchi Alfredo With Vegetables

Servings:6 | Cooking Time: 3 Minutes

Ingredients:
- 1 package gnocchi
- 1 jar Alfredo sauce
- ½ cup chicken broth
- 1 cup chopped cooked chicken
- 1 can mushroom stems and pieces, drained
- 1 can sweet peas and carrots, drained

Directions:
1. In the Instant Pot, add gnocchi and sauce. Pour broth into empty sauce jar, close lid of jar, and shake. Pour mixture into pot. Stir in remaining ingredients. Lock lid.
2. Press the Manual or Pressure Cook button and adjust time to 3 minutes. When timer beeps, let pressure release naturally for 5 minutes. Quick-release any additional pressure until float valve drops. Unlock lid.
3. Transfer to bowls. Serve warm.

Filipino-style Chicken Congee

Servings: 6 | Cooking Time: 55 Minutes

Ingredients:
- 6 chicken drumsticks
- 1 cup Jasmine rice
- 1 tbsp fresh ginger, grated
- 1 tbsp fish sauce
- 4 green onions, chopped
- 3 hard-boiled eggs, halved

Directions:
1. Place chicken, rice, 6 cups of water, fish sauce, and ginger in your Instant Pot and stir. Seal the lid, select Manual, and cook for 25 minutes on High pressure.

2. When done, allow a natural release for 10 minutes. Remove the chicken and shred it. Put shredded chicken back in the pot and cook for 10 minutes on Sauté. Top with eggs and green onions and serve.

Korean-style Chicken

Servings: 6 | Cooking Time: 35 Minutes

Ingredients:
- 3 green onions, sliced diagonally
- 3 chicken breasts, halved
- 5 tbsp sweet chili sauce
- 5 tbsp sriracha sauce
- 1 tbsp grated ginger
- 4 garlic cloves
- 1 tbsp rice vinegar
- 2 tbsp sesame seeds
- 1 tbsp soy sauce
- ½ cup chicken stock

Directions:
1. Combine chili sauce, sriracha sauce, ginger, garlic, vinegar, sesame seeds, soy sauce, and chicken stock in a bowl. Add in the chicken fillets and toss to coat. Transfer to your Instant Pot. Seal the lid, select Manual, and cook for 15 minutes on High pressure. Once ready, allow a natural release for 10 minutes and unlock the lid. Top with green onions and serve.

Insalata Caprese Chicken Bowls

Servings:4 | Cooking Time: 5 Minutes

Ingredients:
- 1 ½ pounds boneless, skinless chicken breasts, cut into 1" cubes
- 1 can diced tomatoes, including juice
- ½ teaspoon salt
- ½ teaspoon ground black pepper
- 1 container fresh ciliegine mozzarella, drained and halved
- 1 tablespoon olive oil
- 2 tablespoons balsamic vinegar
- ½ cup julienned fresh basil leaves

Directions:
1. In the Instant Pot, add chicken and tomatoes. Lock lid.
2. Press the Manual or Pressure Cook button and adjust time to 5 minutes. When timer beeps, let pressure release naturally for 10 minutes. Quick-release any additional pressure until float valve drops. Unlock lid. Check chicken using a meat thermometer to ensure internal temperature is at least 165°F.
3. Using a slotted spoon, transfer chicken and tomatoes to four bowls. Season with salt and pepper. Add mozzarella halves. Drizzle with oil and balsamic vinegar. Garnish with basil. Serve immediately.

Buttered Chicken With Artichokes

Servings: 4 | Cooking Time: 35 Minutes

Ingredients:
- 1 lb chicken breasts, chopped
- 2 artichokes, trimmed, halved
- 3 tbsp butter, melted
- 1 lemon, juiced
- Salt and pepper to taste
- 1 tbsp rosemary, chopped

Directions:
1. Heat 1 tbsp butter on Sauté in your Instant Pot and cook the chicken for a minute per side until slightly golden. Pour in 1 cup of water, seal the lid, and cook on High Pressure for 13 minutes. Do a quick release. Set aside.
2. Insert a trivet in the pot. Rub the artichoke halves with half of the lemon juice and arrange on the trivet. Seal the lid and cook on Steam for 3 minutes. Do a quick release. Combine artichoke and chicken in a large bowl. Stir in salt, pepper, and lemon juice. Drizzle the remaining butter over and sprinkle with rosemary to serve.

Savory Tropical Chicken

Servings: 4 | Cooking Time: 20 Minutes

Ingredients:
- 4 boneless, skinless chicken thighs
- 2 tbsp olive oil
- ¼ cup pineapple juice
- 2 tbsp ketchup
- 2 tbsp Worcestershire sauce
- 1 garlic clove, minced
- 1 tsp cornstarch
- 2 tsp water
- 2 tbsp cilantro, chopped

Directions:
1. Warm oil on Sauté in your Instant Pot. In batches, sear the chicken in oil for 3 minutes until golden brown and set aside on a plate. Mix pineapple juice, Worcestershire sauce, garlic, and ketchup. Add to the pot to deglaze, scraping the bottom to get rid of any browned bits of food. Place the chicken into the sauce and stir well to coat. Seal the lid cook for 5 minutes on High Pressure.
2. Release the pressure quickly. In a bowl, mix water and cornstarch until well dissolved. Press Cancel and set to Sauté. Stir the cornstarch slurry into the sauce and cook for 2 minutes until the sauce is well thickened. Sprinkle with cilantro to serve.

Sticky Teriyaki Chicken

Servings: 4 | Cooking Time: 30 Minutes

Ingredients:
- 1 lb chicken breasts
- 2/3 cup teriyaki sauce
- 1 tsp sesame seeds
- ½ cup chicken stock
- Salt and pepper to taste
- 3 green onions, chopped

Directions:
1. Set your Instant Pot to Sauté. Place in teriyaki sauce and simmer for 1 minute. Stir in chicken stock, salt, and pepper and seal the lid. Select Manual and cook for 12 minutes on High pressure.

Once over, allow a natural release for 10 minutes and unlock the lid. Transfer the chicken to a plate and shred it. Remove 1/2 cup of cooking liquid. Put chicken back in the pot and stir in green onions. Top with sesame seeds and serve.

Peppered Chicken With Chunky Salsa

Servings: 4 | Cooking Time: 30 Minutes

Ingredients:
- 3 mixed-color peppers, cut into strips
- 1 lb chicken breasts
- 2 tbsp olive oil
- 2 jalapeño peppers, sliced
- 1 onion, sliced
- Salt and pepper to taste
- ½ tsp oregano
- ½ tsp cumin
- 2 cups chunky salsa

Directions:
1. Warm the olive oil in your Instant Pot on Sauté. Place in onion, peppers, and jalapeño peppers and sauté for 5 minutes. Sprinkle chicken breasts with salt and pepper and place them in the pot along with oregano, cumin, chunky salsa, and ½ cup of water. Seal the lid and cook for 15 minutes on Manual on High. When ready, perform a quick pressure release. Shred chicken before serving.

Avocado Fajitas

Servings: 4 | Cooking Time: 20 Minutes

Ingredients:
- 4 chicken breasts
- 1 taco seasoning
- 1 tbsp olive oil
- 24-oz can diced tomatoes
- 3 bell peppers, julienned
- 1 shallot, chopped
- 4 garlic cloves, minced
- Juice of 1 lemon
- Salt and pepper to taste
- 4 flour tortillas
- 2 tbsp cilantro, chopped
- 1 avocado, sliced

Directions:
1. In a bowl, mix taco seasoning and chicken until evenly coated. Warm oil on Sauté. Sear chicken for 2 minutes per side until browned. To the chicken, add tomatoes, cilantro, shallot, lemon juice, garlic, and bell peppers. Season with pepper and salt. Seal the lid and press Manual.
2. Cook for 4 minutes on High Pressure. Release the pressure quickly. Move the bell peppers and chicken to tortillas. Add avocado slices and serve.

Chili & Lemon Chicken Wings

Servings: 4 | Cooking Time: 20 Minutes

Ingredients:
- 1 lb chicken wings
- 2 tbsp olive oil
- 1 tbsp honey
- 1 lemon, zested and juiced
- ½ tsp garlic powder
- ½ tsp cayenne pepper
- ½ chili pepper, chopped
- Salt and pepper to taste
- 1 ½ cups chicken broth

Directions:
1. Combine olive oil, lemon zest, lemon juice, red chili pepper, honey, garlic powder, cayenne pepper, black pepper, and salt in a bowl. Brush chicken wings with the mixture on all sides. Place the chicken broth and chicken wings in your Instant Pot. Seal the lid, select Manual, and cook for 10 minutes on High pressure. When over, perform a quick pressure release. Serve warm.

Chicken Sausage & Navy Bean Chili

Servings: 6 | Cooking Time: 50 Minutes

Ingredients:
- 1 can diced tomatoes with green chilies
- 3 tbsp olive oil
- 1 shallot, diced
- ½ cup fennel, chopped
- ¼ cup minced garlic
- 1 tbsp smoked paprika
- 2 tsp chili powder
- 2 tsp ground cumin
- Salt and pepper to taste
- 28-oz can crushed tomatoes
- 2 lb chicken sausages, sliced
- ¾ cup buffalo wing sauce
- 2 cans navy beans

Directions:
1. Warm oil on Sauté in your Instant Pot. Add the sausages and brown for 5 minutes, turning frequently. Set aside on a plate. In the same fat, sauté shallot, roasted fennel, and garlic for 4 minutes until soft. Season with paprika, cumin, pepper, salt, and chili powder.
2. Stir in crushed tomatoes, diced tomatoes with green chilies, buffalo sauce, and navy beans. Return the sausages to the pot. Seal the lid and cook on High Pressure for 30 minutes. Do a quick pressure release. Serve.

Chicken & Quinoa Soup

Servings: 6 | Cooking Time: 30 Minutes

Ingredients:
- 2 tbsp butter
- 1 cup red onion, chopped
- 1 cup carrots, chopped
- 1 cup celery, chopped
- 2 chicken breasts, cubed
- 4 cups chicken broth
- 6 oz quinoa, rinsed
- 2 tbsp parsley, chopped
- Salt and pepper to taste
- 4 oz mascarpone cheese
- 1 cup milk
- 1 cup heavy cream

Directions:
1. Melt butter on Sauté in your Instant Pot. Add carrots, onion, and celery and cook for 5 minutes. Add in broth, parsley, quinoa, and chicken. Season with pepper and salt. Seal the lid. Cook on High Pressure for 10 minutes. Release the pressure quickly. Add mascarpone to the soup and stir to melt it completely. Stir in heavy cream and milk until the soup is thickened and creamy.

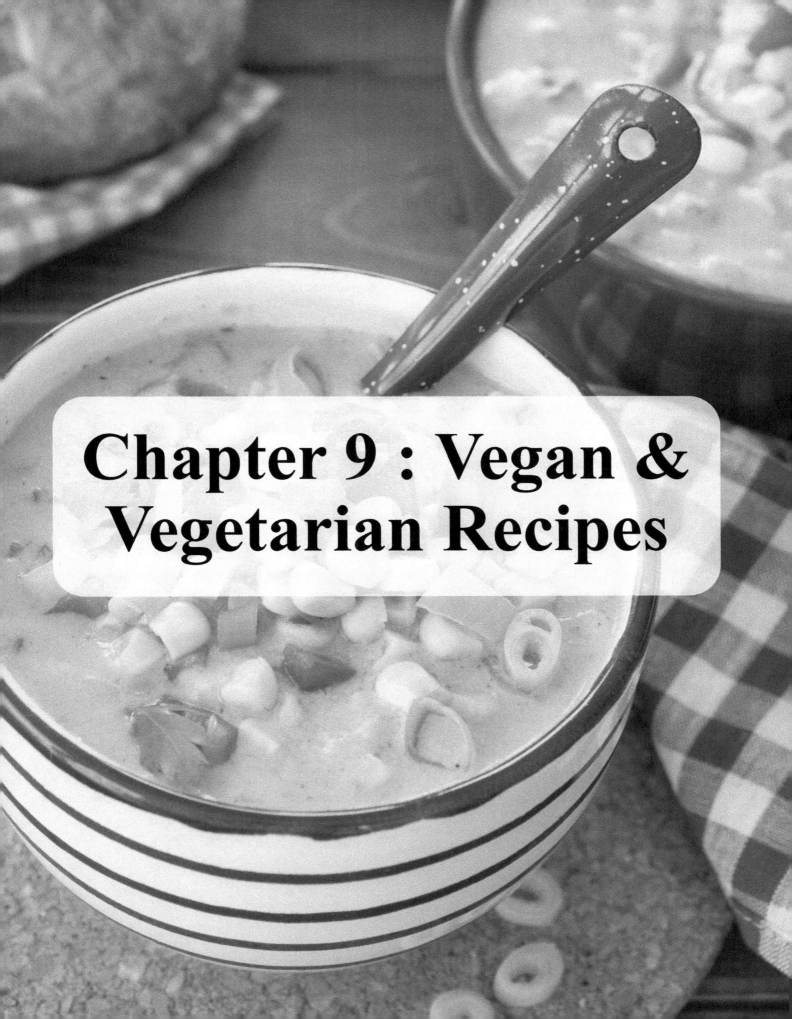

Chapter 9 : Vegan & Vegetarian Recipes

Chapter 9 : Vegan & Vegetarian Recipes

Blood Orange And Goat Cheese Wheat Berry Salad

Servings:6 | Cooking Time: 35 Minutes

Ingredients:
- 3 tablespoons olive oil, divided
- 1 cup wheat berries
- 2 cups water
- ½ cup dried cranberries
- Juice and zest of ½ medium blood orange
- 1 tablespoon balsamic vinegar
- ½ teaspoon salt
- ¼ cup crumbled goat cheese

Directions:
1. Press Sauté button on Instant Pot and heat 1 tablespoon oil. Add wheat berries. Stir-fry 4–5 minutes until browned and fragrant. Add water. Press the Cancel button. Lock lid.
2. Press the Manual or Pressure Cook button and adjust time to 30 minutes. When timer beeps, let pressure release naturally for 10 minutes. Quick-release any additional pressure until float valve drops. Unlock lid.
3. Let cool 10 minutes and drain any additional liquid.
4. Transfer cooled berries to a medium bowl and add remaining ingredients, including remaining oil. Refrigerate covered. Serve chilled.

Coconut Millet Porridge

Servings: 2 | Cooking Time: 25 Minutes

Ingredients:
- ½ cup millet
- ½ cup coconut milk
- 2 tbsp coconut flakes
- 1 tbsp honey

Directions:
1. Place millet, milk, and 1/2 cup of water in your Instant Pot. Seal the lid, select Manual, and cook for 10 minutes on High pressure. When over, allow a natural release for 10 minutes and unlock the lid. Drizzle with honey, top with coconut flakes, and serve.

Grandma's Asparagus With Feta & Lemon

Servings: 4 | Cooking Time: 20 Minutes

Ingredients:
- 1 lb asparagus spears
- 1 tbsp olive oil
- Salt and pepper to taste
- 1 lemon, cut into wedges
- 1 cup feta cheese, cubed

Directions:

1. Into the pot, add 1 cup of water and set trivet over the water. Place steamer basket on the trivet. Place the asparagus into the steamer basket. Seal the lid and cook on High Pressure for 1 minute. Release the Pressure quickly. Add olive oil in a bowl and toss in asparagus until well coated. Season with pepper and salt. Serve with feta and lemon wedges.

Parmesan Topped Vegetable Mash

Servings: 6 | Cooking Time: 15 Minutes

Ingredients:
- 3 lb Yukon gold potatoes, chopped
- 2 cups cauliflower florets
- 1 carrot, chopped
- 1 cup Parmesan, shredded
- ¼ cup butter, melted
- ¼ cup milk
- 1 tsp salt
- 1 garlic clove, minced
- 2 tbsp parsley, chopped

Directions:
1. Into the pot, add potatoes, cauliflower, carrot and salt; cover with enough water. Seal the lid and cook on High Pressure for 10 minutes. Release the pressure quickly. Drain the vegetables and mash them with a potato masher. Add garlic, butter, and milk. Whisk until well incorporated. Top with Parmesan cheese and parsley.

Speedy Mac & Goat Cheese

Servings: 4 | Cooking Time: 20 Minutes

Ingredients:
- 1 lb elbow macaroni
- 2 oz goat's cheese, crumbled
- ½ cup skim milk
- 1 tsp Dijon mustard
- 1 tsp dried oregano
- 1 tsp Italian seasoning
- 2 tbsp olive oil
- 5 oz olives, sliced

Directions:
1. Add macaroni in the Instant Pot and cover with water. Seal the lid and cook on High Pressure for 4 minutes. Do a quick release. Drain the macaroni and set aside. Press Sauté on the pot and add the olive oil, mustard, milk, oregano, and Italian seasoning. Cook for 3 minutes. Stir in macaroni and cook for 2 minutes. Top with fresh goat's cheese and olives and serve.

Chickpea Stew With Onion & Tomatoes

Servings: 4 | Cooking Time: 40 Minutes

Ingredients:
• 6 oz chickpeas, soaked
• 2 tomatoes, chopped
• 1 red onion, chopped
• 1 tbsp cumin seeds
• 2 cups vegetable broth
• 2 tbsp olive oil
• 2 tbsp butter
• 2 tbsp parsley, chopped
• Salt and pepper to taste

Directions:
1. To the Instant Pot, add olive oil, tomatoes, onion, cumin seeds, chickpeas, and pour in the broth. Seal the lid and set the steam handle. Cook on Manual for 30 minutes on High. Do a quick release and set aside to cool for a while.
2. Transfer the soup to a food processor and season with salt and pepper. Process until pureed and spoon onto a serving bowl. Stir in 2 tbsp of butter. Top with freshly chopped parsley and serve.

Savory Spinach With Mashed Potatoes

Servings: 6 | Cooking Time: 20 Minutes

Ingredients:
• 3 lb potatoes, peeled
• ½ cup milk
• ⅓ cup butter
• 2 tbsp chopped chives
• Salt and pepper to taste
• 2 cups spinach, chopped

Directions:
1. Cover the potatoes with salted water in your Instant Pot. Seal the lid and cook on High Pressure for 8 minutes. Release the pressure quickly. Drain the potatoes, and reserve the liquid in a bowl. Mash the potatoes. Mix with butter and milk; season with pepper and salt. With reserved cooking liquid, thin the potatoes to attain the desired consistency. Put the spinach in the remaining potato liquid and stir until wilted; Season to taste. Drain and serve with potato mash. Garnish with chives.

Red Wine And Mushroom Risotto

Servings:4 | Cooking Time: 19 Minutes

Ingredients:
• 2 tablespoons olive oil
• 1 small yellow onion, peeled and finely diced
• 1 cup sliced baby bella mushrooms
• 2 cloves garlic, peeled and minced
• 1 ½ cups Arborio rice
• 3 cups vegetable broth, divided
• 1 cup dry red wine (cabernet sauvignon or pinot noir)
• ½ teaspoon salt
• ¼ teaspoon ground black pepper

Directions:
1. Press the Sauté button on the Instant Pot and heat oil. Add onion and mushrooms and stir-fry 3–5 minutes until onions are translucent. Add garlic and rice and cook an additional 1 minute. Add 1 cup broth and stir 2–3 minutes until it is absorbed by rice.
2. Add remaining 2 cups broth, wine, salt, and pepper. Press the

Cancel button. Lock lid.
3. Press the Manual or Pressure Cook button and adjust time to 10 minutes. When timer beeps, let pressure release naturally for 10 minutes. Quick-release any additional pressure until float valve drops. Unlock lid.
4. Ladle into bowls. Serve warm.

Steamed Artichokes & Green Beans

Servings: 4 | Cooking Time: 20 Minutes

Ingredients:
• 4 artichokes, trimmed
• ½ lb green beans, trimmed
• 1 lemon, halved
• 1 tbsp lemon zest
• 1 tbsp lemon juice
• 3 cloves garlic, crushed
• ½ cup mayonnaise
• Salt to taste
• 2 tbsp parsley, chopped

Directions:
1. Rub the artichokes and green beans with lemon. Add 1 cup water into the pot. Set steamer rack over water and set steamer basket on top. Add in artichokes and green beans and sprinkle with salt. Seal lid and cook on High Pressure for 10 minutes.
2. Release the pressure quickly. In a mixing bowl, combine mayonnaise, garlic, lemon juice, and lemon zest. Season to taste with salt. Serve with warm steamed artichokes and green beans sprinkled with parsley.

Simple Cheese Spinach Dip

Servings: 6 | Cooking Time: 20 Minutes

Ingredients:
• 2 cups cream cheese
• 1 cup baby spinach
• 1 cup mozzarella, grated
• Salt and pepper to taste
• ½ cup scallions
• 1 cup vegetable broth

Directions:
1. Place cream cheese, spinach, mozzarella cheese, salt, pepper, scallions, and broth in a mixing bowl. Stir well and transfer to your Instant Pot. Seal the lid and cook on High Pressure for 5 minutes. Release the steam naturally for 10 minutes. Serve with celery sticks or chips.

Gingery Butternut Squash Soup

Servings: 6 | Cooking Time: 25 Minutes

Ingredients:
• 1 lb peeled and diced Butternut Squash
• 2 garlic cloves, minced
• 1 tbsp Ginger powder
• 4 cups Chicken broth
• 1 cup Heavy cream
• 2 tbsp vegetable oil
• Salt and pepper to taste

Directions:
1. Place the vegetable oil and half of the butternut squash cubes

and cook for 5 minutes until browns on Sauté. Add in the remaining cubes, garlic, ginger powder, chicken broth, heavy cream, salt, and black pepper. Seal the lid, select Manual, and cook for 10 minutes on High pressure. When done, perform a quick pressure release and unlock the lid. Using an immersion blender, pulse until purée. Serve immediately.

Coconut Milk Yogurt With Honey

Servings: 6 | Cooking Time: 15 Hours

Ingredients:
- 2 cans coconut milk
- 1 tbsp gelatin
- 1 tbsp honey
- 1 tbsp probiotic powder
- Zest from 1 lime

Directions:
1. Into the pot, stir in gelatin and coconut milk until well dissolved. Seal the lid, Press Yogurt until the display is reading "Boil". Once done, the screen will then display "Yogurt". Ensure milk temperature is at 180°F. Remove steel pot from Pressure cooker base and place into a large ice bath to cool milk for 5 minutes to reach 112°F.
2. Remove the pot from the ice bath and wipe the outside dry. Into the coconut milk mixture, add probiotic powder, honey, and Lime zest, and stir to combine. Return steel pot to the base of the Instant Pot. Seal the lid, press Yogurt, and cook for 10 hours. Once complete, spoon yogurt into glass jars with rings and lids; place in the refrigerator to chill for 4 hours to thicken.

Parsley Lentil Soup With Vegetables

Servings: 4 | Cooking Time: 20 Minutes

Ingredients:
- 1 tbsp olive oil
- 1 onion, chopped
- 1 cup celery, chopped
- 2 garlic cloves, chopped
- 3 cups vegetable stock
- 1 ½ cups lentils, rinsed
- 4 carrots, halved lengthwise
- ½ tsp salt
- 2 tbsp parsley, chopped

Directions:
1. Warm olive oil on Sauté. Add in onion, garlic, and celery and sauté for 5 minutes until soft. Mix in lentils, carrots, salt, and stock. Seal the lid and cook on High Pressure for 10 minutes. Release the pressure quickly. Serve topped with parsley.

Vegan Lentil & Quinoa Stew

Servings: 4 | Cooking Time: 35 Minutes

Ingredients:
- 10 sun-dried tomatoes, chopped
- 1 cup quinoa
- 1 cup tomatoes, diced
- 1 cup lentils
- 1 tsp garlic, minced
- 4 cups vegetable broth
- 1 tsp salt
- 1 tsp red pepper flakes

Directions:
1. Add sun-dried tomatoes, quinoa, tomatoes, lentils, garlic, broth, salt, and red pepper flakes to your Instant Pot. Seal the lid and adjust the steam release handle. Cook on High Pressure for 20 minutes. Release the steam naturally for about 10 minutes. Carefully unlock the lid.

Mighty "meat"loaf

Servings:4 | Cooking Time: 12 Minutes

Ingredients:
- 1 can cannellini beans, drained and rinsed
- 1 cup finely chopped baby bella mushrooms
- 2 small shallots, minced
- 1 large carrot, peeled and grated
- 2 garlic cloves, minced
- 2 large eggs, whisked
- 1 cup shredded mozzarella cheese
- 1 tablespoon Italian seasoning
- 1 teaspoon sea salt
- ½ teaspoon ground black pepper
- 1 cup old-fashioned oats
- 1 tablespoon Dijon mustard
- 1 can tomato sauce
- 1 cup water

Directions:
1. Add beans to a medium mixing bowl. Using the back of a wooden spoon, smash the beans against the side of the bowl until they all pop open. Add remaining ingredients except water and mix well. Form mixture into a ball and place into a greased 7-cup glass bowl. Slightly press down the top of the ball.
2. Pour 1 cup water into Instant Pot. Insert trivet. Place glass bowl onto trivet. Lock lid.
3. Press the Manual button and adjust time to 12 minutes. When timer beeps, quick-release pressure until float valve drops and then unlock lid. Remove bowl from Instant Pot and let cool for 15 minutes before serving.

Stuffed With Rice Grape Leaves

Servings: 4 | Cooking Time: 50 Minutes

Ingredients:
- 32 wine leaves
- 1 cup long grain rice
- ½ cup olive oil
- 2 garlic cloves, crushed
- ¼ cup lemon juice
- Salt and pepper to taste

Directions:
1. In a bowl, mix rice with 3 tbsp of olive oil, garlic, salt, and pepper. Place 1 wine leaf at a time on a working surface and add 1 tbsp of filling at the bottom. Fold the leaves over the filling towards the center. Bring the 2 sides in towards the center and roll them up tightly.
2. Grease the Instant Pot with 2 tbsp olive oil. Make a layer of wine leaves. Transfer the previously prepared rolls. Add the remaining olive oil, 2 cups water, and lemon juice. Seal the lid and cook on High Pressure for 30 minutes. Do a natural release for 10 minutes. Remove the dolmades from the pot and chill overnight.

Bavarian Kale And Potatoes

Servings:4 | Cooking Time: 10 Minutes

Ingredients:
- 1 tablespoon olive oil
- 1 small onion, peeled and diced
- 1 stalk celery, diced
- 2 cloves garlic, minced
- 4 medium potatoes, peeled and diced
- 2 bunches kale, washed, deveined, and chopped
- 1½ cups vegetable broth
- 2 teaspoons salt
- ½ teaspoon ground black pepper
- ¼ teaspoon caraway seeds
- 1 tablespoon apple cider vinegar
- 4 tablespoons sour cream

Directions:
1. Press the Sauté button on Instant Pot. Heat oil. Add onion and celery and stir-fry 3–5 minutes until onions are translucent. Add garlic and cook for an additional minute. Add potatoes in an even layer. Add chopped kale in an even layer. Add broth. Lock lid.
2. Press the Manual button and adjust time to 5 minutes. Let the pressure release naturally for 10 minutes. Quick-release any additional pressure until float valve drops and then unlock lid; then drain broth.
3. Stir in salt, pepper, caraway seeds, and vinegar; slightly mash the potatoes in the Instant Pot. Garnish each serving with 1 tablespoon sour cream.

Quinoa With Brussels Sprouts & Broccoli

Servings: 2 | Cooking Time: 25 Minutes

Ingredients:
- 1 cup quinoa, rinsed
- Salt and pepper to taste
- 1 beet, peeled, cubed
- 1 cup broccoli florets
- 1 carrot, chopped
- ½ lb Brussels sprouts
- 2 eggs
- 1 avocado, chopped
- ¼ cup pesto sauce
- Lemon wedges, for serving

Directions:
1. In the pot, mix 2 cups of water, salt, quinoa and pepper. Set trivet over quinoa and set steamer basket on top. To the steamer basket, add eggs, Brussels sprouts, broccoli, beet cubes, carrots, pepper, and salt. Seal the lid and cook for 1 minute on High Pressure. Release pressure naturally for 10 minutes. Remove the steamer basket and trivet from the pot and set the eggs in a bowl of ice water. Peel and halve the eggs. Use a fork to fluff the quinoa. Divide quinoa, broccoli, avocado, carrots, beet, Brussels sprouts, eggs between two bowls, and top with a pesto dollop. Serve with lemon wedges.

Cauliflower Charcuterie

Servings:4 | Cooking Time: 2 Minutes

Ingredients:
- ¼ cup hot sauce
- ¼ cup teriyaki sauce
- 1 cup water
- 1 large head cauliflower, chopped into bite-sized florets
- ½ cup ranch dip
- ½ cup blue cheese dip
- 4 medium stalks celery, cut into 1" sections

Directions:
1. Add hot sauce to a medium bowl. Add teriyaki sauce to another medium bowl. Set aside.
2. Add water to the Instant Pot. Add steamer basket to pot and add cauliflower in basket in an even layer. Lock lid.
3. Press the Manual or Pressure Cook button and adjust time to 2 minutes. When timer beeps, quick-release pressure until float valve drops. Unlock lid.
4. Transfer half of cauliflower to bowl with hot sauce and toss. Transfer other half of cauliflower to bowl with teriyaki sauce and toss. Serve warm with dipping sauces and celery.

Wheat Berry Salad

Servings:6 | Cooking Time: 35 Minutes

Ingredients:
- 3 tablespoons olive oil, divided
- 1 cup wheat berries
- 2¼ cups water, divided
- 2 cups peeled and shredded carrots
- 2 apples, peeled, cored, and diced small
- ½ cup raisins
- 2 tablespoons pure maple syrup
- 2 teaspoons orange zest
- ¼ cup fresh orange juice
- 1 tablespoon balsamic vinegar
- ½ teaspoon salt

Directions:
1. Press Sauté button on Instant Pot. Heat 1 tablespoon oil and add wheat berries. Stir-fry for 4–5 minutes until browned and fragrant. Add 2 cups water. Lock lid.
2. Press the Manual button and adjust time to 30 minutes. When timer beeps, let pressure release naturally for 10 minutes. Quick-release any additional pressure until float valve drops and then unlock lid.
3. Let cool for 10 minutes and drain any additional liquid.
4. Transfer cooled berries to a medium bowl and add remaining ingredients. Refrigerate covered overnight until ready to serve chilled.

Corn & Lentil Hummus With Parmesan

Servings: 6 | Cooking Time: 45 Minutes

Ingredients:
- 1 lb lentils, cooked
- 1 cup sweet corn
- 2 tomatoes, diced
- 3 tbsp tomato paste
- ½ tbsp dried oregano
- 2 tbsp Parmesan cheese

- 1 tbsp salt
- ½ tbsp red pepper flakes
- 3 tbsp olive oil
- ¼ cup red wine

Directions:
1. Heat olive oil on Sauté and add tomatoes, tomato paste, and ½ cup of water. Sprinkle with salt, pepper flakes, and oregano and stir-fry for 5 minutes. Add lentils, sweet corn, and red wine. Pour in ½ cup of water and seal the lid. Cook on High Pressure for 2 minutes. Do a quick release. Set aside to cool completely and refrigerate for 30 minutes. Sprinkle with Parmesan cheese before serving.

Saucy Millet And Corn

Servings:4 | Cooking Time: 10 Minutes

Ingredients:
- 2 teaspoons olive oil
- 1 cup millet
- 2 cups vegetable broth
- 1 teaspoon sea salt
- 1 can corn kernels
- 1 can tomato sauce
- ¼ cup grated Gruyère cheese

Directions:
1. Drizzle 2 teaspoons olive oil in Instant Pot. Layer millet into pot. Add vegetable broth and salt. Lock lid.
2. Press the Rice button. When timer beeps, let pressure release naturally for 5 minutes. Quick-release any additional pressure until float valve drops and then unlock lid.
3. Transfer millet to a serving bowl. Toss corn, tomato sauce, and Gruyère cheese in millet. Serve warm.

Indian Dhal With Veggies

Servings: 4 | Cooking Time: 35 Minutes

Ingredients:
- 1 cup lentils
- 2 tbsp almond butter
- 1 carrot, peeled, chopped
- 1 potato, peeled, chopped
- 1 bay leaf
- ¼ tbsp parsley, chopped
- ½ tbsp chili powder
- 2 tbsp ground cumin
- 1 tbsp garam masala
- 3 cups vegetable stock

Directions:
1. Melt almond butter on Sauté. Add carrots, potatoes, and bay leaf. Stir and cook for 10 minutes. Add lentils, chili powder, cumin, garam masala, and stock and press Cancel. If the mixture is very thick, add a bit of water. Seal the lid, select Manual, and cook on High Pressure for 15 minutes. Once the timer goes off, do a quick release. Serve sprinkled with parsley.

Acorn Squash With Sweet Glaze

Servings: 4 | Cooking Time: 15 Minutes

Ingredients:
- 1 lb acorn squash, cut into 2-inch chunks
- 3 tbsp honey
- 2 tbsp butter
- 1 tbsp dark brown sugar
- 1 tbsp cinnamon
- Salt and pepper to taste

Directions:
1. In a small bowl, mix 1 tbsp honey, butter and ½ cup water. Pour into the pot. Add in acorn squash, seal the lid and cook on High Pressure for 4 minutes. Release the pressure quickly. Transfer the squash to a serving dish.
2. Set on Sauté. Mix sugar, cinnamon, the remaining 2 tbsp honey and the liquid in the pot. Cook as you stir for 4 minutes to obtain a thick consistency and turn caramelized and golden. Spread honey glaze over squash; add pepper and salt to taste.

Spicy Vegetable Pilaf

Servings: 4 | Cooking Time: 40 Minutes

Ingredients:
- 3 tbsp olive oil
- 1 tbsp ginger, minced
- 1 cup onion, chopped
- 1 cup green peas
- 1 cup carrots, chopped
- 1 cup mushrooms, chopped
- 1 cup broccoli, chopped
- 1 tbsp chili powder
- ½ tbsp ground cumin
- 1 tbsp garam masala
- ½ tbsp turmeric
- 1 cup basmati rice
- 2 cups vegetable broth
- 1 tbsp lemon juice
- Salt and pepper to taste

Directions:
1. Warm 1 tbsp olive oil on Sauté. Add in onion and ginger and cook for 3 minutes. Stir in broccoli, green peas, mushrooms, and carrots and cook for 5 minutes. Stir in the turmeric, chili powder, garam masala, salt, pepper, and cumin for 1 minute. Add ¼ cup broth and scrape the bottom to get rid of any browned bits. Add the remaining broth and rice. Seal the lid and cook for 20 minutes on High Pressure. Release the pressure quickly. Drizzle with lemon juice and serve.

Black Bean Slider Patties

Servings:8 | Cooking Time: 49 Minutes

Ingredients:
- 1 tablespoon olive oil
- 1 small red bell pepper, seeded and diced small
- 2 cups vegetable broth
- 1 cup dried black beans, rinsed and drained
- 2 teaspoons chili powder
- ½ teaspoon salt
- ½ teaspoon ground black pepper
- 1 large egg

- 1 cup panko bread crumbs

Directions:
1. Press the Sauté button on the Instant Pot and heat oil. Add bell pepper and stir-fry 2–3 minutes until pepper is tender. Add broth and deglaze by scraping the bottom and sides of pot.
2. Add beans, chili powder, salt, and pepper. Press the Cancel button. Lock lid.
3. Press the Bean button and cook for the default time of 30 minutes. When timer beeps, let pressure release naturally for 10 minutes. Quick-release any additional pressure until float valve drops. Press the Cancel button. Unlock lid.
4. Press the Sauté button on the Instant Pot, press the Adjust button to change the heat to Less, and simmer bean mixture unlidded 10 minutes to thicken. Transfer mixture to a large bowl.
5. Once bean mixture is cool enough to handle, quickly mix in egg and bread crumbs. Form into sixteen equal-sized small patties.
6. In a medium skillet over medium heat, cook patties approximately 2–3 minutes per side until browned. Serve warm.

English Vegetable Potage

Servings: 4 | Cooking Time: 50 Minutes

Ingredients:
- 1 lb potatoes, cut into bite-sized pieces
- 2 carrots, peeled, chopped
- 3 celery stalks, chopped
- 2 onions, peeled, chopped
- 1 zucchini, sliced
- A handful of celery leaves
- 2 tbsp butter, unsalted
- 3 tbsp olive oil
- 2 cups vegetable broth
- 1 tbsp paprika
- Salt and pepper to taste
- 2 bay leaves

Directions:
1. Warm olive oil on Sauté and stir-fry the onions for 3-4 minutes until translucent. Add carrots, celery, zucchini, and ¼ cup of broth. Continue to cook for 10 more minutes, stirring constantly. Stir in potatoes, paprika, salt, pepper, bay leaves, remaining broth, and celery leaves. Seal the lid and cook on Meat/Stew for 30 minutes on High. Do a quick release and stir in butter.

Cauliflower & Potato Curry With Cilantro

Servings: 4 | Cooking Time: 40 Minutes

Ingredients:
- 1 tbsp vegetable oil
- 10 oz cauliflower florets
- 1 potato, peeled and diced
- 1 tbsp ghee
- 2 tbsp cumin seeds
- 1 onion, minced
- 4 garlic cloves, minced
- 1 tomato, chopped
- 1 jalapeño pepper, minced
- 1 tbsp curry paste
- 1 tbsp ground turmeric
- ½ tsp chili pepper

- Salt and pepper to taste
- 2 tbsp cilantro, chopped

Directions:
1. Warm oil on Sauté. Add in potato and cauliflower and cook for 8 to 10 minutes until lightly browned; season with salt. Set the vegetables in a bowl. Add ghee to the pot. Mix in cumin seeds and cook for 10 seconds until they start to pop; add onion and cook for 3 minutes until softened. Mix in garlic and pepper; cook for 30 seconds.
2. Add in tomato, curry paste, chili pepper, jalapeño pepper, and turmeric; cook for 4 to 6 minutes. Return potato and cauliflower to the pot. Stir in 1 cup water. Seal the lid and cook on High Pressure for 4 minutes. Quick-release the pressure. Unlock the lid. Top with cilantro and serve.

Amazing Vegetable Paella

Servings: 4 | Cooking Time: 25 Minutes

Ingredients:
- ½ cup green peas
- 2 carrots, chopped
- 1 cup fire-roasted tomatoes
- 1 cup zucchini, chopped
- 3 oz celery root, chopped
- 1 tbsp turmeric
- 2 cup vegetable broth
- 1 cup long-grain rice

Directions:
1. Place green peas, carrots, tomatoes, zucchini, celery, turmeric, and broth in the Instant Pot. Stir well and seal the lid. Cook on Manual for 15 minutes on High. Do a quick release, open the lid, and stir in the rice. Seal the lid and cook on High pressure for 3 minutes. When ready, release the pressure naturally for about 10 minutes.

Tofu With Noodles & Peanuts

Servings: 4 | Cooking Time: 15 Minutes

Ingredients:
- 1 package tofu, cubed
- 8 oz egg noodles
- 2 bell peppers, chopped
- ¼ cup soy sauce
- ¼ cup orange juice
- 1 tbsp fresh ginger, minced
- 2 tbsp vinegar
- 1 tbsp sesame oil
- 1 tbsp sriracha
- ¼ cup roasted peanuts
- 3 scallions, chopped

Directions:
1. In the Instant Pot, mix tofu, bell peppers, orange juice, sesame oil, ginger, egg noodles, soy sauce, vinegar, and sriracha. Cover with enough water. Seal the lid and cook for 2 minutes on High Pressure. Release the pressure quickly. Divide the meal between 4 plates and top with scallions and peanuts to serve.

Millet Eggplant Pilaf

Servings: 4 | Cooking Time: 17 Minutes

Ingredients:
- 1 tablespoon butter
- ¼ cup peeled and diced onion
- 1 cup peeled and diced eggplant
- 1 small Roma tomato, seeded and diced
- 1 cup millet
- 2 cups vegetable broth
- 1 teaspoon sea salt
- ¼ teaspoon ground black pepper
- ⅛ teaspoon saffron
- ⅛ teaspoon cayenne pepper
- 1 tablespoon chopped fresh chives

Directions:
1. Press Sauté button on Instant Pot. Add butter and melt. Add onion and cook 3–5 minutes until translucent. Toss in eggplant and stir-fry for 2 more minutes. Add diced tomato.
2. Add millet to Instant Pot in an even layer. Gently pour in broth. Lock lid.
3. Press the Rice button. When timer beeps, let pressure release naturally for 5 minutes. Quick-release any additional pressure until float valve drops and then unlock lid.
4. Transfer pot ingredients to a serving bowl. Season with salt, pepper, saffron, and cayenne pepper. Garnish with chives.

Creamy Turnips Stuffed With Cheese

Servings: 4 | Cooking Time: 20 Minutes

Ingredients:
- ½ cup chopped roasted red bell pepper
- 4 small turnips
- ¼ cup whipping cream
- ¼ cup sour cream
- 1 tsp Italian seasoning
- 1 ½ cups grated mozzarella
- 4 green onions, chopped
- 1/3 cup grated Parmesan

Directions:
1. Pour 1 cup of water into the pot and insert a trivet. Place the turnips on top. Seal the lid and cook on High for 10 minutes. Do a quick pressure release. Remove the turnips to a cutting board and allow cooling. Cut the turnips in half. Scoop out the pulp into a bowl and mash it with a potato mash. Mix in the whipping and sour cream until smooth. Stir in the roasted bell pepper.
2. Add in Italian seasoning and mozzarella cheese. Fetch out 2 tbsp of green onions and put into the turnips. Fill the turnip skins with the mashed mixture and sprinkle with Parmesan cheese. Arrange on a greased baking dish and place on the trivet. Seal the lid and cook on High pressure for 3 minutes. Do a quick pressure release. Top with the remaining onions to serve.

Celery & Red Bean Stew

Servings: 4 | Cooking Time: 25 Minutes

Ingredients:
- 6 oz red beans, cooked
- 2 carrots, chopped
- 2 celery stalks, chopped
- 1 onion, chopped
- 2 tbsp tomato paste
- 1 bay leaf
- 2 cups vegetable broth
- 3 tbsp olive oil
- 1 tbsp salt
- 2 tbsp parsley, chopped
- 1 tbsp flour

Directions:
1. Warm olive oil on Sauté and stir-fry the onion for 3 minutes. Add celery and carrots. Cook for 5 more minutes. Add red beans, bay leaf, salt, and tomato paste. Stir in 1 tbsp of flour and pour in the vegetable broth. Seal the lid and cook on High Pressure for 5 minutes. Do a natural release for about 10 minutes. Sprinkle with some fresh parsley and serve warm.

Spicy Shiitake Mushrooms With Potatoes

Servings: 4 | Cooking Time: 45 Minutes

Ingredients:
- 1 lb shiitake mushrooms
- 2 potatoes, chopped
- 3 garlic cloves, crushed
- 2 tbsp olive oil
- 1 tsp garlic powder
- 1 tbsp cumin seeds
- ½ tbsp chili powder
- 1 large zucchini, chopped
- 1 cup onions
- 2 cups vegetable stock
- 1 cup tomato sauce

Directions:
1. Warm olive oil on Sauté. Stir-fry cumin seeds for one minute. Add onions, chili powder, garlic, and garlic powder. Cook for 3 minutes, stirring constantly. Add mushrooms and continue to cook on Sauté for 3 more minutes. Add potatoes, zucchini, stock, and tomato sauce and seal the lid. Cook on High Pressure for 20 minutes. When done, release the pressure naturally. Serve warm.

Plant-based Indian Curry

Servings: 4 | Cooking Time: 20 Minutes

Ingredients:
- 1 tsp butter
- 1 onion, chopped
- 2 cloves garlic, minced
- 1 tsp ginger, grated
- 1 tsp ground cumin
- 1 tsp red chili powder
- 1 tsp salt
- ½ tsp ground turmeric
- 1 can chickpeas
- 1 tomato, diced
- 1/3 cup water

- 2 lb collard greens, chopped
- ½ tsp garam masala
- 1 tsp lemon juice

Directions:
1. Melt butter on Sauté. Add in the onion, ginger, cumin, turmeric, red chili powder, garlic, and salt and cook for 30 seconds until crispy. Stir in tomato. Pour in ⅓ cup of water and chickpeas. Seal the lid and cook on High Pressure for 4 minutes. Release the pressure quickly. Press Sauté. Into the chickpea mixture, stir in lemon juice, collard greens, and garam masala until well coated. Cook for 2 to 3 minutes until collard greens wilt on Sauté. Serve over rice or naan.

Five-can Minestrone

Servings:4 | Cooking Time: 3 Minutes

Ingredients:
- 1 can diced, fire-roasted tomatoes, including juice
- 1 can sweet golden corn, drained
- 1 can mixed vegetables
- 1 can cannellini beans, drained and rinsed
- 1 can minestrone soup
- 2 cups vegetable broth

Directions:
1. Add all ingredients to the Instant Pot. Lock lid.
2. Press the Manual button and adjust time to 3 minutes. When timer beeps, quick-release pressure until float valve drops. Unlock lid.
3. Ladle soup into bowls. Serve warm.

Stuffed Avocado Bake

Servings: 2 | Cooking Time: 20 Minutes

Ingredients:
- 1 avocado, halved
- 2 eggs
- 3 tbsp butter, melted
- 1 tbsp dried oregano
- Salt and pepper to taste
- 1 tomato, chopped

Directions:
1. Grease a baking dish with butter. With a spoon, remove some of the avocado flesh to create more space for the eggs. Reserve the flesh for garnish. Place the avocado in the baking dish. Crack an egg into each avocado half. Season with salt and oregano. Add 1 cup of water and place the trivet in the pot. Lower the baking dish on top.
2. Seal the lid, select Manual, and cook on High Pressure for 10 minutes. When done, do a quick release before opening the lid. Mix the reserved avocado flesh with the tomato, season with salt and pepper and serve with the baked avocado.

Curried Red Potatoes

Servings:6 | Cooking Time: 20 Minutes

Ingredients:
- 1 tablespoon olive oil
- 1 small yellow onion, peeled and diced
- 3 pounds small red potatoes, quartered
- 2 tablespoons curry paste
- 1 teaspoon red chile flakes
- 1 teaspoon garlic salt
- 1 teaspoon ground black pepper
- 2 cups vegetable broth
- 2 tablespoons cornstarch

Directions:
1. Press the Sauté button on the Instant Pot and heat oil. Add onion. Stir-fry 3–5 minutes until onions are translucent.
2. Add potatoes, curry paste, red chile flakes, garlic salt, pepper, and broth to pot and stir to combine. Press the Cancel button. Lock lid.
3. Press the Manual or Pressure Cook button and adjust time to 15 minutes. When timer beeps, let pressure release naturally until float valve drops. Unlock lid.
4. Ladle a spoonful of liquid from pot into a small bowl. Whisk in cornstarch until smooth. Add this slurry back to pot and let sit 5 minutes until sauce thickens.
5. Ladle potatoes and sauce into bowls. Serve warm.

Quick Cassoulet

Servings:6 | Cooking Time: 45 Minutes

Ingredients:
- 1 tablespoon olive oil
- 1 medium yellow onion, peeled and diced
- 2 cups dried cannellini beans, rinsed and drained
- 2 medium carrots, peeled and diced small
- 1 tablespoon Italian seasoning
- 1 teaspoon garlic salt
- ½ teaspoon ground black pepper
- 2 ½ cups vegetable broth
- 1 can diced tomatoes, including juice
- 4 vegan smoked apple sausages, each cut into 4 sections

Directions:
1. Press the Sauté button on the Instant Pot and heat oil. Add onion and stir-fry 3–5 minutes until onions are translucent. Add beans and toss.
2. Add carrots, Italian seasoning, garlic salt, and pepper.
3. Gently pour in broth and diced tomatoes. Press the Cancel button. Lock lid.
4. Press the Bean button and cook for the default time of 30 minutes. When timer beeps, let pressure release naturally for 10 minutes. Quick-release any additional pressure until float valve drops. Press the Cancel button. Unlock lid. Add sausage.
5. Press the Sauté button on the Instant Pot, press the Adjust button to change the temperature to Less, and simmer bean mixture unlidded 10 minutes to thicken. Transfer to a serving bowl and carefully toss. Serve warm.

Parsnip & Cauliflower Mash With Chives

Servings: 8 | Cooking Time: 15 Minutes

Ingredients:
- 1 ½ lb parsnips, cubed
- 10 oz cauliflower florets
- 2 garlic cloves
- Salt and pepper to taste
- ¼ cup sour cream
- ¼ cup grated Parmesan
- 1 tbsp butter
- 2 tbsp minced chives

Directions:
1. In the pot, mix parsnips, garlic, 2 cups water, salt, cauliflower, and pepper. Seal the lid and cook on High Pressure for 4 minutes. Release the pressure quickly. Drain parsnips and cauliflower and return to pot. Add Parmesan, butter, and sour cream. Use a potato masher to mash until the desired consistency is attained. Top with chives and place to a serving plate. Serve.

Tortellini In Brodo

Servings:4 | Cooking Time: 15 Minutes

Ingredients:
- 1 tablespoon olive oil
- 1 small yellow onion, peeled and diced
- 1 large carrot, peeled and diced small
- 1 medium stalk celery, diced
- 1 package dried three-cheese tortellini
- 4 cups vegetable broth
- ½ teaspoon salt
- ½ teaspoon ground black pepper
- 1 cup baby spinach

Directions:
1. Press the Sauté button on the Instant Pot and heat oil. Stir-fry onion, carrot, and celery 3–5 minutes until onions are translucent.
2. Add tortellini, broth, salt, and pepper. Press the Cancel button. Lock lid.
3. Press the Manual or Pressure Cook button and adjust time to 10 minutes. When timer beeps, let pressure release naturally for 5 minutes. Quick-release any additional pressure until float valve drops. Unlock lid. Add baby spinach and stir until wilted.
4. Ladle portions into bowls. Serve warm.

Sautéed Spinach With Roquefort Cheese

Servings: 2 | Cooking Time: 10 Minutes

Ingredients:
- ½ cup Roquefort cheese, crumbled
- 9 oz fresh spinach
- 2 leeks, chopped
- 2 red onions, chopped
- 2 garlic cloves, crushed
- 3 tbsp olive oil

Directions:
1. Grease the inner pot with oil. Stir-fry leeks, garlic, and onions for about 5 minutes on Sauté. Add spinach and give it a good stir. Press Cancel, transfer to a serving dish, and sprinkle with Roquefort cheese. Serve right away.

Minestrone Soup With Green Vegetables

Servings: 4 | Cooking Time: 15 Minutes

Ingredients:
- 2 tbsp olive oil
- 10 oz broccoli florets
- 4 celery stalks, chopped
- 1 leek, chopped thinly
- 1 zucchini, chopped
- 1 cup green beans
- 2 cups vegetable broth
- 2 cups chopped kale

Directions:
1. Add broccoli, leek, beans, zucchini, and celery. Mix in vegetable broth, oil, and enough water to cover. Seal the lid and cook on High Pressure for 4 minutes. Release pressure naturally for 5 minutes, then release the remaining pressure quickly. Stir in kale on Sauté and cook until tender. Serve.

Mixed Vegetables Medley

Servings: 4 | Cooking Time: 20 Minutes

Ingredients:
- 10 oz broccoli florets
- 16 asparagus, trimmed
- 10 oz cauliflower florets
- 5 oz green beans
- 2 carrots, cut on bias
- Salt to taste

Directions:
1. Add 1 cup of water and set trivet on top. Place a steamer basket over the water. In an even layer, spread green beans, broccoli, cauliflower, asparagus, and carrots in the steamer basket. Seal the lid and cook on Steam for 3 minutes on High. Release the pressure quickly. Remove basket from the pot and season with salt.

Traditional Italian Pesto

Servings: 4 | Cooking Time: 20 Minutes

Ingredients:
- 3 zucchini, peeled, chopped
- 1 eggplant, peeled, chopped
- 3 red bell peppers, chopped
- ½ cup basil-tomato juice
- ½ tbsp salt
- 2 tbsp olive oil

Directions:
1. Add zucchini, eggplant, bell peppers, basil-tomato juice, salt, and olive oil to the pot and give it a good stir. Pour 1 cup of water. Seal the lid and cook on High Pressure for 15 minutes. Do a quick release. Set aside to cool completely. Serve as a cold salad or a side dish.

Ravioli Lasagna

Servings:4 | Cooking Time: 20 Minutes

Ingredients:
- 1 jar marinara sauce
- 1 package fresh or frozen cheese ravioli
- 1 cup grated mozzarella cheese
- ½ cup grated vegetarian Parmesan cheese
- 2 cups water
- ¼ cup fresh basil chiffonade

Directions:
1. Grease a 7" springform pan. Add ⅓ of marinara sauce to bottom of pan. Add half of ravioli in an even layer(s). Layer ⅓ of marinara sauce over ravioli. Add ½ cup mozzarella cheese in an even layer. Sprinkle with ¼ cup Parmesan cheese. Add remaining ravioli. Pour remaining sauce over ravioli. Add remaining mozzarella and Parmesan cheese.
2. Place a square of aluminum foil along the outside bottom of the pan and crimp up around the edges.
3. Add water to the Instant Pot and insert steam rack. Place pan on steam rack. Lock lid.
4. Press the Manual or Pressure Cook button and adjust time to 20 minutes. When timer beeps, let pressure release naturally for 10 minutes. Quick-release any additional pressure until float valve drops. Unlock lid.
5. Remove pan from pot. Carefully pour off any water/steam from top of lasagna. Place on a cooling rack for 30 minutes before removing sides of springform pan.
6. Slice and garnish with basil. Serve warm.

Cali Dogs

Servings:4 | Cooking Time: 0 Minutes

Ingredients:
- 2 cups water
- 8 meat-free, plant-based hot dogs
- 8 hot dog buns
- ½ cup alfalfa sprouts
- 1 medium avocado, peeled, pitted, and diced
- ½ cup crumbled goat cheese

Directions:
1. Pour water into the Instant Pot. Add hot dogs. Lock lid.
2. Press the Manual or Pressure Cook button and adjust time to 0 minutes. When timer beeps, quick-release pressure until float valve drops. Unlock lid.
3. Assemble hot dogs by placing them in buns and topping with remaining ingredients. Serve warm.

Penne Pasta With Shiitake & Vegetables

Servings: 4 | Cooking Time: 20 Minutes

Ingredients:
- 6 oz shiitake mushrooms, chopped
- 6 oz penne pasta
- 2 garlic cloves, crushed
- 1 carrot, chopped into strips
- 6 oz zucchini cut into strips
- 6 oz finely chopped leek
- 4 oz baby spinach
- 3 tbsp oil
- 2 tbsp soy sauce
- 1 tbsp ground ginger
- ½ tbsp salt

Directions:
1. Heat oil on Sauté and stir-fry carrot and garlic for 3-4 minutes. Add mushrooms, penne, zucchini, leek, spinach, soy sauce, ginger, and salt and pour in 2 cups of water. Cook on High Pressure for 4 minutes. Quick-release the pressure and serve.

Sweet Polenta With Pistachios

Servings: 4 | Cooking Time: 20 Minutes

Ingredients:
- ½ cup honey
- 5 cups water
- 1 cup polenta
- ½ cup heavy cream
- ¼ tsp salt
- ¼ cup pistachios, toasted

Directions:
1. Set your Instant Pot to Sauté. Place honey and water and bring to a boil, stirring often. Stir in polenta. Seal the lid, select Manual, and cook for 12 minutes on High.
2. When ready, perform a quick pressure release and unlock the lid. Mix in heavy cream and let sit for 1 minute. Sprinkle with salt to taste. Top with pistachios and serve.

Turmeric Stew With Green Peas

Servings: 4 | Cooking Time: 35 Minutes

Ingredients:
- 2 cups green peas
- 1 onion, chopped
- 4 cloves garlic, minced
- 3 oz of olives, pitted
- 1 tbsp ginger, shredded
- 1 tbsp turmeric
- 1 tbsp salt
- 4 cups vegetable stock
- 3 tbsp olive oil

Directions:
1. Heat olive oil on Sauté. Stir-fry the onion and garlic for 2-3 minutes, stirring a few times. Add peas, olives, ginger, turmeric, salt, and stock and press Cancel. Seal the lid, select Manual, and cook on High Pressure for 20 minutes. Once the timer goes off, do a quick release before opening the lid. Serve with a dollop of yogurt.

Cauliflower Rice With Peas & Chili

Servings: 2 | Cooking Time: 20 Minutes

Ingredients:
- 10 oz cauliflower florets
- 2 tbsp olive oil
- Salt to taste
- 1 tsp chili powder
- ¼ cup green peas
- 1 tbsp chopped parsley

Directions:
1. Add 1 cup water, set rack over water and place the steamer basket onto the rack. Add cauliflower into the steamer basket.

Seal the lid and cook on High Pressure for 1 minute. Release the pressure quickly. Remove rack and steamer basket. Drain water from the pot. Set it to Sauté and warm oil. Add in cauliflower and stir to break into smaller pieces like rice. Stir in chili powder, peas and salt. Serve the cauliflower topped with parsley.

2. Seal the lid and cook for 7 minutes on High Pressure. Release the pressure quickly. Open the lid and let sit for 6 minutes until flavors combine. Use a fork to fluff quinoa and season with pepper and salt. Stir in cilantro and divide into plates. Top with cheese and avocado slices and serve.

Mushroom Risotto

Servings:4 | Cooking Time: 20 Minutes

Ingredients:
- 4 tablespoons butter
- 1 small onion, peeled and finely diced
- 4 cups sliced baby bella mushrooms
- 2 cloves garlic, minced
- 1½ cups Arborio rice
- 4 cups vegetable broth, divided
- 3 tablespoons grated Parmesan cheese
- ½ teaspoon salt
- ¼ teaspoon ground black pepper
- 2 tablespoons fresh thyme leaves

Directions:
1. Press the Sauté button on the Instant Pot. Add the butter and melt. Add the onion and stir-fry for 3–5 minutes until onions are translucent. Add mushrooms, garlic, and rice and cook for an additional minute. Add 1 cup broth and stir unlidded until liquid is absorbed by the rice.
2. Add remaining 3 cups broth, Parmesan cheese, salt, and pepper. Lock lid.
3. Press the Rice button. Let pressure release naturally for 10 minutes. Quick-release any additional pressure until float valve drops and then unlock lid.
4. Transfer to a serving bowl and garnish with thyme and serve.

Weekend Burrito Bowls

Servings: 4 | Cooking Time: 30 Minutes

Ingredients:
- 2 tbsp olive oil
- 1 onion, chopped
- 2 garlic cloves, minced
- 1 tbsp chili powder
- 2 tbsp ground cumin
- 2 tbsp paprika
- Salt and pepper to taste
- ¼ tbsp cayenne pepper
- 1 cup quinoa, rinsed
- 14.5-oz can diced tomatoes
- 1 can black beans
- 1 ½ cups vegetable stock
- 1 cup frozen corn kernels
- 2 tbsp chopped cilantro
- 2 tbsp cheddar, grated
- 1 avocado, chopped

Directions:
1. Warm oil on Sauté. Add in onion and stir-fry for 3-5 minutes until fragrant. Add garlic and Sauté for 2 more minutes until soft and golden brown. Add in chili powder, paprika, cayenne pepper, salt, cumin, and black pepper and cook for 1 minute until spices are soft. Pour quinoa into onion and spice mixture and stir to coat quinoa thoroughly in spices. Add tomatoes, black beans, vegetable stock, and corn; stir to combine.

Baby Bella Burgundy

Servings:4 | Cooking Time: 17 Minutes

Ingredients:
- 4 tablespoons olive oil
- 3 medium shallots, peeled and diced
- 4 cups sliced baby bella mushrooms
- 1 cup dry red wine
- 2 medium carrots, peeled and thinly sliced
- 2 tablespoons Italian seasoning
- 1 teaspoon garlic salt
- 1 cup vegetable broth
- 2 tablespoons tomato paste

Directions:
1. Press the Sauté button on the Instant Pot and heat oil. Add shallots and mushrooms and cook 3–5 minutes until shallots are translucent.
2. Deglaze pot by adding red wine, scraping any bits from bottom and sides of pot. Cook an additional 2 minutes to allow alcohol to cook off.
3. Add carrots, Italian seasoning, garlic salt, broth, and tomato paste to pot. Press the Cancel button. Lock lid.
4. Press the Manual or Pressure Cook button and adjust time to 10 minutes. When timer beeps, quick-release pressure until float valve drops. Unlock lid.
5. Ladle mixture into bowls. Serve warm.

Mushroom & Gouda Cheese Pizza

Servings: 4 | Cooking Time: 30 Minutes

Ingredients:
- 4 oz button mushrooms, chopped
- ½ cup grated gouda cheese
- 1 pizza crust
- ½ cup tomato paste
- 1 tbsp sugar
- 1 tbsp dried oregano
- 2 tbsp olive oil
- 12 olives
- 1 cup arugula

Directions:
1. Grease the bottom of a baking dish with one tbsp of olive oil. Line some parchment paper. Flour the working surface and roll out the pizza crust to the approximate size of your Instant Pot. Gently fit the dough in the previously prepared baking dish.
2. In a bowl, combine tomato paste, ¼ cup water, sugar, and oregano. Spread the mixture over the crust, make a layer with button mushrooms and grated gouda. Add a trivet inside the pot and pour in 1 cup water. Seal the lid and cook for 15 minutes on High Pressure. Do a quick release. Sprinkle the pizza with the remaining oil and top with olives and arugula. Serve.

One-pot Swiss Chard & Potatoes

Servings: 4 | Cooking Time: 15 Minutes

Ingredients:
- 1 lb Swiss chard, chopped
- 2 potatoes, peeled, chopped
- ¼ tsp oregano
- 1 tsp salt
- 1 tsp Italian seasoning

Directions:
1. Add Swiss chard and potatoes to the pot. Pour water to cover all and sprinkle with salt. Seal the lid and select Manual. Cook for 3 minutes on High. Release the steam naturally for 5 minutes. Transfer to a serving plate. Sprinkle with oregano and Italian seasoning and serve.

Steamed Artichokes With Lime Aioli

Servings: 4 | Cooking Time: 20 Minutes

Ingredients:
- 2 large artichokes
- 2 garlic cloves, smashed
- ½ cup mayonnaise
- Salt and pepper to taste
- Juice of 1 lime

Directions:
1. Using a serrated knife, trim about 1 inch from the top of the artichokes. Into the pot, add 1 cup of water and set trivet over. Lay the artichokes on the trivet. Seal lid and cook for 14 minutes on High Pressure. Release the pressure quickly. Mix the mayonnaise, garlic, and lime juice. Season with salt and pepper. Serve artichokes on a platter with garlic mayo on the side.

Sweet Potato Chili

Servings:4 | Cooking Time: 17 Minutes

Ingredients:
- 1 tablespoon olive oil
- 1 small yellow onion, peeled and diced
- 2 medium sweet potatoes, peeled and diced
- 1 can kidney beans, drained and rinsed
- 2 tablespoons chili powder
- 1 tablespoon hot sauce
- 1 teaspoon garlic salt
- 1 can fire-roasted diced tomatoes, including juice
- 2 cups vegetable broth

Directions:
1. Press the Sauté button on the Instant Pot and heat oil. Add onion. Stir-fry 3–5 minutes until onions are translucent.
2. Add remaining ingredients to pot and stir to combine. Press the Cancel button. Lock lid.
3. Press the Manual or Pressure Cook button and adjust time to 12 minutes. When timer beeps, let pressure release naturally until float valve drops. Unlock lid.
4. Ladle chili into bowls. Serve warm.

Stuffed Bell Peppers

Servings:4 | Cooking Time: 15 Minutes

Ingredients:
- 4 large bell peppers
- 2 cups cooked white rice
- 1 medium onion, peeled and diced
- 3 small Roma tomatoes, diced
- ¼ cup marinara sauce
- 1 cup corn kernels (cut from the cob is preferred)
- ¼ cup sliced black olives
- ¼ cup canned cannellini beans, rinsed and drained
- ¼ cup canned black beans, rinsed and drained
- 1 teaspoon sea salt
- 1 teaspoon garlic powder
- ½ cup vegetable broth
- 2 tablespoons grated Parmesan cheese

Directions:
1. Cut off the bell pepper tops as close to the tops as possible. Hollow out and discard seeds. Poke a few small holes in the bottom of the peppers to allow drippings to drain.
2. In a medium bowl, combine remaining ingredients except for broth and Parmesan cheese. Stuff equal amounts of mixture into each of the bell peppers.
3. Place trivet into the Instant Pot and pour in the broth. Set the peppers upright on the trivet. Lock lid.
4. Press the Manual button and adjust time to 15 minutes. When timer beeps, let pressure release naturally until float valve drops and then unlock lid.
5. Serve immediately and garnish with Parmesan cheese.

Macaroni And Cheese

Servings:6 | Cooking Time: 4 Minutes

Ingredients:
- 1 pound elbow macaroni
- ¼ cup milk
- 1 cup shredded sharp Cheddar
- ¼ cup ricotta cheese
- 2 tablespoons grated Parmesan cheese
- 2 tablespoons butter
- ½ teaspoon ground mustard
- 2 teaspoons salt
- ½ teaspoon ground black pepper

Directions:
1. Place macaroni in an even layer in Instant Pot. Pour enough water to come about ¼" over pasta. Lock lid.
2. Press the Manual button and adjust time to 4 minutes. When the timer beeps, let the pressure release naturally for 3 minutes. Quick-release any additional pressure until float valve drops and then unlock lid.
3. Drain any residual water. Add milk, Cheddar, ricotta, Parmesan, butter, mustard, salt, and pepper. Stir in the warmed pot until well-combined. Serve warm.

Chapter 10 : Desserts & Drinks Recipes

Chapter 10 : Desserts & Drinks Recipes

Lemon-apricot Compote

Servings: 6 | Cooking Time: 20 Minutes

Ingredients:
- 2 lb fresh apricots, sliced
- 1 lb sugar
- 2 tbsp lemon zest
- 1 tsp ground nutmeg
- 10 cups water

Directions:
1. Add apricots, sugar, water, nutmeg, and lemon zest. Cook, stirring occasionally until half of the water evaporates, on Sauté. Press Cancel and transfer the apricots and the remaining liquid into glass jars. Let cool. Refrigerate.

Orange New York Cheesecake

Servings: 6 | Cooking Time: 1 Hour + Freezing Time

Ingredients:
- For the crust
- 1 cup graham crackers crumbs
- 2 tbsp butter, melted
- 1 tsp sugar
- For the filling
- 2 cups cream cheese
- ½ cup sugar
- 1 tsp vanilla extract
- Zest from 1 orange
- A pinch of salt
- 2 eggs

Directions:
1. Fold a 20-inch piece of aluminum foil in half lengthwise twice and set on the Instant Pot. Grease a parchment paper and line it to a cake pan. In a bowl, combine melted butter, sugar, and graham crackers. Press into the bottom and about ⅓ up the sides of the pan. Transfer the pan to the freezer as you prepare the filling.
2. In a separate bowl, beat sugar, cream cheese, salt, orange zest, and vanilla until smooth. Beat eggs into the filling, one at a time. Stir until combined. Add the filling over the chilled crust in the pan. Add 1 cup water and set a trivet into the pot. Put the pan on the trivet.
3. Seal the lid, press Cake, and cook for 40 minutes on High. Release the pressure quickly. Cool the cheesecake and then transfer it to the refrigerator for 3 hours. Use a paring knife to run along the edges between the pan and cheesecake to remove the cheesecake and set to the plate.

Pearberry Crisp

Servings:4 | Cooking Time: 8 Minutes

Ingredients:
- Pearberry Filling
- 6 medium pears, peeled, cored, and diced
- 1 cup thawed frozen mixed berries
- ¼ cup water
- 1 tablespoon fresh lemon juice
- 2 tablespoons pure maple syrup
- 1 teaspoon ground cinnamon
- ¼ teaspoon ground nutmeg
- Pinch of salt
- Topping
- 4 tablespoons melted butter
- 1 cup old-fashioned oats
- ⅛ cup all-purpose flour
- ¼ cup chopped almonds
- ¼ cup packed light brown sugar
- ¼ teaspoon sea salt

Directions:
1. For Pearberry Filling: Place Pearberry Filling ingredients in Instant Pot. Stir to distribute ingredients.
2. For Topping: Mix Topping ingredients together in a small bowl. Spoon drops of topping over the filling. Lock lid.
3. Press the Manual button and adjust time to 8 minutes. When the timer beeps, let pressure release naturally until float valve drops and then unlock lid. Spoon into bowls and enjoy.

Simple Apple Cinnamon Dessert

Servings: 6 | Cooking Time: 30 Minutes

Ingredients:
- Topping:
- ½ cup rolled oats
- ½ cup oat flour
- ½ cup granulated sugar
- ¼ cup olive oil
- Filling:
- 5 apples, cored, and halved
- 2 tbsp arrowroot powder
- ½ cup water
- 1 tsp ground cinnamon
- ¼ tsp ground nutmeg
- ½ tsp vanilla paste

Directions:
1. In a bowl, combine sugar, oat flour, rolled oats, and olive oil to form coarse crumbs. Spoon the apples into the Instant Pot. Mix water with arrowroot powder in a bowl. Stir in nutmeg, cinnamon, and vanilla. Toss in the apples to coat. Apply oat topping to the apples. Seal the lid and cook on High Pressure for 10 minutes. Release the pressure naturally for 10 minutes.

Pineapple Upside-down Cake

Servings:4 | Cooking Time: 35 Minutes

Ingredients:
- ½ cup drained crushed pineapple
- 12 maraschino cherries
- 1 large egg
- 2 tablespoons melted butter
- ⅓ cup sugar
- 1 teaspoon vanilla extract
- 1 cup ricotta cheese
- 1 cup flour
- 2 teaspoons baking powder
- 1 teaspoon baking soda
- Pinch of salt
- 1½ cups water

Directions:
1. Grease a 6" cake pan. Place a circle of parchment paper in the bottom. Add a layer of pineapple and distribute cherries evenly among the pineapple.
2. In a medium bowl, beat egg. Whisk in butter, sugar, and vanilla until smooth. Add remaining ingredients except water. Pour into pan over pineapple and cherries.
3. Pour water into Instant Pot. Add trivet. Lower cake pan onto trivet. Lock lid.
4. Press the Manual button and adjust time to 35 minutes. When the timer beeps, quick-release pressure until float valve drops and then unlock lid.
5. Remove cake pan from the pot and transfer to a rack to cool. Flip cake onto a serving platter. Remove parchment paper. Slice and serve.

Stuffed Apples

Servings:4 | Cooking Time: 10 Minutes

Ingredients:
- 4 Granny Smith apples
- 5 tablespoons unsalted butter, softened
- 2 teaspoons ground cinnamon
- ¼ cup packed light brown sugar
- ¼ teaspoon vanilla extract
- ¼ cup chopped walnuts
- ⅛ teaspoon salt
- 2 cups water

Directions:
1. Core apples, leaving some skin on bottom of hole to hold filling in place. Using a paring knife, remove just a little more of the apple center for a bigger area to fill.
2. In a medium bowl, combine butter, cinnamon, brown sugar, vanilla, walnuts, and salt. Stuff apples with this mixture. Place apples in a 7-cup baking dish.
3. Add water to the Instant Pot and insert steam rack. Place baking dish on steam rack.
4. Press the Manual or Pressure Cook button and adjust time to 10 minutes. When timer beeps, quick-release pressure until float valve drops. Unlock lid.
5. Allow apples to cool in pot 20 minutes. Serve warm.

Pie Cups With Fruit Filling

Servings: 6 | Cooking Time: 40 Minutes + Chilling Time

Ingredients:
- For the crust:
- 2 cups flour
- ¾ tsp salt
- ¾ cup butter, softened
- 1 tbsp sugar
- ½ cup ice water
- For the filling:
- ½ fresh peach
- ½ cup apples, chopped
- ¼ cup cranberries
- 2 tbsp flour
- 1 tbsp sugar
- ½ tsp cinnamon
- 1 egg yolk, for brushing

Directions:
1. Place flour, salt, butter, sugar, and water in a food processor and pulse until dough becomes crumbly. Remove to a lightly floured work surface. Divide among 4 equal pieces and wrap in plastic foil. Refrigerate for an hour. Place apples, peach, cranberries, flour, sugar, and cinnamon in a bowl. Toss to combine and set aside. Roll each piece into 6-inch round discs. Add 2 tablespoons of the apple mixture at the center of each disc and wrap to form small bowls. Brush each bowl with egg yolk and gently Transfer to an oiled baking dish. Pour 1 cup of water into the pot and insert the trivet. Place the pan on top. Seal the lid, and cook for 25 minutes on High Pressure. Release the pressure naturally. Serve cool.

Banana & Walnut Oatmeal

Servings: 2 | Cooking Time: 20 Minutes

Ingredients:
- 1 banana, chopped
- 1 cup rolled oats
- 1 cup milk
- ¼ teaspoon cinnamon
- 1 tbsp chopped walnuts
- ½ tsp white sugar

Directions:
1. Pour 1 cup of water into your Instant Pot and fit in a steam rack. Place oats, sugar, milk, cinnamon, and ½ of water in a bowl. Divide between small-sized cups. Place on the steam rack. Seal the lid, select Manual, and cook for 5 minutes on High pressure. When done, allow a natural release for 10 minutes and unlock the lid. Top with banana and walnuts and serve.

Carrot Coconut Cake

Servings:4 | Cooking Time: 20 Minutes

Ingredients:
- ¼ cup coconut oil, melted
- ½ cup sugar
- 1 large egg
- ½ teaspoon ground cinnamon
- Pinch of ground nutmeg
- ½ teaspoon vanilla extract
- ¼ cup peeled, grated carrot

- ¼ cup unsweetened coconut flakes
- ½ cup all-purpose flour
- ½ teaspoon baking powder
- ¼ cup chopped pecans
- 1 cup water

Directions:
1. In a medium bowl, whisk together oil, sugar, egg, cinnamon, nutmeg, vanilla, carrot, coconut flakes, flour, and baking powder. Do not overmix. Fold in pecans. Pour batter into a greased 6" cake pan.
2. Pour water into the Instant Pot. Set trivet in pot. Place cake pan on top of the trivet. Lock lid.
3. Press the Manual button and adjust time to 20 minutes. When timer beeps, let pressure release naturally for 5 minutes. Quick-release any additional pressure until float valve drops and then unlock lid.
4. Remove cake pan from the pot and transfer to a rack until cool. Flip cake onto a serving platter.

Simple Apple Cider With Orange Juice

Servings: 6 | Cooking Time: 20 Minutes

Ingredients:
- 6 green apples, chopped
- ¼ cup orange juice
- 2 cinnamon sticks

Directions:
1. In a blender, add orange juice, apples, and 3 cups water and blend until smooth; use a fine-mesh strainer to strain and press using a spoon. Get rid of the pulp. In the pot, mix the apple puree and cinnamon sticks. Seal the lid and cook for 10 minutes on High Pressure. Release the Pressure naturally. Strain again and do away with the solids.

Homemade Lemon Cheesecake

Servings: 6 | Cooking Time: 1 Hour + Chilling Time

Ingredients:
- Crust:
- 4 oz graham crackers
- 1 tsp ground cinnamon
- 3 tbsp butter, melted
- Filling:
- 1 lb mascarpone cheese, softened
- ¾ cup sugar
- ¼ cup sour cream, at room temperature
- 2 eggs
- 1 tsp vanilla extract
- 1 tsp lemon zest
- 1 tbsp lemon juice
- A pinch of salt
- 1 cup strawberries, halved

Directions:
1. In a food processor, beat cinnamon and graham crackers to attain a texture almost same as sand; mix in melted butter. Press the crumbs into the bottom of a 7-inch springform pan in an even layer. In a stand mixer, beat sugar, mascarpone cheese, and sour cream for 3 minutes to combine well and have a fluffy and smooth mixture. Scrape the bowl's sides and add eggs, lemon zest, salt, lemon juice, and vanilla. Carry on to beat the mixture until you obtain a consistent color and all ingredients are completely com-

bined. Pour filling over crust.
2. Into the inner pot, add 1 cup water and set in a trivet. Place the springform pan on the trivet. Seal the lid, press Cake, and cook for 40 minutes on High. Release the pressure quickly. Remove the cheesecake and let it cool. Garnish with strawberry halves on top. Use a paring knife to run along the edges between the pan and cheesecake to remove it and set it to a plate. Serve.

Walnut & Dark Chocolate Brownies

Servings: 6 | Cooking Time: 30 Minutes

Ingredients:
- 2 eggs
- 1/3 cup granulated sugar
- ¼ cup olive oil
- 1/3 cup flour
- 1/3 cup cocoa powder
- 1/3 cup dark chocolate chips
- 1/3 cup chopped walnuts
- 1 tbsp milk
- ½ tsp baking powder
- 1 tbsp vanilla extract

Directions:
1. Add 1 cup of water and set a steamer rack into the cooker. Line a parchment paper on the steamer basket. In a bowl, beat eggs and sugar to mix until smooth. Stir in oil, cocoa, milk, baking powder, chocolate chips, flour, walnuts, vanilla, and sea salt. Transfer the batter to the prepared steamer basket. Arrange into an even layer. Seal the lid, press Cake, and cook for 20 minutes on High. Release the pressure quickly. Let cool before cutting into squares. Use powdered sugar to dust and serve.

Spiced & Warming Mulled Wine

Servings: 6 | Cooking Time: 20 Minutes

Ingredients:
- 3 cups red wine
- 2 tangerines, sliced
- ¼ cup honey
- 6 whole cloves
- 6 whole black peppercorns
- 2 cardamom pods
- 8 cinnamon sticks
- 1 tsp fresh ginger, grated
- 1 tsp ground cinnamon

Directions:
1. Add red wine, honey, cardamom, 2 cinnamon sticks, cloves, tangerine slices, ginger, and peppercorns. Seal the lid and cook for 5 minutes on High Pressure. Release pressure naturally for 10 minutes. Using a fine mesh strainer, strain the wine. Discard spices. Divide the warm wine into glasses. Garnish with cinnamon sticks to serve.

Strawberry Upside-down Cake

Servings:4 | Cooking Time: 35 Minutes

Ingredients:
- 2 cups diced strawberries
- 1 cup plus 1 tablespoon all-purpose flour, divided
- ⅓ cup plus 1 tablespoon granulated sugar, divided
- 1 large egg
- 2 tablespoons unsalted butter, melted
- 1 teaspoon vanilla extract
- 1 cup ricotta cheese
- 2 teaspoons baking powder
- 1 teaspoon baking soda
- ⅛ teaspoon salt
- 1 ½ cups water

Directions:
1. Grease a 6" cake pan. Place a circle of parchment paper in the bottom.
2. In a medium bowl, toss strawberries in 1 tablespoon flour and 1 tablespoon sugar. Add strawberries to pan in an even layer.
3. In a medium bowl, beat egg. Whisk in butter, ⅓ cup sugar, and vanilla until smooth. Add remaining ingredients, including remaining flour, except water. Pour batter into pan over strawberry layer.
4. Add water to the Instant Pot and insert steam rack. Lower cake pan onto steam rack. Lock lid.
5. Press the Manual or Pressure Cook button and adjust time to 35 minutes. When timer beeps, quick-release pressure until float valve drops. Unlock lid.
6. Remove cake pan from pot and transfer to a cooling rack to cool for 30 minutes. Flip cake onto a serving platter. Remove parchment paper. Slice and serve.

Pumpkin Cheesecake

Servings:6 | Cooking Time: 30 Minutes

Ingredients:
- Crust
- 20 gingersnaps
- 3 tablespoons melted butter
- Cheesecake Filling
- 1 cup pumpkin purée
- 8 ounces cream cheese, cubed and room temperature
- 2 tablespoons sour cream, room temperature
- ½ cup sugar
- Pinch of salt
- 2 large eggs, room temperature
- ¼ teaspoon ground cinnamon
- ⅛ teaspoon ground nutmeg
- ½ teaspoon vanilla extract
- 2 cups water

Directions:
1. Grease a 7" springform pan and set aside.
2. For Crust: Add gingersnaps to a food processor and pulse to combine. Add in melted butter and pulse to blend. Transfer crumb mixture to springform pan and press down along the bottom and about ⅓ of the way up the sides of the pan. Place a square of aluminum foil along the outside bottom of the pan and crimp up around the edges.
3. For Cheesecake Filling: With a hand blender or food processor, cream together pumpkin, cream cheese, sour cream, sugar, and salt. Pulse until smooth. Slowly add eggs, cinnamon, nutmeg,

and vanilla. Pulse for another 10 seconds. Scrape the bowl and pulse until batter is smooth.
4. Transfer the batter into springform pan.
5. Pour water into the Instant Pot. Insert the trivet. Set the springform pan on the trivet. Lock lid.
6. Press the Manual button and adjust time to 30 minutes. When timer beeps, quick-release pressure until float valve drops and then unlock lid. Lift pan out of Instant Pot. Let cool at room temperature for 10 minutes.
7. The cheesecake will be a little jiggly in the center. Refrigerate for a minimum of 2 hours to allow it to set. Release side pan and serve.

Amazing Fruity Cheesecake

Servings: 6 | Cooking Time: 35 Minutes

Ingredients:
- 1 ½ cups graham cracker crust
- 1 cup raspberries
- 3 cups cream cheese
- 1 tbsp fresh orange juice
- 3 eggs
- ½ stick butter, melted
- ¾ cup sugar
- 1 tsp vanilla paste
- 1 tsp orange zest

Directions:
1. Insert the tray into the pressure cooker, and add 1 cup of water. Grease a springform. Mix in graham cracker crust with sugar and butter in a bowl. Press the mixture to form a crust at the bottom. Blend the raspberries and cream cheese with an electric mixer. Crack in the eggs and keep mixing until well combined. Mix in orange juice, vanilla paste, and orange zest. Pour this mixture into the pan, and cover the pan with aluminum foil. Lay the springform on the tray. Select Pressure Cook and cook for 20 minutes on High. Once the cooking is complete, do a quick pressure release. Refrigerate the cheesecake.

Butterscotch Crème Brûlée

Servings:4 | Cooking Time: 20 Minutes

Ingredients:
- 4 large egg yolks
- 2 tablespoons sugar
- Pinch of salt
- ¼ teaspoon vanilla extract
- 1½ cups half-and-half
- ¾ cup butterscotch chips
- 2 cups water
- ½ cup superfine sugar

Directions:
1. In a small bowl, whisk together egg yolks, sugar, salt, and vanilla. Set aside.
2. In saucepan over medium-low heat, heat half-and-half until you reach a low simmer. Whisk a spoonful into the egg mixture to temper the eggs, then slowly add the egg mixture back into the saucepan with remaining half-and-half. Add butterscotch chips and continually stir on simmer until butterscotch is melted, about 10 minutes. Remove from heat and evenly distribute butterscotch mixture among four custard ramekins.
3. Pour water into Instant Pot. Insert trivet. Place silicone steamer

basket onto trivet. Place ramekins onto steamer basket. Lock lid.

4. Press the Manual button and adjust time to 6 minutes. When the timer beeps, let pressure release naturally for 10 minutes. Quick-release any additional pressure until float valve drops and then unlock lid.

5. Transfer custards to a plate and refrigerate covered for 2 hours.

6. Right before serving, top custards with equal amounts superfine sugar. Blow-torch the tops to create a caramelized shell. Serve.

Chocolate Quinoa Bowl

Servings: 4 | Cooking Time: 15 Minutes

Ingredients:
- 12 squares dark chocolate, shaved
- 2 tbsp cocoa powder
- 1 cup quinoa
- 2 tbsp maple syrup
- ½ tsp vanilla
- A pinch of salt
- 1 tbsp sliced almonds

Directions:
1. Put the quinoa, cocoa powder, maple syrup, vanilla, 2 ¼ cups water, and salt in your Instant Pot. Seal the lid, select Manual, and cook for a minute on High pressure. When ready, allow a natural release for 10 minutes and unlock the lid. Using a fork, fluff the quinoa. Top with almonds and dark chocolate and serve.

Creme Caramel With Whipped Cream

Servings: 4 | Cooking Time: 30 Minutes + Cooling Time

Ingredients:
- ½ cup granulated sugar
- 4 tbsp caramel syrup
- 3 eggs
- ½ tsp vanilla extract
- ½ tbsp milk
- 5 oz whipping cream

Directions:
1. Combine milk, whipping cream, and vanilla extract in your Instant Pot. Press Sauté, and cook for 5 minutes, or until small bubbles form. Set aside. Using an electric mixer, whisk the eggs and sugar. Gradually add the cream mixture and whisk until well combined. Divide the caramel syrup between 4 ramekins. Fill with egg mixture and place them on the trivet. Pour in 1 cup water. Seal the lid and cook for 15 minutes on High Pressure. Do a quick release. Remove the ramekins and cool.

Chocolate Chip Cheesecake

Servings:6 | Cooking Time: 30 Minutes

Ingredients:
- Crust
- 22 chocolate wafer cookies
- 4 tablespoons unsalted butter, melted
- Cheesecake Filling
- 14 ounces cream cheese, cubed and softened
- ½ cup granulated sugar
- ⅛ teaspoon salt
- 2 large eggs, room temperature
- ½ cup mini semisweet chocolate chips

- 1 cup water

Directions:
1. Grease a 7" springform pan and set aside.

2. Add chocolate wafers to a food processor and pulse to combine. Add in butter. Pulse to blend. Transfer crumb mixture to prepared springform pan and press down along the bottom and about ⅓ of the way up sides of pan. Place a square of aluminum foil along the outside bottom of pan and crimp up around edges.

3. With a hand blender or food processor, cream together cream cheese, sugar, and salt. Pulse until smooth. Slowly add eggs. Pulse another 10 seconds. Scrape bowl and pulse until batter is smooth. Fold in chocolate chips.

4. Pour mixture over crust in springform pan.

5. Add water to the Instant Pot and insert steam rack. Set springform pan on steam rack. Lock lid.

6. Press the Manual or Pressure Cook button and adjust time to 30 minutes. When timer beeps, quick-release pressure until float valve drops. Unlock lid.

7. Lift pan out of pot. Let cool at room temperature 10 minutes. The cheesecake will be a little jiggly in the center. Refrigerate a minimum of 2 hours or up to overnight to allow it to set. Release sides of pan and serve.

Banana Chocolate Bars

Servings: 6 | Cooking Time: 25 Minutes

Ingredients:
- ½ cup almond butter
- 3 bananas
- 2 tbsp cocoa powder

Directions:
1. Place the bananas and almond butter in a bowl and mash finely with a fork. Add the cocoa powder and stir until well combined. Grease a baking dish. Pour the banana and almond butter into the dish. Pour 1 cup water into the cooker and lower a trivet. Place the baking dish on the trivet and seal the lid. Select Pressure Cook for 15 minutes on High. When it goes off, do a quick release. Let cool for a few minutes before cutting into squares.

Hot Cocoa Brownies

Servings:6 | Cooking Time: 25 Minutes

Ingredients:
- 2 large eggs, beaten
- ¼ cup all-purpose flour
- 2 packets instant hot cocoa mix
- ⅓ cup granulated sugar
- 2 teaspoons baking powder
- 1 teaspoon baking soda
- ⅛ teaspoon salt
- 4 tablespoons unsalted butter, melted
- ⅓ cup mini marshmallows
- 1 cup water

Directions:
1. Grease a 6" cake pan.

2. In a large bowl, combine eggs, flour, hot cocoa mix, sugar, baking powder, baking soda, and salt. Stir in butter and then fold in mini marshmallows. Do not overmix. Pour batter into prepared cake pan.

3. Add water to the Instant Pot and insert steam rack. Place cake pan on top of steam rack. Lock lid.

4. Press the Manual or Pressure Cook button and adjust time to 25 minutes. When timer beeps, let pressure release naturally for 10 minutes. Quick-release any additional pressure until float valve drops. Unlock lid.
5. Remove cake pan from pot and transfer to a cooling rack to cool 10 minutes.
6. Flip brownies onto a serving platter. Let cool completely 30 minutes. Slice and serve.

Banana Bread Pudding

Servings:4 | Cooking Time: 20 Minutes

Ingredients:
- 4 cups cubed French bread, dried out overnight
- 2 small bananas, peeled and sliced
- ¼ cup granulated sugar
- 2 cups whole milk
- 3 large eggs
- ⅛ teaspoon salt
- 3 tablespoons unsalted butter, cut into 4 pats
- 1 ½ cups water

Directions:
1. Grease a 7-cup glass baking dish. Add bread, then banana slices. Sprinkle sugar evenly over bananas. Set aside.
2. In a small bowl, whisk together milk, eggs, and salt. Pour over ingredients in glass baking dish and place butter pats on top.
3. Add water to the Instant Pot and insert steam rack. Place glass baking dish on top of steam rack. Lock lid.
4. Press the Manual or Pressure Cook button and adjust time to 20 minutes. When timer beeps, quick-release pressure until float valve drops. Unlock lid.
5. Remove glass bowl from pot. Transfer to a cooling rack for 30 minutes until set. Serve.

Plum & Almond Dessert

Servings: 6 | Cooking Time: 1 Hour 50 Minutes

Ingredients:
- 6 lb sweet ripe plums, pits removed and halved
- 2 cups white sugar
- 1 cup almond flakes

Directions:
1. Drizzle the plums with sugar. Toss to coat. Let it stand for about 1 hour to allow plums to soak up the sugar. Transfer the plum mixture to the Instant Pot and pour 1 cup of water. Seal the lid and cook on High Pressure for 30 minutes. Allow the Pressure to release naturally for 10 minutes. Serve topped with almond flakes.

Festive Fruitcake

Servings:8 | Cooking Time: 20 Minutes

Ingredients:
- 1 can crushed pineapple, including juice
- ½ cup raisins
- ½ cup dried unsweetened cherries
- ½ cup pitted and diced dates
- 1 cup pecan halves
- ½ cup chopped walnuts
- ½ cup unsweetened coconut flakes
- ½ cup sugar
- ¼ cup melted butter, cooled
- 2 teaspoons vanilla extract
- 2 tablespoons fresh orange juice
- 4 large eggs
- 1 cup all-purpose flour
- 2 teaspoons baking powder
- ¼ teaspoon salt
- ¼ teaspoon ground nutmeg
- 1 cup water

Directions:
1. In a medium bowl, combine all ingredients except water until well mixed. Grease a 6" cake pan. Press mixture into the pan.
2. Pour 1 cup water into the Instant Pot. Insert trivet. Lower 6" pan onto trivet. Lock lid.
3. Press the Manual button and adjust time to 20 minutes. When timer beeps, let pressure release naturally for 10 minutes. Quick-release any additional pressure until float valve drops and then unlock lid.
4. Remove fruitcake from Instant Pot and transfer to a cooling rack. Refrigerate covered overnight. Flip onto a cutting board, slice, and serve.

Chocolate Custard

Servings:4 | Cooking Time: 20 Minutes

Ingredients:
- 4 large egg yolks
- 2 tablespoons sugar
- Pinch of salt
- ¼ teaspoon vanilla extract
- 1½ cups half-and-half
- ¾ cup semisweet chocolate chips
- 2 cups water

Directions:
1. In a small bowl, whisk together egg yolks, sugar, salt, and vanilla. Set aside.
2. In saucepan over medium-low heat, heat half-and-half to a low simmer. Whisk a spoonful into the egg mixture to temper the eggs, then slowly add the egg mixture back into the saucepan with remaining half-and-half. Add chocolate chips and continually stir on simmer until chocolate is melted, about 10 minutes. Remove from heat and evenly distribute chocolate mixture among four custard ramekins.
3. Pour water into Instant Pot. Insert trivet. Place silicone steamer basket onto trivet. Place ramekins onto steamer basket. Lock lid.
4. Press the Manual button and adjust time to 6 minutes. When timer beeps, let pressure release naturally for 10 minutes. Quick-release any additional pressure until float valve drops and then unlock lid.
5. Transfer custards to a plate and refrigerate covered for 2 hours. Serve.

Peachy Crisp

Servings:4 | Cooking Time: 12 Minutes

Ingredients:
- 3 cups peeled, pitted, and diced peaches
- 4 tablespoons unsalted butter, melted
- ½ cup old-fashioned oats
- ⅛ cup all-purpose flour
- ¼ cup chopped almonds
- ⅓ cup granulated sugar
- ¼ teaspoon ground allspice
- ¼ teaspoon salt
- 1 cup water

Directions:
1. Place peaches in a 7-cup glass baking dish.
2. In a food processor, pulse together butter, oats, flour, almonds, sugar, allspice, and salt until butter is well distributed.
3. Preheat oven to broiler at 500°F.
4. Add water to the Instant Pot and insert steam rack. Lower glass baking dish onto steam rack. Lock lid.
5. Press the Manual or Pressure Cook button and adjust time to 8 minutes. When timer beeps, let pressure release naturally until float valve drops. Unlock lid.
6. Place dish under broiler 3–4 minutes until browned.
7. Serve warm or chilled.

Catalan-style Crème Brûlée

Servings: 4 | Cooking Time: 15 Minutes

Ingredients:
- 5 cups heavy cream
- 8 egg yolks
- 1 cup honey
- 4 tbsp sugar
- 1 vanilla extract
- 1 cup water

Directions:
1. In a bowl, combine heavy cream, egg yolks, vanilla, and honey. Beat well with an electric mixer. Pour the mixture into 4 ramekins. Set aside. Pour water into the pot and insert the trivet. Lower the ramekins on top. Seal the lid and cook for 10 minutes on High Pressure. Do a quick pressure release. Remove the ramekins from the pot and add a tablespoon of sugar to each ramekin. Burn evenly with a culinary torch until brown. Chill well and serve.

Root Beer Float Cupcakes

Servings:12 | Cooking Time: 18 Minutes

Ingredients:
- Cupcakes
- ½ box moist vanilla cake mix
- 6 ounces (½ can) root beer
- 2 cups water
- Vanilla Buttercream
- 1 cup confectioners' sugar
- ⅓ cup unsalted butter, softened
- ½ teaspoon vanilla extract
- 1 tablespoon whole milk

Directions:
1. Grease twelve silicone cupcake liners.
2. In a medium bowl, combine cake mix and root beer. Spoon mixture into cupcake liners.
3. Add water to the Instant Pot and insert steam rack. Place six cupcake liners on steam rack. Lock lid.
4. Press the Manual or Pressure Cook button and adjust time to 9 minutes. When timer beeps, quick-release pressure until float valve drops. Unlock lid. Transfer cupcakes to a cooling rack. Repeat cooking process with remaining six cupcake liners.
5. To make buttercream, cream together vanilla buttercream ingredients in a medium mixing bowl. If buttercream is too loose, add a little more confectioners' sugar. If buttercream is too thick, add a little more milk.
6. Let cupcakes cool for at least 30 minutes until they reach room temperature, then spread buttercream on cooled cupcakes. Serve.

Chocolate Glazed Cake

Servings: 6 | Cooking Time: 40 Minutes + Chilling Time

Ingredients:
- 3 cups yogurt
- 3 cups flour
- 2 cups granulated sugar
- 1 cup oil
- 2 tsp baking soda
- 3 tbsp cocoa
- For the glaze:
- 7 oz dark chocolate
- 10 tbsp sugar
- 10 tbsp milk
- 5 oz butter, unsalted

Directions:
1. In a bowl, combine yogurt, flour, sugar, oil, baking soda, and cocoa. Beat well with an electric mixer. Transfer a mixture to a large springform pan. Wrap the pan in foil. Insert a trivet in the Instant Pot. Pour in 1 cup water and place the pan on top. Seal the lid and cook for 30 minutes on High Pressure. Do a quick release, remove the pan, and unwrap. Chill well. Microwave the chocolate and whisk in butter, milk, and sugar. Beat well with a mixer and pour the mixture over the cake. Refrigerate for at least two hours before serving.

Chocolate Cherry Soda Pop Cupcakes

Servings:12 | Cooking Time: 18 Minutes

Ingredients:
- Cupcakes
- ½ box moist chocolate cake mix
- 6 ounces (½ can) cherry soda
- 2 cups water
- Chocolate Icing
- 4 ounces cream cheese, softened
- ¼ cup unsweetened cocoa powder
- 4 tablespoons unsalted butter, softened
- ½ teaspoon vanilla extract
- ⅛ teaspoon salt
- 2 cups confectioners' sugar

Directions:
1. Grease twelve silicone cupcake liners.
2. In a medium bowl, combine cake mix and cherry soda. Spoon mixture into prepared cupcake liners.
3. Add water to the Instant Pot and insert steam rack. Place six cupcake liners on steam rack. Lock lid.

4. Press the Manual or Pressure Cook button and adjust time to 9 minutes. When timer beeps, quick-release pressure until float valve drops. Unlock lid. Transfer cupcakes to a cooling rack. Repeat cooking process with remaining six cupcake liners.

5. In a medium mixing bowl, cream together cream cheese, cocoa powder, butter, vanilla, and salt. Blend in sugar until smooth. If icing is too loose, add a little more sugar. If icing is too thick, add a little milk.

6. Let cupcakes cool for at least 30 minutes until they reach room temperature, then spread icing on cooled cupcakes. Serve.

Cottage Cheesecake With Strawberries

Servings: 6 | Cooking Time: 35 Minutes +cooling Time

Ingredients:
- 10 oz cream cheese
- ¼ cup sugar
- ½ cup cottage cheese
- 1 lemon, zested and juiced
- 2 eggs, cracked into a bowl
- 1 tsp lemon extract
- 3 tbsp sour cream
- 1 cup water
- 10 strawberries, halved to decorate

Directions:
1. Blend with an electric mixer, the cream cheese, quarter cup of sugar, cottage cheese, lemon zest, lemon juice, and lemon extract until a smooth consistency is formed. Adjust the sweet taste to liking with more sugar. Add the eggs. Fold in at low speed until incorporated. Spoon the mixture into a greased baking pan. Level the top with a spatula and cover with foil. Fit a trivet in the pot and pour in water. Place the cake pan on the trivet.

2. Seal the lid. Select Manual and cook for 15 minutes. Mix the sour cream and 1 tbsp of sugar. Set aside. Once the timer has gone off, do a natural pressure release for 10 minutes. Use a spatula to spread the sour cream mixture on the warm cake. Let cool. Top with strawberries.

Cornmeal Cake

Servings:6 | Cooking Time: 20 Minutes

Ingredients:
- 2 cups milk
- ¼ cup packed light brown sugar
- 1 teaspoon orange zest
- ½ cup self-rising cornmeal
- 1 large egg
- 2 egg yolks
- 2 tablespoons melted butter
- 2 tablespoons orange marmalade
- 1 cup water

Directions:
1. Heat the milk in a saucepan over medium heat until it reaches a simmer. Stir in the brown sugar; simmer and stir until the milk is at a low boil, about 2–3 minutes. Whisk in the orange zest and cornmeal. Simmer and stir for 2 minutes or until thickened. Remove from heat.

2. In a small bowl, whisk together egg, egg yolks, butter, and orange marmalade. Add a spoonful of the cornmeal mixture into the egg mixture and quickly stir to temper the eggs. Slowly add the egg mixture into the cornmeal mixture.

3. Grease a 6" baking pan. Transfer the cornmeal batter to the prepared pan.

4. Pour water into Instant Pot and insert trivet. Place the cake pan on trivet. Lock lid.

5. Press the Manual button and adjust time to 15 minutes. When timer beeps, quick-release pressure until float valve drops and then unlock lid. Transfer cake pan to a cooling rack. Serve when cooled.

Walnut & Pumpkin Tart

Servings: 6 | Cooking Time: 70 Minutes

Ingredients:
- 1 cup packed shredded pumpkin
- 3 eggs
- ½ cup sugar
- 1 cup flour
- ½ cup half-and-half
- ¼ cup olive oil
- 1 tsp baking powder
- 1 tsp vanilla extract
- 1 tsp ground cinnamon
- ½ tsp ground nutmeg
- ½ cup chopped walnuts
- 2 cups water
- Frosting:
- 4 oz cream cheese, room temperature
- 8 tbsp butter
- ½ cup confectioners sugar
- ½ tsp vanilla extract
- ½ tsp salt

Directions:
1. In a bowl, beat eggs and sugar to get a smooth mixture. Mix in oil, flour, vanilla extract, cinnamon, half-and-half, baking powder, and nutmeg. Stir well to obtain a fluffy batter. Fold walnuts and pumpkin through the batter. Add batter into a cake pan and cover with aluminum foil. Into the pot, add 1 cup water and set a trivet. Lay cake pan onto the trivet.

2. Seal the lid, select Manual, and cook on High Pressure for 40 minutes. Release pressure naturally for 10 minutes. Beat cream cheese, confectioners' sugar, salt, vanilla, and butter in a bowl until smooth. Place in the refrigerator until needed. Remove cake from the pan and transfer to a wire rack to cool. Over the cake, spread frosting and apply a topping of shredded carrots.

Late Night Brownies

Servings:6 | Cooking Time: 25 Minutes

Ingredients:
- 2 large eggs, whisked
- 1 teaspoon vanilla extract
- ¼ cup all-purpose flour
- ¼ cup unsweetened cocoa powder
- ⅓ cup granulated sugar
- 2 teaspoons baking powder
- 1 teaspoon baking soda
- ⅛ teaspoon salt
- 4 tablespoons unsalted butter, melted
- 2 tablespoons whole milk
- 1 cup water
- 2 tablespoons confectioners' sugar

Directions:

1. Grease a 6" cake pan.

2. In a large bowl, combine eggs, vanilla, flour, cocoa powder, granulated sugar, baking powder, baking soda, and salt. Stir in butter and milk. Do not overmix. Pour batter into prepared pan.

3. Add water to the Instant Pot and insert steam rack. Place cake pan on top of steam rack. Lock lid.

4. Press the Manual or Pressure Cook button and adjust time to 25 minutes. When timer beeps, let pressure release naturally for 10 minutes. Quick-release any additional pressure until float valve drops. Unlock lid.

5. Remove cake pan from pot and transfer to a cooling rack to cool 10 minutes.

6. Flip brownies onto a serving platter. Let cool completely 30 minutes. Garnish with confectioners' sugar. Slice and serve.

After-dinner Boozy Hot Cocoa

Servings:4 | Cooking Time: 5 Minutes

Ingredients:
- 6 cups whole milk
- ¼ cup unsweetened cocoa powder
- ¼ cup mini chocolate chips
- ¼ cup granulated sugar
- ½ cup Irish cream
- ⅛ teaspoon salt
- 2 teaspoons vanilla extract

Directions:

1. Place all ingredients in the Instant Pot. Lock lid.

2. Press the Steam button and adjust time to 5 minutes. When timer beeps, quick-release pressure until float valve drops. Unlock lid. Whisk ingredients to ensure smoothness.

3. Ladle cocoa into four mugs. Serve warm.

Stuffed "baked" Apples

Servings:4 | Cooking Time: 5 Minutes

Ingredients:
- ½ cup fresh orange juice
- ½ teaspoon orange zest
- ¼ cup packed light brown sugar
- ¼ cup golden raisins
- ¼ cup chopped pecans
- ¼ cup quick-cooking oats
- ½ teaspoon ground cinnamon
- 4 cooking apples
- 4 tablespoons butter, divided
- 1 cup water

Directions:

1. In a small bowl, mix together orange juice, orange zest, brown sugar, raisins, pecans, oats, and cinnamon. Set aside.

2. Rinse and dry the apples. Cut off the top fourth of each apple. Peel the cut portion of the apple. Dice it and then stir into the oat mixture. Hollow out and core the apples by cutting to, but not through, the apple bottoms.

3. Place each apple on a piece of aluminum foil that is large enough to wrap the apple completely. Fill the apple centers with the oat mixture. Top each with 1 tablespoon butter. Wrap the foil around each apple, folding the foil over at the top and then pinching it firmly together.

4. Pour the water into Instant Pot. Set in trivet. Place the apple packets on the rack. Lock lid.

5. Press the Manual button and adjust time to 5 minutes. When timer beeps, let pressure release naturally for 10 minutes. Quick-release any additional pressure until float valve drops and then unlock lid.

6. Carefully unwrap apples and transfer to serving plates.

Cinnamon Brown Rice Pudding

Servings:4 | Cooking Time: 25 Minutes

Ingredients:
- 1 cup short-grain brown rice
- 1⅓ cups water
- 1 tablespoon vanilla extract
- 1 cinnamon stick
- 1 tablespoon butter
- 1 cup raisins
- 3 tablespoons honey
- ½ cup heavy cream

Directions:

1. Add rice, water, vanilla, cinnamon stick, and butter to Instant Pot. Lock lid.

2. Press the Manual button and adjust time to 20 minutes. When timer beeps, let pressure release naturally for 10 minutes. Quick-release any additional pressure until float valve drops and then unlock lid.

3. Remove the cinnamon stick and discard. Stir in the raisins, honey, and cream.

4. Press Sauté button on Instant Pot, press Adjust button to change the temperature to Less, and simmer unlidded for 5 minutes. Serve warm.

Quick Coconut Treat With Pears

Servings: 2 | Cooking Time: 15 Minutes

Ingredients:
- ¼ cup flour
- 1 cup coconut milk
- 2 pears, peeled and diced
- ¼ cup shredded coconut

Directions:

1. Combine flour, milk, pears, and shredded coconut in your Pressure cooker. Seal the lid, select Pressure Cook and set the timer to 5 minutes at High pressure. When ready, do a quick pressure release. Divide the mixture between two bowls. Serve.

Homemade Walnut Layer Cake

Servings: 6 | Cooking Time: 25 Minutes

Ingredients:
- ½ cup vanilla pudding powder
- 3 standard cake crusts
- ¼ cup granulated sugar
- 4 cups milk
- 10.5 oz chocolate chips
- ¼ cup walnuts, minced

Directions:

1. Combine vanilla powder, sugar, and milk in the inner pot. Cook until the pudding thickens, stirring constantly on Sauté. Remove from the steel pot. Place one crust into a springform pan.

Pour half of the pudding and sprinkle with minced walnuts and chocolate chips. Cover with another crust and repeat the process. Finish with the final crust and wrap in foil.

2. Insert the trivet, pour in 1 cup of water, and place springform pan on top. Seal the lid and cook for 10 minutes on High Pressure. Do a quick release. Refrigerate.

White Chocolate Pots De Crème

Servings:4 | Cooking Time: 20 Minutes

Ingredients:
- 4 large egg yolks
- 2 tablespoons sugar
- Pinch of salt
- ¼ teaspoon vanilla extract
- 1½ cups half-and-half
- ¾ cup white chocolate chips
- 2 cups water

Directions:
1. In a small bowl, whisk together egg yolks, sugar, salt, and vanilla. Set aside.
2. In saucepan over medium-low heat, heat half-and-half to a low simmer. Whisk a spoonful into the egg mixture to temper the eggs, and then slowly whisk that egg mixture into the saucepan with remaining half-and-half. Add white chocolate chips and continually stir on simmer until chocolate is melted, about 10 minutes. Remove from heat and evenly distribute white chocolate mixture among four custard ramekins.
3. Pour water into Instant Pot. Insert trivet. Place silicone steamer basket onto trivet. Place ramekins onto steamer basket. Lock lid.
4. Press the Manual button and adjust time to 6 minutes. When timer beeps, let pressure release naturally for 10 minutes. Quick-release any additional pressure until float valve drops and then unlock lid.
5. Transfer custards to a plate and refrigerate covered for 2 hours. Serve.

Cinnamon Applesauce

Servings:8 | Cooking Time: 8 Minutes

Ingredients:
- 3 pounds apples (any variety), cored and chopped
- 1 teaspoon ground cinnamon
- ½ teaspoon ground allspice
- ½ cup granulated sugar
- ⅛ teaspoon salt
- ½ cup freshly squeezed orange juice
- ⅓ cup water

Directions:
1. Place all ingredients in the Instant Pot.
2. Press the Manual or Pressure Cook button and adjust time to 8 minutes. When timer beeps, quick-release pressure until float valve drops. Unlock lid.
3. Use an immersion blender to blend ingredients in pot until desired consistency is reached. Serve warm or cold.

Rice Pudding

Servings:4 | Cooking Time: 25 Minutes

Ingredients:
- 1 cup Arborio rice
- 1 ½ cups water
- 1 tablespoon vanilla extract
- 1 cinnamon stick
- 1 tablespoon unsalted butter
- 1 cup golden raisins
- ¼ cup granulated sugar
- ½ cup heavy cream

Directions:
1. Add rice, water, vanilla, cinnamon stick, and butter to the Instant Pot. Lock lid.
2. Press the Manual or Pressure Cook button and adjust time to 20 minutes. When timer beeps, let pressure release naturally for 10 minutes. Quick-release any additional pressure until float valve drops. Press the Cancel button. Unlock lid.
3. Remove cinnamon stick and discard. Stir in raisins, sugar, and heavy cream.
4. Press the Sauté button on the Instant Pot, press Adjust button to change temperature to Less, and simmer unlidded 5 minutes. Serve warm.

Nutty Brownie Cake

Servings:6 | Cooking Time: 20 Minutes

Ingredients:
- 4 tablespoons butter, room temperature
- 2 large eggs
- ⅓ cup all-purpose flour
- ½ teaspoon baking powder
- ⅓ cup unsweetened cocoa powder
- Pinch of sea salt
- ⅓ cup sugar
- ⅓ cup semisweet chocolate chips
- ⅓ cup chopped pecans
- 1 cup water
- 2 tablespoons powdered sugar

Directions:
1. In a large bowl, whisk together butter, eggs, flour, baking powder, cocoa powder, salt, and sugar. Do not overmix. Fold in chocolate chips and pecans. Pour batter into a greased 6" cake pan. Cover pan with a piece of aluminum foil.
2. Pour water into the Instant Pot. Set trivet in pot. Place cake pan on top of the trivet. Lock lid.
3. Press the Manual button and adjust time to 20 minutes. When timer beeps, let pressure release naturally for 5 minutes. Quick-release any additional pressure until float valve drops and then unlock lid.
4. Remove cake pan from the Instant Pot and transfer to a rack to cool. Sprinkle with powdered sugar and serve.

Peanut Butter Chocolate Cheesecake

Servings: 6 | Cooking Time: 30 Minutes

Ingredients:
- Crust
- 20 vanilla wafers
- 2 tablespoons creamy peanut butter
- 3 tablespoons melted butter
- Cheesecake Filling
- 12 ounces cream cheese, cubed and room temperature
- 2 tablespoons sour cream, room temperature
- ½ cup sugar
- ¼ cup unsweetened cocoa
- 2 large eggs, room temperature
- 1 teaspoon vanilla extract
- 2 cups water
- ¼ cup mini semisweet chocolate chips
- ¼ cup chopped peanuts
- 2 tablespoons chocolate syrup
- 1 cup whipped cream

Directions:
1. For Crust: Grease a 7" springform pan and set aside.
2. Add vanilla wafers to a food processor and pulse to combine. Add in peanut butter and melted butter. Pulse to blend. Transfer crumb mixture to springform pan and press down along the bottom and about ⅓ of the way up the sides of the pan. Place a square of aluminum foil along the outside bottom of the pan and crimp up around the edges.
3. For Cheesecake Filling: With a hand blender or food processor, cream together cream cheese, sour cream, sugar, and cocoa. Pulse until smooth. Slowly add eggs and vanilla extract. Pulse for another 10 seconds. Scrape the bowl and pulse until batter is smooth. Transfer the batter into springform pan.
4. Pour water into the Instant Pot. Insert the trivet. Set the springform pan on the trivet. Lock lid.
5. Press the Manual button and adjust time to 30 minutes. When timer beeps, quick-release pressure until float valve drops and then unlock lid. Lift pan out of Instant Pot. Garnish immediately with chocolate chips and chopped peanuts. Let cool at room temperature for 10 minutes.
6. The cheesecake will be a little jiggly in the center. Refrigerate for a minimum of 2 hours to allow it to set. Release side pan and serve with drizzled chocolate syrup and whipped cream.

Classic French Squash Tart

Servings: 6 | Cooking Time: 35 Minutes

Ingredients:
- 15 oz mashed squash
- 6 fl oz milk
- ½ tsp cinnamon, ground
- ½ tsp nutmeg
- ½ tsp salt
- 3 large eggs
- ½ cup granulated sugar
- 1 pack pate brisee

Directions:
1. Place squash puree in a large bowl. Add milk, cinnamon, eggs, nutmeg, salt, and sugar. Whisk together until well incorporated. Grease a baking dish with oil. Gently place pate brisee creating the edges with hands. Pour the squash mixture over and flatten the surface with a spatula. Pour 1 cup of water into the pot and insert

the trivet. Lay the baking dish on the trivet. Seal the lid, and cook for 25 minutes on High Pressure. Do a quick release. Transfer the pie to a serving platter. Refrigerate.

Vanilla Cheesecake With Cranberry Filling

Servings: 8 | Cooking Time: 1 Hour + Chilling Time

Ingredients:
- 1 cup coarsely crumbled cookies
- 2 tbsp butter, melted
- 1 cup mascarpone cheese
- ½ cup sugar
- 2 tbsp sour cream
- ½ tsp vanilla extract
- 2 eggs
- 1/3 cup dried cranberries

Directions:
1. Fold a 20-inch piece of aluminum foil in half lengthwise twice and set on the Instant Pot. In a bowl, combine butter and crumbled cookies. Press firmly to the bottom and about 1/3 of the way up the sides of a cake pan. Freeze the crust. In a separate bowl, beat mascarpone cheese and sugar to obtain a smooth consistency. Stir in vanilla and sour cream. Beat one egg and add into the cheese mixture to combine well. Do the same with the second egg.
2. Stir cranberries into the filling. Transfer the filling into the crust. Into the pot, add 1 cup water and set the steam rack. Center the springform pan onto the prepared foil sling. Use the sling to lower the pan onto the rack.
3. Fold foil strips out of the way of the lid. Seal the lid, press Manual, and cook on High Pressure for 40 minutes. Release the pressure quickly. Transfer the cheesecake to a refrigerator for 3 hours. Use a paring knife to run along the edges between the pan and cheesecake to remove the cheesecake and set to the plate.

Chocolate Mint Chip Pots De Crème

Servings: 4 | Cooking Time: 18 Minutes

Ingredients:
- 4 large egg yolks
- 2 tablespoons granulated sugar
- ⅛ teaspoon salt
- ¼ teaspoon vanilla extract
- 1 ½ cups heavy whipping cream
- ¾ cups mint chocolate chips
- 2 cups water

Directions:
1. In a small bowl, whisk together egg yolks, sugar, salt, and vanilla. Set aside.
2. In a small saucepan over medium-low heat, heat whipping cream to a low simmer, about 2 minutes. Take out a spoonful and whisk it into egg mixture in bowl to temper eggs. Then slowly whisk egg mixture into saucepan with remaining whipping cream.
3. Add mint chocolate chips and continually stir on simmer until chocolate is melted, about 8–10 minutes. Remove from heat and evenly distribute mixture among four custard ramekins.
4. Add water to the Instant Pot and insert steam rack. Place steamer basket on steam rack. Place ramekins into basket. Lock lid.
5. Press the Manual or Pressure Cook button and adjust time to 6 minutes. When timer beeps, let pressure release naturally for 10

minutes. Quick-release any additional pressure until float valve drops. Unlock lid.

6. Transfer ramekins to a plate and refrigerate covered at least 2 hours or up to overnight. Serve chilled.

Best Tiramisu Cheesecake

Servings: 6 | Cooking Time: 35 Minutes + Chilling Time

Ingredients:
- 1 ½ cups ladyfingers, crushed
- 1 tbsp Kahlua liquor
- 1 tbsp granulated espresso
- 1 tbsp butter, melted
- 16 oz cream cheese
- 8 oz mascarpone cheese
- 2 tbsp powdered sugar
- ½ cup white sugar
- 1 tbsp cocoa powder
- 1 tsp vanilla extract
- 2 eggs

Directions:
1. In a bowl beat the cream cheese, mascarpone, and white sugar. Gradually beat in the eggs, the powdered sugar, cocoa powder, and vanilla. Combine Kahlua liquor, espresso, butter, and ladyfingers, in another bowl. Press the ladyfinger crust at the bottom. Pour the filling on a greased cake pan. Cover the pan with aluminum foil. Pour 1 cup of water into your pressure cooker and lower a trivet. Place the pan inside and seal the lid. Select Manual and set to 25 minutes at High pressure. Release the pressure quickly. Allow cooling completely.

Peanut Butter Custards

Servings:4 | Cooking Time: 18 Minutes

Ingredients:
- 4 large egg yolks
- 2 tablespoons granulated sugar
- ⅛ teaspoon salt
- ¼ teaspoon vanilla extract
- 1 ½ cups heavy whipping cream
- ¾ cup peanut butter chips
- 2 cups water

Directions:
1. In a small bowl, whisk together egg yolks, sugar, salt, and vanilla. Set aside.
2. In a small saucepan over medium-low heat, heat cream to a low simmer, about 2 minutes. Whisk a spoonful of warm cream mixture into egg mixture to temper eggs. Then slowly add egg mixture back into saucepan with remaining cream.
3. Add peanut butter chips and continually stir on simmer until chips are melted, about 8–10 minutes. Remove from heat and evenly distribute mixture among four custard ramekins.
4. Add water to the Instant Pot and insert steam rack. Place steamer basket on steam rack. Place ramekins into basket. Lock lid.
5. Press the Manual or Pressure Cook button and adjust time to 6 minutes. When timer beeps, let pressure release naturally for 10 minutes. Quick-release any additional pressure until float valve drops. Unlock lid.
6. Transfer ramekins to a plate and refrigerate covered at least 2 hours or up to overnight. Serve chilled.

Homemade Spanish-style Horchata

Servings: 4 | Cooking Time: 20 Minutes

Ingredients:
- 4 cups cold water
- ½ cup short-grain rice
- ¼ stick cinnamon
- Zest from 1 lemon
- 2 tbsp sugar
- 1 tbsp cinnamon powder

Directions:
1. In the pot, combine cinnamon stick, rice and 2 cups of water. Seal the lid cook on High Pressure for 5 minutes. Release pressure naturally for 10 minutes. In a blender, puree the rice mixture with the lemon zest and sugar. Strain the blended mixture into the remaining water. Mix well and place in the refrigerator until ready for serving. Serve sprinkled with cinnamon.

Simple Lemon Cheesecake

Servings:6 | Cooking Time: 30 Minutes

Ingredients:
- Crust
- 22 vanilla wafer cookies
- 4 tablespoons unsalted butter, melted
- Cheesecake Filling
- 14 ounces cream cheese, cubed and softened
- ½ cup granulated sugar
- ⅛ teaspoon salt
- Juice and zest of 1 large lemon
- 2 large eggs, room temperature
- 1 cup water

Directions:
1. Grease a 7" springform pan and set aside.
2. Add vanilla wafers to a food processor and pulse to combine. Add butter. Pulse to blend. Transfer crumb mixture to prepared springform pan and press down along the bottom and about ⅓ of the way up sides of pan. Place a square of aluminum foil along the outside bottom of pan and crimp up around edges.
3. With a hand blender or food processor, cream together cream cheese, sugar, salt, lemon juice and zest. Pulse until smooth. Slowly add eggs. Pulse another 10 seconds. Scrape bowl and pulse until mixture is smooth.
4. Pour mixture over crust in springform pan.
5. Add water to the Instant Pot and insert steam rack. Set springform pan on steam rack. Lock lid.
6. Press the Manual or Pressure Cook button and adjust time to 30 minutes. When timer beeps, quick-release pressure until float valve drops. Unlock lid.
7. Lift pan out of pot. Let cool at room temperature 10 minutes. The cheesecake will be a little jiggly in the center. Refrigerate a minimum of 2 hours or up to overnight to allow it to set. Release sides of pan and serve.

Pumpkin Pudding With Apple Juice

Servings: 4 | Cooking Time: 20 Minutes

Ingredients:
- 1 lb pumpkin, chopped
- 1 cup granulated sugar
- ½ cup cornstarch
- 4 cups apple juice
- 1 tsp cinnamon, ground
- 3-4 cloves

Directions:
1. In a bowl, combine sugar and apple juice until sugar dissolves completely. Pour the mixture into the pot and stir in cornstarch, cinnamon, cloves, and pumpkin. Seal the lid, and cook for 10 minutes on High Pressure. Do a quick release. Pour in the pudding into 4 serving bowls. Let cool at room temperature and refrigerate overnight.

Molten Chocolate Cake

Servings: 6 | Cooking Time: 40 Minutes

Ingredients:
- 1 cup butter
- 4 tbsp milk
- 2 tsp vanilla extract
- 1 ½ cups chocolate chips
- 1 ½ cups sugar
- Powdered sugar to garnish
- 7 tbsp flour
- 5 eggs
- 1 cup water

Directions:
1. Grease the cake pan with cooking spray and set aside. Fit the trivet at the pot, and pour in water. In a heatproof bowl, add the butter and chocolate and melt them in the microwave for about 2 minutes. Stir in sugar. Add eggs, milk, and vanilla extract and stir again. Finally, add the flour and stir it until smooth. Pour the batter into the greased cake pan and use a spatula to level it. Place the pan on the trivet, inside the pot, seal the lid, and select Manual at High for 15 minutes.
2. Do a natural pressure release for 10 minutes. Remove the trivet with the pan on it and place the pan on a flat surface. Put a plate over the pan and flip the cake over onto the plate. Pour the powdered sugar in a fine sieve and sift over the cake. Cut the cake into slices and serve.

Individual Cheesecakes

Servings:6 | Cooking Time: 20 Minutes

Ingredients:
- Crust
- 18 gingersnaps
- 3 tablespoons granulated sugar
- 3 tablespoons unsalted butter, melted
- ⅛ teaspoon salt
- Cheesecake Filling
- 8 ounces cream cheese, cubed and softened
- ¼ teaspoon vanilla extract
- ¼ cup granulated sugar
- ⅛ teaspoon salt
- 1 large egg, room temperature

- 1 cup water

Directions:
1. Grease six silicone cupcake liners.
2. In a small food processor, pulse together crust ingredients. Transfer crumb mixture to liners and press down along bottom and one-third of the way up sides of liners.
3. With a hand blender or food processor, cream together cream cheese, vanilla, sugar, and salt. Pulse until smooth. Slowly add egg. Pulse 10 seconds. Scrape bowl and pulse until mixture is smooth.
4. Pour mixture into prepared cupcake liners.
5. Add water to the Instant Pot. Insert steam rack. Place steamer basket on steam rack. Carefully place cupcake liners in basket. Lock lid.
6. Press the Manual or Pressure Cook button and adjust time to 20 minutes. When timer beeps, quick-release pressure until float valve drops. Unlock lid.
7. Remove basket from pot. Let cheesecakes cool at room temperature 10 minutes.
8. Cheesecakes will be a little jiggly in the center. Refrigerate at least 1 hour or up to overnight to allow them to set. Serve chilled.

Blueberry-orange Quick Jam

Servings:4 | Cooking Time: 7 Minutes

Ingredients:
- 1 pound fresh blueberries
- 1 cup granulated sugar
- Juice and zest from ½ medium orange
- ⅛ teaspoon salt
- ½ cup water, divided
- 2 tablespoons cornstarch

Directions:
1. Add blueberries, sugar, orange juice and zest, salt, and ¼ cup water to the Instant Pot. Lock lid.
2. Press the Manual or Pressure Cook button and adjust time to 4 minutes. When timer beeps, let pressure release naturally for 10 minutes. Quick-release any additional pressure until float valve drops. Press the Cancel button. Unlock lid.
3. Create a slurry by whisking together remaining ¼ cup water and cornstarch.
4. Add slurry to berry mixture to thicken, smooshing blueberries against sides of pot as you stir.
5. Press the Sauté button on the Instant Pot and cook an additional 3 minutes. Allow mixture to cool for at least 30 minutes until it reaches room temperature.
6. Transfer jam to an airtight container and refrigerate until ready to eat. Serve warmed or chilled.

Spiced Red Wine–poached Pears

Servings:4 | Cooking Time: 13 Minutes

Ingredients:
- 4 ripe but still firm pears
- 2 tablespoons fresh lemon juice
- 4 cups dry red wine
- ½ cup freshly squeezed orange juice
- 2 teaspoons grated orange zest
- ¼ cup sugar
- 1 cinnamon stick
- ½ teaspoon ground cloves
- ½ teaspoon ground ginger
- 1 sprig fresh mint

Directions:
1. Rinse and peel the pears leaving the stem. Using a corer or melon baller, remove the cores from underneath without going through the top so you can maintain the stem. Brush the pears inside and out with the lemon juice.
2. Combine the wine, orange juice, orange zest, sugar, cinnamon stick, cloves, and ginger in Instant Pot. Press the Sauté button and then hit the Adjust button to change the temperature to More. Bring to a slow boil in about 3–5 minutes; stir to blend and dissolve the sugar. Carefully place the pears in liquid. Press Adjust button to change temperature to Less and simmer unlidded for 5 additional minutes. Lock lid.
3. Press Manual button and adjust time to 3 minutes. Use the Pressure button to set the pressure to Low. When the timer beeps, quick-release pressure until float valve drops and then unlock lid.
4. Use a slotted spoon to transfer the pears to a serving platter. Garnish with mint sprig.

Grandma's Fruit Compote

Servings: 6 | Cooking Time: 45 Minutes

Ingredients:
- 7 oz Turkish figs
- 7 oz fresh cherries
- 7 oz plums
- 3 ½ oz raisins
- 3 large apples, chopped
- 3 tbsp cornstarch
- 1 tsp cinnamon, ground
- 1 cup sugar
- 1 lemon, juiced

Directions:
1. Combine figs, cherries, plums, raisins, apples, cornstarch, cinnamon, sugar, and lemon juice in the Instant Pot. Pour in 3 cups water. Seal the lid and cook for 30 minutes on High pressure. Release the pressure naturally for 10 minutes. Store in big jars.

Honey Homemade Almond Milk

Servings: 4 | Cooking Time: 15 Minutes

Ingredients:
- 1 cup raw almonds, peeled
- 2 dried apricots, chopped
- 2 tbsp honey
- 1 vanilla bean
- ½ tsp almond extract

Directions:
1. In the Instant Pot, mix a cup of water with almonds and apricots. Seal the lid and cook for 1 minute on High. Release the pressure quickly. The almonds should be soft and plump, and the water should be brown and murky. Use a strainer to drain almonds and apricots. Rinse with cold water. To a blender, add the rinsed almonds and apricots, almond extract, vanilla bean, honey, and 4 cups water. Blend for 2 minutes until well combined and frothy. Line a cheesecloth to the strainer. Place the strainer over a bowl and strain the milk. Use a wooden spoon to press milk through the cheesecloth and get rid of solids. Place almond milk in an airtight container and refrigerate.

Easy Lemon Cake

Servings: 6 | Cooking Time: 30 Minutes

Ingredients:
- 2 eggs
- 2 cups sugar
- 1 cup vegetable oil
- ½ cup flour
- 1 tsp baking powder
- Lemon topping:
- 1 cup sugar
- 1 cup lemon juice
- 1 tbsp lemon zest
- 1 lemon, sliced

Directions:
1. In a bowl, combine eggs, sugar, oil, and baking powder. Gradually add flour until the mixture is thick and slightly sticky. Shape balls with hands and flatten them to half-inch thick. Place in a baking pan. Pour 1 cup of water, insert a trivet, and lower the pan onto the trivet. Cover the pan with foil and seal the lid. Cook on High Pressure for 20 minutes. Do a quick release. Let cool at room temperature. Add sugar, lemon juice, lemon zest, and lemon slices to the Instant Pot. Press Sauté and stir until the sugar dissolves. Pour the hot topping over the cake.

APPENDIX : Recipes Index

T

Z

CPSIA information can be obtained
at www.ICGtesting.com
Printed in the USA
BVHW012200170922
647318BV00004B/101